MW00422903

THE
GREAT
BLACK
HOPE

Louis Moore

**Doug Williams, Vince Evans, and the
Making of the Black Quarterback**

THE
GREAT
BLACK
HOPE

PUBLICAFFAIRS

New York

PublicAffairs
Hachette Book Group
1290 Avenue of the Americas, New York, NY 10104
www.publicaffairsbooks.com
@Public_Affairs

Printed in the United States of America

First Edition: September 2024

Published by PublicAffairs, an imprint of Hachette Book Group, Inc. The PublicAffairs name and logo is a registered trademark of the Hachette Book Group.

The Hachette Speakers Bureau provides a wide range of authors for speaking events. To find out more, go to hachettespeakersbureau.com or email HachetteSpeakers@hbgusa.com.

PublicAffairs books may be purchased in bulk for business, educational, or promotional use. For more information, please contact your local bookseller or the Hachette Book Group Special Markets Department at special.markets@hbgusa.com.

The publisher is not responsible for websites (or their content) that are not owned by the publisher.

Print book interior design by Amy Quinn.

Library of Congress Cataloging-in-Publication Data has been applied for.

ISBNs: 9781541705098 (hardcover), 9781541705111 (ebook)

LSC-C

Printing 2, 2024

CONTENTS

INTRODUCTION

WITH 11:04 LEFT IN THE GAME AND TRAILING TAMPA BAY 10–6, Chicago's quarterback Vince Evans jogged onto Soldier Field ready to lead a comeback. The Bears' offense had been hibernating all game, and they needed just the right jolt. Few quarterbacks were as electrifying as Vince Evans. In the three games he had played in that 1979 season, he already recorded three touchdowns of more than 50 yards. As Evans gathered his teammates for the impending drive, CBS went to commercial.

The commercial highlighted Ford's future. The car company touted a ceramic gas turbine engine that would improve gas mileage by 30 percent, a turbocharged four-cylinder Mustang with the power of eight cylinders, and a hybrid vehicle that ran on gas and battery power. This vehicle existed because Ford was facing multiple market challenges and knew it had to innovate.

Like Ford, the NFL was on the cusp of change. The difference was—its leaders and financiers didn't know it yet. After fifty-nine years of the NFL, it was still a foreign concept that Black men could be the field generals. At the conclusion of that 1979 season,

1

in fact, Ed Garvey, the head of the NFL Players Association (NFLPA), looked at the lack of Black coaches, Black general managers, and Black quarterbacks and labeled the league a "monument of racism." But monuments crumble—or at least some racist relics are hidden from the public—and so too would the racist belief that Black men couldn't lead or think well enough to play professional quarterback. Just when that day would come was unknown, but if one looked hard enough on September 30, 1979, they could see the future of football on Soldier Field. And the future was Black. For the first time in the modern NFL, in a contest that CBS called "the battle of the bombers," two Black quarterbacks started against each other.

With a low-cut Afro, caramel-colored skin, and Hollywood good looks, Vince Evans was set to be the change. In college, the ex-USC quarterback had appeared in bit roles in episodes of *The Six Million Dollar Man* and *Rich Man, Poor Man*, and now he was ready for top billing. Like Hollywood, however, the NFL had few leading roles for Black men. He was one of four Black quarterbacks in the league, and one of two starters. The other starter, Doug Williams, was on the opposing sidelines.

Evans had crossover appeal. As one *Chicago Sun-Times* headline simply stated, he was BOUND FOR STARDOM. In just his third week as a starter, the onetime Rose Bowl MVP was the toast of the town. The car dealers wanted him, the sporting goods stores gave his phone a ring, Saks and Sears tried to get a piece, and the radios and local TV stations always inquired about his availability. Even little white boys on the north side of town argued among themselves over who got to play Evans in their sandlot games. Had things gone the way folks thought they might, Evans was poised to enter that rarified Chicago sports air that was reserved for only a select few Black athletes. If he kept gunning the ball like Al Capone, he'd be untouchable. He'd join Chicago's pantheon of

Black athletes, with Ernie Banks, Gale Sayers, Walter Payton, and later Michael Jordan.

At six foot two and 220 pounds, Evans had a combination of arm strength and speed that brought creativity from the world of sportswriters. At times, this writing dipped into racial stereotypes, but the point was made: he was a dual threat. He could "heave a football from Chi-town to China and run like the cops are after him even when they aren't," and he had "an arm modeled after a bazooka and feet that would do Fred Astaire proud." It was true. Evans could throw the ball over Lake Michigan and run to the other side in time to catch it. If a coach used Evans correctly, he was the perfect weapon. The future of football.

When play resumed after the commercial break with the Bears on the Bucs' 35-yard line, Evans set up in the I formation and surveyed the Bucs' dominating 3-4 defense—three defensive linemen on the line of scrimmage with four linebackers behind them. Would he have time to get off his play-action screen pass to Walter Payton? To run a screen pass, the quarterback had to have quick feet, because the offensive linemen left the quarterback unprotected so that they could set up blocks for the intended receiver. Adding a play-action fake to a screen pass would take even more time. But with Evans behind the line, offensive coordinator Ken Meyer had faith. Evans was the fastest quarterback in football. When he called hike, he faked the run to Payton, dropped back 10 yards with a Bucs defender closing in on him, and lofted a perfect pass to Payton on the left side of the field. "Sweetness" did the rest. A 65-yard touchdown put the Bears up 13–10. Your turn, Doug Williams.

Doug Williams had grown up in rural Louisiana, where the Klan spent their weekends trying to intimidate Black citizens. A 3-point deficit was nothing to him. At six foot four and 212 pounds, he was cast in the mold of a perfect pro quarterback. The biggest quarterback in the league and the second fastest behind Evans, Williams also had the best arm. He just had the wrong paint job. With his dark skin, big brown eyes, and a deep and slow Southern accent, some pundits thought his all-white offensive line would not be able to understand him, let alone take orders from him. But his linemen understood football, and they knew Doug Williams was a football player. He had an arm made by God and a gun company. He could loft the ball 70 yards in the air and have it smoothly drop into his receiver's hands like one would toss a toy to a baby.

With a rocket launcher for an arm, Williams had the ability to score quickly, so all game long, the Bears defense had been playing to prevent the deep passes. For this fourth-quarter drive, he responded by deftly taking the Bucs up the field, mixing in short passes to go along with the Bucs' punishing rushing game. Sitting at the Bears' 8-yard line and staring at third and 2, everyone expected Bucs coach John McKay would call another run to get the first down and take time off the clock before going for a game-winning touchdown. Instead, he put the ball and the game in Williams's large black hands. From the split back set, McKay called a quick slant/corner route for receiver Isaac Hagins. Calling for a double move meant the play would take time to develop. Williams would have to be patient and poised, characteristics critics claimed that Black quarterbacks lacked. He'd also have to help sell the inside route. Williams called hike, took a classic quarterback drop, and stood tall in the pocket. As Hagins broke inside for his slant, Williams made the defender jump the slant route by pump-faking a pass. In the NFL, few quarterbacks dared do that for fear of the ball slipping out. Besides, old-school coaches thought it was hotdogging. Doug Williams was new school. As the defender bit on the fake, Hagins faded to the corner of the end zone, where Williams lofted a pass in to his hands. Touchdown.

"Being a black quarterback," Jim Murray of the *Los Angeles Times* once wrote, "is like being a member of the bomb squad. You're allowed one mistake." Right as Evans's career was ready to take off in that September 30 game against the Bucs, his time as an NFL quarterback almost imploded. In his last two drives of the game, Evans threw two interceptions on passes that sailed over his receivers' heads. The last interception brought a chorus of boos. Would Evans ever get another chance to prove himself? A staph infection that sent him to the hospital and ended his season put that question to bed for the moment, but to most people watching, it looked like Evans would be another victim of the Black quarterback syndrome, a belief that many Black people shared, inside and outside of football. The Black quarterback syndrome suggested that despite how good a Black person was, he or she would never be good enough for their white employers. Because of their visibility, the Black quarterback became the barometer of how many Black folks gauged gradual improvement in American society.

The matchup between Williams and Evans was one of the most significant games in regular season history. After years of denying Black men a chance to succeed in the sport's most important position, the NFL had finally been unable to ignore the sheer talents of these two Black players. And they were two different types of quarterbacks. Williams was big and strong, and although he could run, his mentor, Eddie Robinson, taught him to stand in the pocket like a classic quarterback, so NFL teams would not try to switch his position like they did with so many other Black men. Evans had blazing speed and was more comfortable rolling outside of the pocket and presenting himself as a dual threat to the defense, where he could run or pass.

But few reporters or pundits could give the game proper social context. Clearly, the game meant something, but just how much? "There will be no speeches or blare of trumpets, but mankind will take another step forward Sunday at Chicago's Soldier Field," one writer chimed. Another added, "There was no need to start marching down the streets singing 'We HAVE Overcome.'" True, Vince Evans wasn't John Lewis and Doug Williams wasn't Martin Luther King Jr., but what the game represented, and what the starting Black quarterback symbolized, was the true promise of civil rights: that merit would matter. One's abilities and work ethic would finally cut through the racist stereotypes that for so long strangled the aspirations and advancement of too many Black Americans.

The pro quarterback was a symbol that carried weight in America. More than just a position in a popular sport, team owners, coaches, media, and the fans celebrated the quarterback as the ultimate sign of leadership and intelligence. As one white writer put it in the mid-1960s, "This is the glamour position. This is where the money goes. This is, most of all, the job which requires great physical skills, high intelligence, and the ability to lead. And this is where the Negro has never been given a complete chance."

As modern pro football slowly started to integrate after World War II, there was a small window when the possibility of a Black quarterback didn't seem so far-fetched. In fact, two pro teams, the 1946 Los Angeles Rams (Kenny Washington), and the 1949 Brooklyn–New York Yankees of the AAFC (Alva Tabor), had Black quarterbacks. But just as Black players reintegrated pro football, starting with Kenny Washington in 1946, the quarterback also became the most important position on the field. And very quickly, quarterbacking became the domain of white men. To protect that privilege, white coaches built nearly impenetrable defenses of stereotypes, excuses, and flat-out refusals to give Black men a chance. As Pittsburgh sportswriter Phil Musick once mused, "There are, of course, no such things as black quarterbacks; only figments of the liberal imagination. Somewhere on their way to the pocket—poof!—they became defensive backs, flankers, pulling guards, automobile mechanics, insurance salesmen." He was right. For far too many Black quarterbacks, the NFL stood for "not for long." That's because pro football protected the position like a precious heirloom. Black quarterbacks, Kevin Lamb of the *Chicago Sun-Times* observed, "had to swim the moat white folks had built around the football position that stood for leadership and glory." He added, "They've struggled more than most quarterbacks just for the opportunity to struggle at being a pro quarterback." In other words, pro football had a caste system, and quarterbacks were a white-only class.

This was intentional. White owners, general managers, coaches, and scouts did not believe the Black quarterback belonged in the league, and they found all manner of rationalizations. They said he was not smart enough to read a defense, his white teammates would not follow his leadership, and he did not have the courage to stand in the pocket and deliver an accurate pass with a defender barreling down on him. One unnamed coach even claimed in 1968, "I don't know quite how to describe it, but the Negro is often sort of loosey-goosey. He seems to throw the ball a little differently. He doesn't seem to keep his forearm as rigid. He tends to snap his wrist like he's throwing a curveball. A pass thrown like this wobbles. It doesn't have as much speed on it. It's less accurate." Then there was the Black quarterback's vernacular. With most Black quarterbacks coming from the South, the stereotype suggested that white players would not be able to understand his Black Southern accent. One white writer wrote of Doug Williams, "In truth, Williams' sentences are filled with a combination of black jargon and Louisiana bayou slang and it all adds up to distinctive listening." Williams heard the nonsense and chided, "I know I have bad English, but I think everybody understands me."

Then there was the Black quarterback's speed. In a nation where racial stereotypes ran ripe, the Black quarterback could never outrun the belief that his speed was more valuable at any other position than quarterback. So, they threw him at receiver or tossed him in the secondary. If he wanted to play pro ball, he had no choice. When asked about what happened to him, Cornell Gordon, who starred at North Carolina A&T in the mid-1960s before playing defensive back on the 1968 Super Bowl Champion New York Jets, emphatically put it, "Sure, I wanted a chance to play quarterback, but they wouldn't give it to me." Most coaches had a special formula they used to evaluate Black quarterbacks: Black + quarterback = defensive back.

Why the secondary? Speed. Football experts believed cornerbacks had all brawn and little brain. According to the white power structure in pro football, cornerback was the opposite of the quarterback; there was no thinking involved. Very quickly, the cornerback became thought of as the domain for the Black athlete. In 1968, *Sports Illustrated*'s Jack Olsen vividly explained, "The cornerback areas resembled the middle of a cotton field in Crumrod, Ark. Three-fourths of the starting cornerbacks, 24 out of 32, were black." An amazing stat considering the league was only 25 percent Black. As one ex-player once put it, "Cornerback is not a brains position. You pick up the split end or the flanker and you stay with him all the way. That's it. There's very little judgement required." In the period between 1955, when Charlie "Choo Choo" Brackins played three snaps at quarterback for the Green Bay Packers, and 1968, when Marlin Briscoe became the Denver Broncos' starting QB, pro teams switched the positions of every Black college quarterback that made a roster. The great majority of them became cornerbacks. It did not matter if they went to a big-time white school or a small Black college. Pro football had no use for them as signal callers. The list included men like Sid Williams (Wisconsin),

8

Willie Wood (USC), Mike Howell (Grambling), Pete Hall (Marquette), Jim Kearney (Prairie View), Ken Riley (FAMU), Cornell Gordon (North Carolina A&T), Brigman Owens (Cincinnati), Ken Reaves (Norfolk State), Freddie Summers (Wake Forest), Charlie Stukes (Maryland State College), and Jimmy Raye (Michigan State). After seeing too many Black quarterbacks switched to defense, Black sportswriter Sam Skinner complained, "That's the trouble with Negro quarterbacks. They're blessed with this thing called speed. So they wind up somewhere else. A white boy comes along, he can only run the 100 in 11 seconds, so they have to let him play quarterback."

There is a name for this phenomenon—moving people of color into specific roles. It's called *stacking*. By the late 1960s, pro football looked as if Bull Connor was forced to pick an integrated team. All the so-called thinking positions down the middle of the field—quarterback, center, middle linebacker, and free safety—were reserved for white players. The positions that required speed and reaction were reserved for Black players. In a study conducted by *Sports Illustrated*, they showed that on one pro football Sunday in 1967, no Black quarterback or center played, and only three of the thirty-two offensive guards were Black. At linebacker, the numbers were just as bad. Only three of the forty-eight starters were Black. The middle linebacker, the so-called quarterback of the defense, had to wait until 1967, when Willie Lanier became the first Black starting middle linebacker. Walter Highsmith was the first Black starting center in 1968, the same year Marlin Briscoe became the first modern Black quarterback to start a pro game.

No position or player mattered more than the Black quarterback. When combined, the two words, *Black* and *quarterback*, hold a significant meaning in American society. They tell a story of race relations in post–World War II America. Understanding the history of the making of the Black quarterback is as much of a story about prejudices as it is promises of a future free from discrimination.

Both born in the Jim Crow South in 1955, Vince Evans and Doug Williams came into the world at the dawn of the modern civil rights movement. The Supreme Court overturned separate but equal in education with the *Brown* decision in 1954. Buses were next, then Black Americans would take their fight to restaurants, employment, housing, social rights, and the vote. In the meantime, as sports became more integrated after the Dodgers signed Jackie Robinson in 1945, and then Kenny Washington, Woody Strode, Marion Motley, and Bill Willis reintegrated pro football in 1946, activists fought for Black men to field leadership positions in sports—like coaches, managers, general managers, and of course the ultimate position of authority: pro quarterback.

As the civil rights movement progressed, the absence of a Black leader on the professional gridiron grew increasingly conspicuous. As a Maryland economics professor wrote about the position in 1958, "There have been great strides in abolishing barriers in football [but] it seems . . . one particular spot appears to be reserved 'for whites only'—the quarterback. No doubt [this is due to] rationalizations about confidence in leadership and the necessity for harmony. When a pro team or even a major college team entrusts the signal calling and team leadership to a colored boy, then integration can be said to have been firmly established." A decade later, sociologist Dan D. Dodson observed, "Sports and exhibitionistic professions such as show business have been used in this country for years by minority groups to come into the mainstream of American life." He continued, "What is new today is the feeling on the part of the Negro leadership that they are going to come into the mainstream—not in the stereotyped job but in the jobs that require intelligence." As Dodson put it, "The black players in professional football in the past have held the beef and brawn jobs, like being linemen, and now they want to demonstrate intelligence and nimbleness. And they are doing it in the name of race." Seeing a Black pro quarterback signaled to White America that beyond the field, Blacks could lead and whites would willingly follow. That's what Williams and Evans symbolized.

When Doug Williams and Vince Evans marched onto Soldier Field on September 30, 1979, they represented so much more than themselves. "Historians will remember Sunday's game for a reason other than who wins and loses," one reporter predicted. "When two black men start and not much of a fuss is raised about it, the National Football League will show it is, by one yardstick, in better shape than ever before." For this historian, the game measures as one of the most monumental contests in NFL history. It was a promissory note from professional football that one day things would change in the game and in society.

CHAPTER 1

In early December 1942, the ranks of UCLA football fans were engaged in a long debate about quarterbacking. If Kenny Washington and Bob Waterfield played on the same team, they wondered, who would you start as your quarterback? It was a tough hypothetical question, because the two stars had quarterbacked under different offensive systems. Waterfield was UCLA's current quarterback and played in the T formation, and a few years earlier, in 1939, Washington had led the team to national prominence as a single-wing quarterback. (In a single-wing offense, the quarterback often runs with the football, putting less emphasis on passing.) While Waterfield had star potential, many believed Washington was the greatest player to ever lace up cleats on the West Coast. A year removed from the attack on Pearl Harbor and in a city where the threat of a Japanese assault still felt very real, it may have seemed a trivial question. But it was a conversation that many fans and coaches would continue to have about other quarterbacks without admitting to themselves what they were really asking. Because in the end, this was not a question about skills and character; this was a question about color. Waterfield was white, and Washington was Black.

In 1942, UCLA head coach Babe Horrell thought he had the answer when asked the question by a local reporter. Horrell had coached both quarterbacks, as well as one other athlete whose potential at the position he had quickly dismissed: Jackie Robinson. After giving it a moment's thought, he went with his current quarterback, Waterfield. Why? Speed. While Washington could throw the ball farther than anyone in the history of college football, Horrell would rather have the ball in his hands as a running back or a flanker. Waterfield was a passer. Washington was an athlete. It was an innocent answer, but a choice that countless coaches over the years would make. Put the Black guy in a position where he could be a natural athlete. Put the white guy where he can think and lead. Few could have known it at the time, but switching from the single wing to the T formation had devastating consequences for the Black quarterback.

THE BLACK MAN AND THE T

POLITICAL PRESSURE BROUGHT KENNY WASHINGTON INTO PRO ball. Although the NFL had started out integrated in 1920, a "gentlemen's agreement" kept the league segregated from 1933 to 1945. In 1946, however, when the lily-white Cleveland Rams moved to Los Angeles with the intent of playing in the Coliseum, Halley Harding, a local Black sportswriter, saw their move as an opportunity to score a point for integration. Once the Rams had signed a contract with the Coliseum to play their home games, Harding forcefully argued to city officials that because the stadium was a public facility with a nondiscrimination clause, the Rams would have to integrate or lose access to the stadium. The city agreed. The Rams conceded. To help the Rams in their search, Harding suggested Washington.

Although Washington was six years removed from his college glory days at UCLA, Harding's decision to push Washington as the first Black player to reintegrate the league was calculated. Kenny Washington was a quarterback. In the late 1930s at UCLA, flanked by Jackie Robinson and Woody Strode, the Black trio dominated the competition and dazzled the crowds with their athleticism and gracefulness on the field. As a Bruin, Washington played quarterback in the single-wing offense, that day's most popular set. Used by more than 90 percent of teams before 1940, in the single wing, the quarterback was more like a running back who would throw the ball. But he was still the leader of the team. On offense, he stood a few yards behind the center, like one would in today's shotgun offense, and had a fullback to his slight right; he also had an additional blocker lined up behind the right tackle, a tight end, and a receiver at the end of the offensive line. After the snap, he could hand the ball off to the fullback or throw a pass to one of his receiving options, but as the best athlete on the field, the quarterback usually found himself running forward behind his mass of blockers. With Washington taking the snaps, the Bruins also emphasized the deep ball. "Kenny was the greatest long passer ever," Jackie Robinson claimed. Known for his long bombs, Washington completed six passes over 60 yards, including a 66-yard touchdown to Jackie Robinson. In 1937, he broke the college record for the longest pass from point of throw to catch when one of his moon shots traveled 62 yards. When the Jim-Crowed NFL rejected his services in 1940, he continued to play football with the semipro Hollywood Bears, where he wowed crowds with his running and throwing abilities.

Understanding their limited options in 1946, the reluctant Rams leadership signed Washington. Unfortunately for Washington, the NFL had waited too long to give him his break. Those seasons in semipro football tore up his knees, and he needed offseason surgery before the 1946 season. Still recovering, he'd have to navigate the rough terrain of a racial pioneer on bad knees. The transition from the Hollywood Bears to the Rams as a quarterback would be even tougher, because when the NFL initially pushed Washington away in 1940, the game also changed. The Rams had no use for a single-wing quarterback. Like most pro teams, they ran a modern T formation.

Before it had a name, the T formation was just the "regular" offense that most teams used in the early days of football. In the T, the quarterback lined up directly behind the center and had three running backs behind him in a straight line, forming a T. Back then, the term *quarterback* had nothing to do with throwing ability, because until 1906, forward passes were not permitted. The quarterback got its name because he was a quarter between the center and the halfback. Teams ran the T because it was practical. Before the advent of the forward pass, the first player to touch the ball after the snap could not advance it, so they snapped the ball to the quarterback, and then he handed it off to one of the backs behind him.

Once the rules changed to allow the forward pass, the game and formations quickly shifted. Led by innovators like Pop Warner, who coached the Carlisle Indians, teams started to employ the single wing and variations of that set, like the double wing. The quarterback in the wing became a dual threat on the field as a passer and a runner. Most teams that ran the wing depended on size up front and speed in the backfield. Coaches started to look for the biggest players they could find to block for all their running plays. The game was played in a small space that formed around the offensive line and seldom used the whole field. Once players got to the pros, however, the single wing ran into problems. Plays of mass and might worked at the college level, but at the pros, when the defenders were bigger and stronger, offenses struggled to generate big chunk plays.

For most of its early history, pro football offenses were stagnant and dull, because few teams employed the pass as their main weapon, but in the 1930s, the league made changes to help the quarterback. First, they allowed the quarterback to throw the ball from anywhere behind the line of scrimmage. Prior to 1933, he had to be 5 yards behind the line, and while most quarterbacks dropped that far back anyway, lifting the restrictions allowed for more mobility like rollouts and bootlegs. In addition, the league decreased the size of the ball by two inches. This gave the quarterback better grip and control to throw the ball farther and with more accuracy. And finally, the league added inbound lines for where a ball had to be placed after it went out-of-bounds. Placing these lines 10 yards away from the out-of-bounds line opened play even more. Once teams got comfortable with the rules, the forward pass took off. By the mid-1930s, if a team didn't have a top quarterback, they weren't going to win a championship.

In 1940, the game changed even more when Coaches Clark Shaughnessy and George Halas reintroduced the T at the college and pro levels. Shaughnessy fashioned himself a scientist of the game and believed football should be wide open on offense, use the whole field, and rely on speed and deception. No longer should coaches just depend on big brutes; they needed nimble brainy guys too. According to football analyst Doug Farrar, Shaughnessy "did more to establish concepts that are still seen today than anybody else." In the mid-1930s, noticing that Halas and the Bears were struggling in their T to generate offense, Shaughnessy, who coached football at the University of Chicago, offered Halas help, which Halas gladly accepted. Shaughnessy would spend all day working on formations, then come to Halas with a full briefcase bearing gifts of new plays. During summers, Shaughnessy would even send his wife away because he would rather fool around with Halas and the T. He kept the basic concepts the same. The quarterback was directly behind the center with three backs lined up behind him, but then the coach added more creative twists. Shaughnessy put a man in motion so the quarterback could read the defense better, he added more feints and deceptions from the handoff from quarterback to running back, added an end split farther from the offensive line, and emphasized that teams should pass more. The T just needed proof of concept.

In 1940, Shaughnessy packed up, headed west, and implemented his T at Stanford. With his new T, and a small, brainy quarterback named Frank Albert, Stanford caught western America by surprise and rattled off nine straight wins, including a 1941 Rose Bowl victory over Nebraska. During that same 1940 season, with Shaughnessy's T concept, Coach Halas and his Bears won the NFL championship, concluding the season with a 73–0 shellacking over Washington. The modern quarterback was born.

Unlike the single wing, the T formation's success depended on the quarterback's brain and arm. The T quarterback had to master the feints to the running backs, he had to turn his head quickly to assess the defense to find an open receiver, he had to call the plays, he needed to know everything each offensive player was supposed to do, and he had to know what the defense would do to counter their plays. Or as Shaughnessy said, "They are fakers, deceptive, quick reacting type. They are smart, thoughtful, courageous, and never get rattled. They look for opportunities, recognize them." No longer was he just the best athlete lining up behind the line and taking a snap like he had done in the single wing; he now had to be the smartest man on the field too. "The T is a great formation," one college coach put it in 1946, "if you have the material, but without a brainy quarterback who can pass, you are playing under a handicap."

The Bears' Sid Luckman was that man. The Columbia-educated intellectual became the early prototype of what a modern quarterback should be. He was smart, agile, and accurate. With Luckman leading the show, the Bears won the NFL championship three of the next four seasons, and Luckman was named MVP in 1943.

In a copycat game, teams at all levels of play and from across the country soon implemented the T. By 1945, it was estimated that 90 percent of colleges were using Shaughnessy's version of the T, and by 1952, every NFL team ran the T after the Steelers stopped being the last holdout. Very quickly, innovators started to tinker with the T. In college came the split T, then the winged T, and in the pros, Paul Brown removed a running back from the backfield and put him as a receiver and split the other two backs wide behind the quarterback. With quarterback Otto Graham leading the way, Brown's Cleveland teams revolutionized the game of football. In what became known as the pro-style offense, his teams thrashed the AAFC, winning four championships in the 1940s, and when they merged into the NFL in 1950, they won championships in 1950, 1954, and 1955. The success of the Bears and Browns, and more specifically Luckman and Graham, centered the T quarterback as the most important person on the field—and in all of sport.

Could a Black man run the T formation? While nobody openly asked this question in the early 1940s, people wanted to know. This was a query about what Americans thought of race, brains, and brawn that would shape the course of the history of the position. When the new T came into vogue, American sports fans were coming to terms with a trope about Black athletes. The success of Jesse Owens at the 1936 Olympics solidified a thought that had been percolating in white minds for quite some time: Black people were fast. But what explained Black speed? Was it nature or nurture? Some well-intentioned (though misguided) whites suggested that it was nurture. The migration from the South to the North gave guys like Owens (from Alabama to Ohio) an opportunity to leave the cotton fields, go to school, and get real athletic training. Then there were the not-so-well-intentioned whites, some say downright racists, that tried to say the Black athlete had natural speed. All brawn and no brains. Some believed the Black athlete acquired speed because they had different muscles, perhaps extra muscles. Some said they were even less developed in evolution. Some used the theory of "survival of the fittest" and slavery to explain Black speed, while others said that enslavers bred the enslaved to be big. Whatever the case, the stereotype of Black speed stuck. In football, this meant that if you had one on your team—and very few college teams had Black players in the 1930s and 1940s—you gave him the ball. Before the advent of the modern T, the Black athlete could be a single-wing quarterback like Kenny Washington because the offense got the ball in his hands primarily as a runner, and when he passed, he would just chuck it deep. He was not a thinker, just an athlete.

In the pros, in 1946, for a moment, Washington tried to be the guy when the Rams converted him to a T quarterback to back up Bob Waterfield. Understanding Washington had bad knees that would not allow him to play receiver, Coach Adam Walsh reasoned, "We have plays that would allow Washington to pass from either halfback or from fullback. We also have plays that allow the quarterback to carry the ball. . . . But because the quarterback does a minimum of running, and seldom gets mixed up in close formation play where he is liable to take a battering, I am going to try Washington at that position until I see how his knees that were operated on recently hold up." With limited experience with the T and busted knees, the prognosis for Washington was bad. Here he was, a racial pioneer, the most popular Black player in football, the one who was supposed to be the best Black player ever, and now the football world waited and watched to see if Washington could master the thinking position.

To be sure, Washington failed at the T, but this was not a fair fight. And it had nothing to do with race. He would have had an easier time beating Joe Louis than trying to conquer the T. Even before he tried to be a T quarterback, Washington had his struggles. For one, the single wing did not rely on precision passing. Washington could throw the ball long but lacked touch and accuracy on intermediate passes. According to his college teammate Jackie Robinson, "He threw the ball so hard that receivers just couldn't catch it." Of course, this would be a stereotype the Black quarterback continued to hear. Doug Williams heard it. Vince Evans heard it. Every Black quarterback heard it. The stereotype just sounded worse when it came from a white coach or a white reporter, and not Jackie Robinson. As time went by and white coaches made conscious decisions to keep Black men from the position, it meant that the Black quarterback used his natural athleticism to throw, but never put in the hard work to learn how to be a real quarterback.

For Washington, trying to learn the T would take more than passing skills. He needed a crash course in football speak. Washington told the press the T was like learning Chinese. He didn't know how to line up under center, he couldn't figure out the feints, and worst of all, the press and his teammates mocked him as a signal caller. The Black man could not get the signals right. "When the Rams come out of the huddle the quarterback rattles off a series of code words that tell certain men what to do. Kenny's teammates got a big laugh out of Washington when, to show his confusion, he inserted punctuation marks into his signal calling: 'Ready, 75, 14, period, 26, down, comma, semicolon, right." His teammates might have laughed at his self-mocking joke, but the perception of the unthinking Black quarterback was no laughing matter.

Regardless of his early struggles, Washington became the first Black quarterback to throw and complete a pass in the modern NFL, when he went 1 of 7 for 19 yards in the opening game against the Eagles on September 29, 1946. Given more time at the position, he could have been a great T quarterback. But the Rams did not want to spend more time teaching Washington to play quarterback. The Rams soon switched him to fullback, where he could use his athleticism. Reflecting on the old debate about the two quarterbacks, Waterfield and Washington, a writer stated, "today little green-eyed grid followers of the two former UCLA heroes now with the Rams can traverse their respective paths in comparative peace and safety for the argument has been settled, once and for all." First one up, first one down. Who was next?

WILLIE THROWER

TWO YEARS AFTER THE RAMS SWITCHED WASHINGTON, THE New York Yankees of the AAFC signed Tom Casey, a single-wing quarterback from Hampton, but switched him to the secondary, and the following year, they signed Nevada's Alva Tabor to play as their T quarterback, but Tabor never saw action in the 1949 regular season. In 1951, the Browns became the first team to draft a Black T quarterback when they selected Syracuse's Bernie Custis in the eleventh round, but after one day, Paul Brown switched him to safety, telling him, "Bernie, we've decided you'll fit in best on the Cleveland Browns as a free safety. You've got the speed." Instead of facing the indignity of being switched, Custis headed to Canada to play quarterback in the CFL. For those waiting to see if a Black quarterback would ever get a chance to play professional quarterback, they would have to wait until 1953, when the Bears signed Willie Thrower from Michigan State.

Thrower had played sparingly at MSU, but with his large hands that made a football look like an orange and his moon shot throws that made one Lansing scribe rave, "Willie can pitch a football with the ease of a kid eating ice cream," the Bears and George Halas decided to take a chance in making a Black man a T quarterback.

Thrower had potential, but he didn't have time. Pro quarterbacks took at least three to five years to develop into stars, and no team was going to give a Black man that long to learn. The media knew there was a long learning curve, but it didn't stop them from jumping all over Thrower early. "They are shoving things at Willie pretty fast," a reporter noted. "I think at this stage he is just a little confused, but they told us he was getting along well."

Despite his early struggles, Thrower made the team and made his first appearance against the San Francisco 49ers on October 18, 1953. Coming off the bench, Thrower gave his team a spark, bringing the Bears to the 49ers' 15-yard line. Although Thrower skillfully moved the Bears to the red zone, Coach Halas reinserted starter George Blanda to lead the team to a touchdown. *I know I would have gotten the team in for that touchdown*, Thrower thought. Thrower only played in one more game before being cut at the end of the season.

While today, many remember and celebrate Thrower as the first modern Black quarterback—it's actually Kenny Washington— what was said and remembered during his time is just as important to the story of the Black quarterback. On the one hand, it was clear Black fans understood the meaning of the moment. "A lot of blacks from around Chicago went to the games then and I remember them cheering when I went out there," Thrower recalled. He continued, "I think a lot of them remember me from playing on a national championship team at Michigan State and they were excited and proud to see me step in. They knew I was a passer supreme." On the other hand, his white teammates looked at his Blackness and assessed he did not have what it took. All brawn and no brains. Years later, team captain George Connor told a reporter, "In the excitement and pressure of a game—even an exhibition game—the complex assortment of Bear plays froze in his mind. He was hopeless as a quarterback." He continued to explain, "I found that out that first time the Papa Bear used him in an exhibition." According to Connor, Thrower took too long to call the plays, and he seemed unsure of himself. "'I think I'll call,' began Willie, groping frantically for a play to call. We waited and waited until I began to worry that we'd be penalized for unnecessary delay. Then he blurted out, 'I think I'll call 43 left on 3.'" Eventually, Connor went to Coach Halas and told him, "We need a new quarterback. This one has just exhausted his repertoire." Connor continued to tell this story, but as years went by, he switched the game in the story from a meaningless exhibition contest to the match against the 49ers that everyone considers the first time a Black quarterback played in the NFL. Once again, Thrower's life was adapted to fit an unkind stereotype, rather than the other way around.

CHARLIE "CHOO CHOO" BRACKINS

In the summer of 1955, just as Vince Evans and Doug Williams were coming into the world, Charlie "Choo Choo" Brackins tried to make his own breakthrough. Drafted in the sixteenth round by the Green Bay Packers, the Black two-time all-American from Prairie View A&M was forecast by some pundits to "become the first full-time Negro quarterback in the modern history of professional football." At six foot two and 200 pounds, the T formation quarterback had the tools and makings of a professional quarterback: height, leadership, arm, brain. As one white writer put it, "Brackins has tremendous qualifications for the role of 'first quarterback.' In addition to his mechanical skill—throwing, punting, and running, Brackins is highly courageous and, according to scouts, an 'excellent team leader.'" Black sportswriter Bill Nunn Jr. described Brackins as a "clever quarterback who ran and passed the opposition dizzy, can do everything with a football but eat it." Packers coach Liz Blackbourn once said Brackins had a better arm than Bart Starr. But as Brackins discovered in just a matter of months, he had one disqualifying deficiency—his skin color.

When Brackins entered his first professional training camp, everything seemed to be headed in the right direction. Within weeks, he surpassed two other quarterbacks on the depth chart to win the backup role behind Tobin Rote. Brackins played well in training camp, throwing for 180 yards in an intra-squad game. He also saw action in all six preseason games, showing enough promise for Packers fans to envision a future with a Black quarterback. Unfortunately, the team saw other possibilities.

Brackins quickly ran up against the old stereotypes that would typecast Black athletes into specific roles for their speed. Although only a few Black players had made NFL rosters at that time—the Packers had three the previous season—Black players' immense athletic talent was undeniable. The previous year, despite being a small percentage of the league, Black skill players led the NFL in three of the eight offensive categories. This meant that for Black quarterbacks like Brackins, the league would value their brawn and not their brains. During the regular season, he punted, they tried him at wide receiver, but he saw little action at quarterback. His only playing time at quarterback came during a 41–10 drilling by the Cleveland Browns on October 23. Backed up on his own 10-yard line, against the best defense in the league, he went 0 of 3.

On November 8, the Packers waived Brackins for undisclosed reasons. "Well, Brackins," his coach said, "I think we've given you an equal shot to make the football team. You don't seem like you've arrived!" A frustrated Brackins pleaded that he had only played in one game, a contest against the defending champions, where he had to battle their top defense while being buried near his end zone. That was hardly a fair shot. When asked for a comment after Brackins was let go, Coach Blackbourn cryptically claimed, "There are certain things you can't talk about in public. All I can tell you is it had nothing to do with his football."

Nearly a quarter of a century later, Coach Blackbourn told the truth. It had nothing to do with Brackins's brain or brawn, but it had everything to do with his Blackness. "He wasn't bad until he made the ball club," the coach claimed. "But then he went hot dog on me. He ordered a lot of stuff at the tailor; he acted up pretty good." Blackbourn continued, "The night before the Bear game Borden and Switzer [Nate Borden and Veryl Switzer, two Black Packers players] reported him as going out all hours. That's when I let him go. I knew he was getting a little hot doggish and his play was running down a little bit." *Hot dog*, of course, was a coded phrase. It meant that Brackins did not know his place. In other words, Charlie "Choo Choo" Brackins was too Black to lead a team. During the civil rights movement, it would be hard to convince any Black kid growing up in America that they'd have a chance to play quarterback at the highest level.

CHAPTER 2

Born on August 9, 1955, to Robert and Laura Williams, Douglas Lee Williams came into the world at the dawn of the modern civil rights movement. His dreams of playing quarterback sprouted in a rural community so small, he once put it, "it doesn't have a name." He and his friends couldn't hang out on the corner because "there was only one road running straight through." So sure that folks would not even know where he was from, Williams often told people he was raised in Zachary, Louisiana, the closest town to Chaneyville.

Chaneyville wasn't a city. Chaneyville wasn't a town. Chaneyville was a community, a fiercely independent Black community whose origins can only be told in oral histories from the Black elders who held on to memories of a prideful place built to protect them from prejudice. This is where Doug Williams, the Black Hope, was made.

The area known as Chaneyville is a rural community that sits roughly twenty-five miles northeast of Baton Rouge. In the late 1700s, white enslavers from the Carolinas and Georgia settled that territory to grow cotton. Outside government had little influence over rural Baton Rouge. The large plantation owners, the Drehs, Kellys, Norwoods, Carneys, and the Chaneys, ruled. By the 1850s, the area was half free whites and half enslaved Black people.

After emancipation, Black families like the Squares, Thompsons, Franklins, Moores, Shanklins, Barbers, Whitleys, Matthewses, Dyers, Davises, Wallaces, and Williamses stayed around the plantations they were once forced to labor on. Like many newly freed people, Black folks in that area defined freedom by their ability to control land, protect their families, and finally receive proper educations. In short, they wanted to be as independent from the former enslavers as possible. Landownership would be central to this quest for independence, but the combination of President Andrew Johnson's administration and white violence ended most hope of Black landownership in Louisiana. By the end of the decade, only two hundred Black families in Louisiana received land throughout the Southern Homestead Act. During Reconstruction, only one Black family in the Chaneyville area owned land, siblings Buckner and Sarah Florida.

In the meantime, those who stayed had two options to work the land: tenant farming or sharecropping. At first, the former attracted most Black families, as they hoped that through hard work and cooperative weather, paying a predetermined rent or lease amount to the white landowner would be more profitable and provide a bit more independence than sharecropping. As tenants, they didn't have to worry about the trap of perpetual debt that came with sharecropping, the exploitive system most Black Southerners had to settle for. In sharecropping, the sharecropper agreed to split all his profits with the landowner fifty-fifty. A typical sharecropper would work from 50 to 250 acres of land, but to do that, they needed supplies, food for their families, clothes, work tools, and a mule if they could get one. That all added up to debt, and debt came with white control. The tenant farmer could leave after his lease was up. The sharecropper had to work off his debt. If he chose to escape, the local authorities were ready to nab him, throw him in jail, and force him to work off his court costs and fines as part of the racially exploitive convict lease system.

No matter what system they chose, the white man was there to cheat them at the scales. Longtime Chaneyville resident Johnnie Hughes remembered going to the scales in Zachary with his grandfather George Hughes:

> He was selling cotton at Zachary. He taught me how to read the cotton scale. We went in there where you read the scales. The man was weighing Grandpa's cotton, and he says, "Will, you got about 700 pounds of cotton." I said, "Grandpa, the scale says 900." The old man pulled his glasses off, he rubbed his glasses, and said, "Let me check. That's right, it really was on 9." He was going to take 200 pounds from Grandpa because my grandpa couldn't read. After that, Grandpa made sure I went so I could read the scale to him.

Hughes was lucky that the clerk only put on his glasses instead of pulling out his pistol. Countless Black men lost their lives in the South trying to make sure they were not cheated at the scales.

Despite the obstacles, the Black families in the area had no intention of leaving. The white families had no intention of leaving either. Each formed their own communities. The white families that stayed closest to the old plantations formed Pride. Other white families moved a bit farther and created Central. The more well-to-do white families moved even farther away and established Zachary. The Black families that stayed on the white-controlled land created their own community around three old white plantations: the Norwoods', the Carneys', and the Chaneys'. Either out of benevolence or to make sure cheap Black labor stayed around the area, or a bit of both, the white landowners gifted land to the local Black residents. In 1886, James J. B. Chaney gave a small portion of his land for a school, which the residents named Chaneyville. A few years later, in 1890, James Carney gave a small portion of his land to a Black family so they could build a church, which they called Philadelphia. The church ran the K–6 one-room school, and thus these two places became the center of the community. And that's how Chaneyville was born. There was no post office or any other government recognition that this was an incorporated town. It became a community named after its most important institution, the school.

The Black families in Chaneyville prided themselves on independence. They built their school. They built their homes. They built their roads. As one elder put it, "They wanted to build a community of working and industrious people who would work and make their living on their own, and stay, and build the community up. They strictly believed in farming. No public work. They were interested in the children going to school. Becoming producing, self-supporting."

True independence and autonomy in that Black community rested on landownership. They knew the exploitive nature of sharecropping and how it made them subordinate to local whites. Back then, the elders would go around telling the young men to save their money and buy land. As a youngster, Doug's dad heard that message, and then he instilled it in Doug. "My daddy told me, 'Always own land. Nothing is more valuable,'" Doug said during his playing days. After the quarterback made it to the pros, he came back and did just that. He built his parents a new home on their property, he bought eight acres across from their house and built a $120,000 house, and then he bought another twenty-three acres. Doug was the wildest dreams come true of many generations of Black men in Chaneyville.

THE GREAT BLACK HOPE

Most families in Chaneyville only had the basics. This included Doug Williams and his family. His dad, a World War II veteran with a bad back and swollen joints, worked construction until his disabilities forced him to stop, and his mom was an orderly at a local hospital and a cook for the local schools. By the time Doug was a teen, his father was on government disability, so they had to get by on the twenty dollars a week his mom brought home and money from his dad's government assistance. They had a small three-bedroom house with six kids to feed (they had two other children who were adults living outside the house). Doug shared a room with three of his brothers, where two sets of bunk beds were crammed next to each other. They had hand-me-down clothes, and although they never missed a meal, the family was on welfare, receiving powdered eggs, milk, and whatever the government called their meat. To Doug and his siblings, it looked like horsemeat. A luxury was a "jam sandwich," or two pieces of bread jammed together.

Ironically, the poverty and years of neglect from the white power base in Baton Rouge helped build Doug's arm strength. Until he was fourteen, his house did not have running water. Doug and his siblings had to take turns getting water from a well to meet his family's basic needs. This also meant there was no indoor plumbing. Each morning, Doug would have to take out the slop jar to dump it out in the outhouse. To avoid splashing the excrement on himself, he held the slop jar as far away from his body as possible. The technique protected his body from the splash but also made him stronger. According to Williams, the combination of throwing rocks from the unpaved gravel roads and years of having to carry pails of water from the well into their house built up his arm and shoulder strength. "I really don't know for sure what it is about Louisiana," Williams once said. "Maybe it's all the gravel roads. When I was a kid, I was always picking up stones and throwing them at mailboxes, stop signs, freight trains . . . I may have even broken a few windows."

By high school, he could whip a football in the air 70 yards. One bomb he threw against Cottonport his senior year had fans debating whether it went 70, 73, or 78 yards in the air. There wasn't a level of football—high school, college, or pro—where onlookers weren't awed by the way his pretty passes floated in the air until dropping at the right time into a receiver's hands.

But even Doug's miraculous arm couldn't meet all his family's needs. As one Chaneyville elder recalled, "No electricity. If the good Lord didn't let his moon shine at night, and we couldn't see any stars, we had to know where we were to make any headway at night." The darkness also brought trouble. Doug recalled, "There was great fear in our community, especially at night. My mom always preached to us, 'You'd better be here by night fall.' Walking the road was dangerous." Danger also meant the Klan, who on Friday nights burned crosses at the end of the roads surrounding the community. Black elders like Doug's father would chase them away and put out the flames, but the message was sent; Blacks need not go beyond their own community.

This type of violent racial intimidation had existed throughout Jim Crow, but the threats and appearance of the Klan started to intensify after World War II, when Black veterans, like Doug's dad, came home and started to demand their rights. During the war, Black Americans fought for a double V—victory abroad and victory at home—and in the proud Chaneyville community, this had a profound impact. Violence and Jim Crow laws had stripped the vote away from nearly 95 percent of Black Louisiana voters, but in post–World War II America, Black Americans demanded their full constitutional rights. Chaneyville saw an upswing in registered voters, and to make sure folks could pass the racist literacy test adopted to screen out Black voters, the community formed a voter registration league. As the community pushed for the vote for adults, they pushed for better education for their children. To this proud Black community, better education didn't mean integration, it meant equal education and the same opportunities that white students had.

The school was the heart of the community. The community built the first two Chaneyville schools (1886 and 1924) by hand because the East Baton Rouge School Board denied them funds for a new school. Finally, in 1949, the local school board built the community a new school that for the first time went to the twelfth grade. The modernity of the school caught many by surprise. So few houses had indoor plumbing that when the Chaneyville school put in flushing toilets in the 1950s, students did not know how to use them. In fact, as their principal remembered, many were so scared to mess them up, they went on the floors. The Williams kids were part of the first generation of Chaneyville residents to have the chance to complete a high school education.

Sports were a big part of the community. It started with baseball. That's the game the men played. Since the men played the game, the boys did too. In the independent-minded Chaneyville community, landowner Len Whitley built a baseball field on his property, Whitley Park, so the townsfolk would have a place to play. Chaneyville had their own all-Black team and played other all-Black teams from around the area. Until his body quit on him, Doug's dad, Robert Sr., was the star catcher of the team. His mom was even better at softball. Their dad loved baseball, so the Williams boys loved baseball. "When I was real young, I liked to go out in the woods all day," Doug reflected. "But once I started playing ball, that's what I wanted to do all the time."

At home, poverty forced the Williams boys to be creative with their athletics. Balls were a luxury. When they played baseball in the yard, they used a hardened berry, a cucklebug, as a ball and a mop handle as a bat. They used a clothes hanger and aluminum foil for a basketball hoop and a ball. As their mom remembered, "They would break things in my house. And if they ever had the luxury of having a real ball, they would play with that in the house too. They would get in the house and throw a football just as hard as they did outside."

Doug's older brother Robert Jr. was the best athlete in the family. He also happened to be Chaneyville High's first quarterback in 1959, when the school started their football program. But with no Black pro quarterbacks to look up to, he followed the path Black baseball stars lit. A hard-throwing right-hander who could hit 90 mph with his fastball, he took his pitching talents to Grambling after high school and compiled a 31–3 record, including 3 no-hitters, and led the team to four straight Southwestern Athletic Conference (SWAC) titles. After going 7–1 with a 1.30 ERA his senior year, the Cleveland Indians signed Robert to their farm system for $15,000. He topped out at Triple-A, when an arm injury derailed his career. Robert came back home to work as a teacher and a coach, and he taught Doug and his friends the finer points of the game.

Learning from Robert was a lesson in toughness. He taught by doing and through tough love. The ex-pro pitcher made the kids act as his catchers as he fired 90 mph fastballs at them. If they didn't want to catch those fireballs, "you had him to fight." With Robert as his teacher and the Dodgers' Don Drysdale as his idol, Doug grew into a top-notch pitcher. With long, lanky fingers, he could grip a ball and throw three different elite-level pitches; a fastball, a breaking ball, and an un-hittable curve. Starting at eight years old, when he was eligible for Little League ball, he played on all-Black teams until his senior year in high school. In one Little League playoff game, he played the maximum allowed fifteen innings and fanned all but one batter. As a college freshman playing for his American Legion team, he struck out seventeen of eighteen batters in one game, prompting one scout to call him the best prospect in America.

Baseball also happened to be Doug's first run-in with integration, giving him a stark reminder that he would never be just an ordinary player; he was a Black player. During his senior season, the local American Legion league finally integrated, and Doug joined two other Black players on the team. At one practice, he heard one of his white teammates say *nigger*, although the player apologized later. Until that moment, he had never been a minority in sports. He had grown up in an all-Black community. "Right then," he said, "I knew what I was up against." To make matters worse, the league played their games in Denham Springs, the home of the grand wizard of the KKK. The fans hurled racial vitriol at the young pitcher. This was his first introduction with racist fandom, but even back then, he would never back down. After one incident when a catcher for Denham Springs intentionally landed on him with full force trying to injure him, Doug plotted to exact revenge. Playing second base at that time, when the offending catcher attempted to slide while trying to steal, Doug slapped him across the face with his glove.

Despite his success on the diamond, Doug cut short his baseball career early. After his freshman year in college, his football coach, Eddie Robinson, gave him an ultimatum: baseball or football. Baseball, his older brother told him, was not worth his troubles. Doug Williams was a football player.

CHAPTER 3

On September 22, 1967, 7,500 fans jammed into Greensboro High School Stadium to witness local history. Thirteen years after the *Brown v. Board of Education* decision, Dudley High battled Grimsley High in the first contest between all-Black and all-white teams in the city. Although Dudley had a tradition of success, none of that mattered in previous years to white onlookers in Greensboro. Dudley was still Black, and thus white observers figured Dudley played inferior Black competition. Years of segregation blinded local whites to the reality of Dudley's superiority. Led by two touchdown runs from their Black quarterback, Stahle Vincent, Dudley defeated Grimsley 19–7. Vincent's touchdowns were not just touchdowns, however; they were touchdowns against white boys. As one reporter put it years later, "In many ways, that Dudley-Grimsley game represented a turning point, a high-water mark both for sports at Dudley and for athletic fulfillment among blacks in Greensboro."

A young Vince Evans wanted to be like the star football players from Dudley. Two of their quarterbacks, Kenneth Henry (Wake Forest) and Vincent (Rice), signed with big-time white schools. As a young kid, Vince dabbled in baseball and was an excellent high school hooper, but those sports never took hold. It was football that had his heart from the beginning. Comparing the movement of a football to a basketball and baseball, he simply said, "That's just beauty. It was always something special to me. It gave football almost a sort of mystique." Every Christmas, he received a new football. "It was the highlight of my year," he recalled. With those balls, he taught himself how to throw a tight spiral. "I would marvel at the way the ball went through the air, the spiral." Self-taught, he did not use the laces to guide his throwing, a fact that would continue to haunt him throughout his career.

Born on June 14, 1955, in Lancaster, South Carolina, to Robert and Reva Evans, Vincent Tobias Evans and his family moved to Greensboro, North Carolina, when he was still a toddler. They lived on the southeast side of town, the Black side. The second oldest of four boys, Vince grew up in a middle-class Black home to parents who were educators. Although segregated and chronically underfunded, Greensboro had a strong Black school system. The community took pride in the schools, seeing education as a means to combat the restraints of Jim Crow, and Dudley High School had a national reputation as one of the best Black schools in the nation. By the 1950s, every Black teacher had at least a BA, and 65 percent of those teachers also had a master's, including Vince's parents, who attended the all-Black North Carolina A&T. Along with A&T, Greensboro was home to Bennett College, a Black women's school with a strong reputation.

As educators, the Evanses worked in one of the few jobs that allowed Black economic advancement in Greensboro. As the city transitioned from agriculture to industry after Reconstruction, Black workers constituted 50 percent of all skilled workers in 1900, but by 1910, that number drastically dropped to 8 percent as the white power system excluded Black workers from the economic change. City ordinances also decreed that those Blacks that eventually found work at a factory were not allowed to work next to a white worker. By mid-century, 40 percent of all Black workers in Greensboro worked in personal service jobs with only 15 percent working in professional jobs, such as teaching.

The same caste system that worked to keep Blacks out of jobs in Greensboro limited their housing options. In 1914, an ordinance ruled that residents could not live on streets where a majority of another race lived. Although a court found that ordinance illegal, the law had its intended effect. Housing segregation remained until the late 1960s. By then, segregation hemmed Black residents into the southeast side by all directions. There was a highway to the north, state-owned land to the east, an industrial area to the south, and downtown to the west. With no room for expansion, that overcrowded section that composed 14 percent of the land in Greensboro held 26 percent of the population.

Due to redlining and racially restrictive covenants, most Black middle-class families who could afford better homes had to pay a premium for those houses. The ones who moved out experienced what was known as *blockbusting*, where a white homeowner sold their home cheap to avoid what they feared was impending integration, and then a white real estate agent turned around and sold the home to a desperate middle-class homebuyer at an exorbitant price.

Black housing options finally started to improve in 1958, when the city approved a new Black middle-class housing subdivision, Benbow Park. They also built commercial real estate featuring a brand-new Kroger supermarket. The white city leaders didn't do this out of benevolence. This came from bigotry. They sent a clear message to upward mobile Black residents: *Stay where you are.* Benbow Park stood out as a remarkable feat. The three hundred houses, built on one hundred acres of land, ranged from $11,000 to $16,000 and were brick with a choice between modern, colonial, or split-level designs. This is where Vince Evans grew up, and this is where his parents tried to raise him on a straight and narrow path.

Whereas Doug Williams came home at night for fear of the Klan, the Evanses feared their son would get trapped by street life. His strict parents made him come inside when it started to get dark. As a kid, he never understood why, but later in life, he appreciated the discipline. "Sometimes, I didn't understand it all, but all the kids who could stay out after the streetlights went on are still on the streets," he reflected. Evans avoided the pitfalls, but he remained close with many of his neighborhood friends, who wrote him from jail. A typical letter would read, "Vince, if I could do it all over again, I'd keep a clean nose, I wouldn't be guided by peer pressure." Years later, as a pro in Chicago, Evans worked tirelessly in his off time to make sure young Black kids would not fall into the same trap. One could often find him at the notorious Cabrini-Green housing projects, mentoring the youth.

Although his parents tried to keep him out of trouble, young Vince was rambunctious. The same attitude that let him put his head down and run through a linebacker made him feel invincible off the field. He frequently received spankings in elementary school for his bad behavior, where his teacher Mrs. Cundiff would "whip" him every day. When he came home from school, his father would take his turn. Once after being caught stealing, his father whipped him so much that Vince thought he "was a slave."

By ninth grade, the pressure of having to live up to the expectations of college-educated parents got the best of him. He ran away. A few days in a detention center helped set him straight. But it wasn't just crime his parents worried about. Greensboro was a rapidly changing city, and they wanted Vince to be prepared for a future where Jim Crow was no longer a barrier. His life would not be restricted by racial covenants, ordinances, and laws. Black people in Greensboro were making sure of that.

In 1954, Greensboro's education leaders positioned the city to be at the forefront of the modern civil rights movement. A day after the *Brown v. Board of Education* ruling, Greensboro became the first Southern school district to claim they would comply. Citing its reputation and place in history as an egalitarian city, and also noting that noncompliance would be the end of American democracy, the Greensboro school board voted 6–1 to follow the law of the land. The school superintendent, Benjamin Smith, whom many viewed as the leading thinker on education in the state, said, "It is unthinkable that we will try to abrogate the laws of the United States of America." While Greensboro was the first to say they would comply, they were one of the last cities to follow orders. Neither the city nor the state would fully obey the *Brown* decision until the federal government forced them to do so in 1971. This decision that led to a slow integration had a monumental impact on the city. As Black citizens fought for civil rights, Greensboro became a hub of the movement. This local activism prepared Evans to cross the moat of whiteness protecting the quarterback position.

From the beginning, most members of the school board and white parents fought the initial decision to integrate. Most board members reasoned that *Brown* simply meant that the school system could not discriminate and argued that the court did not say they had to integrate. Initially, they were not sure how that distinction would work, but they soon found their pathway to compliance without having to comply. Led by Governor Luther Hodges, North Carolina took a two-pronged approach to fighting integration. First, Governor Hodges took the control of the schools from the state and gave authority to the local cities and school boards. In his mind, this meant that the state could not get in trouble with the federal government over noncompliance. If a city wanted to integrate, they could on their terms. Second, if the federal government forced them to integrate, they gave the local school district the okay to completely close their schools. Under this plan, students would receive a voucher to attend a private school.

Worried that a complete rejection of integration would send the federal government after the state and their school boards, North Carolina leaders also believed they needed some sort of token integration. If only a few Blacks integrated, they reasoned, most white students would not be impacted, and the federal government would leave the state alone. In 1957, Greensboro became a city of token integration when the school board allowed six Black students to integrate. One Black student integrated a high school, and the other five went to an elementary school. The students and their parents received a constant barrage of intimidating racist vitriol and threats at school and at their homes, and they needed a police escort to go to school. By the next year, in 1958, only five Black kids were in an integrated school.

In 1959, after agreeing to allow Black children into the previously all-white Caldwell Elementary, the school board called every white parent to teach them how to properly apply for a transfer to another white school. When Caldwell was integrated, it no longer mattered, because no white student or teacher taught there. Just a few years later, Vince started school at the formerly all-white school with his all-Black classmates. In fact, it wasn't until junior high as a teenager at Aycock that Evans interacted with white students. In 1968, he was one of only 176 Black students surrounded by a sea of 940 white pupils. By this time, Greensboro was engulfed in a major struggle for civil rights.

On February 1, 1960, four college students from North Carolina A&T started a movement. One of the Greensboro Four, David Richmond, was a former standout athlete at the all-Black Dudley High and broke the school's high jump record the previous year. Like the other three students that joined him, Richmond had grown tired of the slow progress of integration. As a student athlete, Richmond knew firsthand of the limits and lies of separate but equal. "The opportunities for blacks in sports left something to be desired under the 'separate but equal' doctrine," he recalled. "Our facilities and equipment were inferior." Determined to change the ways of the South, the Greensboro Four marched into a Woolworth's, sat at a counter that had previously only served white patrons, ordered food, and refused to leave until they were served. This brave move sparked the sit-in movement of college students across the South and by April led to the creation of the Student Nonviolent Coordinating Committee (SNCC).

In Greensboro, business managers spent months trying to avoid integration—Woolworth's shut down so they didn't have to deal with the protests and lost $200,000 in business—but eventually, in July 1960, businesses agreed to open their counters to Black patrons. Just like with education, however, words and deeds were two different things. In 1963, disillusioned with the pace of integration, local Black college students started another mass demonstration. During these demonstrations, a local North Carolina A&T student, Jesse Jackson, got his start in protest politics when students tabbed him to help, because he was a popular quarterback. After months of protests, enough businesses pledged to desegregate and hire Blacks that the protests ended. The schools were next.

Unlike business leaders, white parents would not budge. The school district planned to avoid full integration as long as they could. In the summer of 1963, the school board only allowed 128 students to leave their previously all-Black schools. Two years later, after the federal government ruled that the city's school choice plan was in violation of Title VI of the Civil Rights Act of 1964, the school board reluctantly opened freedom of choice to all students. Unwilling to concede more than they had to, the board only opened enrollment for ten days in September. Even with that, the city refused to bus Black students to white schools. But the refusal to implement meaningful integration would not last long. In 1967, in *Green v. County School Board of New Kent County*, the Supreme Court ruled that a school system could not have freedom of choice if that choice operated to maintain segregation. Greensboro, which had eleven all-Black schools, five all-white schools, and only one thousand students integrated—only one white student went to a Black school—was put on official notice by the federal government that they had to integrate. The school board did as little as possible to integrate and had lost nearly a million dollars in federal funds because of their steadfast refusal to comply.

The year 1971 changed everything. In April, in *Swann v. Charlotte-Mecklenburg Board of Education*, the Supreme Court ruled that busing was a legal means to achieve integration. A week after the decision, the federal government ordered Greensboro to integrate. The new school semester started in just four months. To comply, schools had to have at least a 70/30 racial ratio in every school. That summer, the city went on a massive campaign to prepare parents and students for what was to come. With the school year nearing, on August 15, local leaders declared a "Public Sunday School" to emphasize the importance of tolerance and cooperation. Schools held open houses before the school year, which attracted more than thirty thousand nervous parents. As one student pointed out, it was the parents who needed this more than the students. "Students will make the change if parents stand behind them." Everyone was tense about how this would go. It was under this backdrop that high school sports played a lead role in the city.

Before integration, Dudley High School was the center of Greensboro's Black sporting world. "Everybody used the term

'down Dudley,'" one coach said. "If it didn't happen 'down Dudley,'" he concluded, "it just didn't happen in east Greensboro."
As with their textbooks and lab equipment, the sporting facilities at Dudley were separate and unequal. The gym was a small,
cramped place with brick walls sitting just eighteen inches from
the sidelines. After the *Brown* decision, when Dudley's PTA
complained about the inadequate facilities, the school board told
them to just shorten the court. Instead, the Black parents pushed
to use the gym at the all-white senior high. Without even looking at the calendar of events, the school board claimed that all
the gym times were full. But when the Black PTA demanded to
see a schedule, the school board knew their time was up. After all
these years, Dudley finally got to use the white gym. To maintain segregation, however, the school board built a brand-new
gym for Dudley.

The all-Black school sported generational talent like Curly Neal,
who went on to Harlem Globetrotters fame; Lou Hudson, who
starred at Minnesota and later with the Atlanta Hawks in the
NBA; and Charlie Sanders, who also attended Minnesota and then
played tight end for the Detroit Lions during his Hall of Fame
career. Of those segregated days, Hudson remembered, "I grew
up when athletics was not the way out. If it were, no one told me
about it. If you were a good athlete, there was a slight chance some
college would be interested in you. But recruiters didn't beat down
my door." Hudson never had a conversation with a white student
until he got to college. For Evans, however, his fate was different. With integration coming, he would be the Black kid on the
bus. He'd be the Black quarterback at the formerly white school.
He'd be the face of integration. Like every other Black quarterback
entering a white space, he'd be a symbol.

CHAPTER 4

Just days after the 1969 NFL draft, on the streets of Boston, the Boston Patriots' Black executive Rommie Loudd bumped into the Red Sox Black first baseman George Scott. Scott needed to know one thing. "They're not going to switch him?" Scott asked. *Him?* That was Onree Jackson, a Black quarterback out of Alabama A&M. Jackson stood six foot four and could launch the ball 70 yards with accuracy. Plus, he had good speed, but not great speed, with a 4.9 40-yard time, just slow enough that teams would not switch him. There were plenty of white guys who could run a 4.9 40. During training camp, when Jackson ran faster than expected, with a 4.8 40-yard time, one of his Black teammates jokingly shouted that Jackson had better watch out or the team was going to make him a cornerback. But Jackson was too big and slow for that. He was a pure passer. The Patriots' offensive coordinator, John Mazur, compared Jackson's quick release to Joe Namath's. Another scout observed, "Onree's just as accurate deep as he is short. He's already learned when to take something off the ball, when to flatten it out and when to lob it. I'm particularly impressed with his ability to pick out his receivers." Knowing all this, Loudd proudly told Scott, "He's a quarterback prospect all the way." A satisfied Scott shot back, "That's a change." Both Black men knew what was at stake. Picked in the fifth round in a draft that included five other Black college quarterbacks—Freddie Summers (fourth round, Browns), James Harris (eighth round, Bills), Mike Stripling (ninth round, Bengals), Paul Champlin (thirteenth round, 49ers), and Ray Stephens (fourteenth round, Rams)—many thought Jackson had a chance to be the first full-time Black quarterback. Loudd even proclaimed that Jackson "could be the Willie Mays of pro football." The Patriots cut him before the season started.

Why were Loudd and Scott so proud that the Black community finally had a pro quarterback? By the late 1960s, the Black quarterback represented hope to the community that equal opportunities awaited them. As journalist Doc Young once explained, "[James Harris] is very important, because he symbolizes the fight of the qualified Afro-American for equal employment opportunities, because he has been cannibalized by racists." When Black fans saw that a team cut the Black quarterback too early or switched him to another position, the reality that few Black Americans received fair chances in life hit home. And Black fans rarely sat idly by watching teams do their quarterbacks wrong.

POLITICS AND THE POSITION

In 1967, West Texas State's Hank Washington came close to being next, but he was too cocky. He had everything that it took to make it. He had the height and the arm, and he played in a pro-style offense. The six-foot-three Washington could reportedly toss the pigskin 90 yards. Like the old Black lawman Bass Reeves, Washington was a gunslinger. During his senior season, he threw nearly thirty times a game and amassed 2,017 yards with seventeen touchdowns, good for fourth overall for offense and fifth for passing in the nation. Those totals put him ahead of Heisman Trophy winner Steve Spurrier.

Washington could also lead Southern white teammates. Along with playing in Texas on an integrated team, he also participated in the North-South College All-Star game for the South, and for the first time, television viewers saw a Black quarterback lead Southern white men. One Black writer put matters starkly: "It seems we have learned quite well to play together, here at home, and in most cases the combination turns out to be a championship caliber. We seem to be able to die together, far from home, and to fight more effectively as integrated American units. Then when are we going to learn to live in peace together?"

Washington knew he had the goods. "The only thing that can stop me is pro football itself. I can do all the things they want a quarterback to do. The quick release is the difference between a passer and a thrower, and I can get rid of it quick. I can change plays at the line of scrimmage, and I have done it. And I can throw the football." And that was the problem according to pro football. He believed in himself.

A Black man insisting that he was a quarterback was too much for the pros, in an era in which Muhammad Ali shook the foundation of what whites thought Black gratitude and docility should be. The white football world wasn't ready for a Black quarterback who dared to believe in himself by simply insisting he was a quarterback. As one white scout said, "The kid has been cocky all through school. He has always said he won't play anywhere but quarterback." In the 1967 draft, teams drafted soccer players, basketball players, and sprinters, but not a Black quarterback. Unfortunately for Washington, although the New York Giants signed him after the draft, they never gave him a fair shot. "I think I got a raw deal somewhere down the line," Washington complained.

The racial politics of the moment were not lost on the Black press. Black America was itching for a Black man in a leadership position, and they thought Washington would be the man for the job. One writer complained, "How is it when a White player like Ol' Dizzy Dean sounds off, it is 'colorful.' When a Negro, Frank Robinson and now, young Hank Washington, makes it with confidence in his ability he 'has the wrong attitude' or 'he's too cocky'? Why the double standard?" The *Pittsburgh Courier*'s Bill Nunn Jr., wrote, "For you Hank Washington, football player, quarterback, Negro, the American promise of a young man moving ahead on his ability, hasn't been fulfilled." Washington died from cancer in 1971.

As the Black writers who protested Washington's raw deal noted, the Black quarterback represented the promise of civil rights and integration; if one had the mind and merit, nothing else mattered. A starting Black quarterback might seem unimportant in the grand scheme of the civil rights movement when Black protesters were being arrested, beaten, and even killed for fighting for equal rights, but as Black sportswriter Claude Harrison Jr. said about the lack of pro Black quarterbacks in the 1960s, "While this is no secret and no burning issue with the Negro fans, now that there are more important issues such as the Freedom fight, riots and the drive to defeat Barry Goldwater, it does bother me."

Tennessee State coach John Merritt perfectly understood that sentiment. At his school, from 1964 to 1967, Merritt worked with Eldridge Dickey, "the Lord's Prayer." On the football field, his powerful right wrist allowed his six-foot-two frame to reportedly hurl the ball as far as 100 yards. That was just with his right hand. Dickey could also throw accurately with his left hand up to 30 yards. That wasn't all. He had blazing speed, running 100 yards in 9.6 seconds. Running Merritt's pro-style offense at Tennessee State, under Dickey, the Tigers went 33–5, which included a twenty-four-game winning streak. All total, he threw for 6,628 yards and had 74 touchdowns on 430 completions, numbers that brough him into pro teams' sites and Black Americans' hope. And Merritt understood what Dickey meant to the rest of the community. With a clear vision in mind, Merritt once told a reporter, "To us, this has a larger meaning. Eldridge and I have never taken part in demonstrations or things like that—I'm a state employee and he goes to a state school. But we feel we owe something to our people. This is our way of making a contribution."

In preparation, Merritt made sure Dickey had the right temperament to represent the race. As Merritt put it, "Knowing how to play football isn't enough." In other words, he had to be more than just a great athlete, he had to be a person who could lead white men. He enrolled Dickey in public speaking classes and human relations courses and sent him to talk at banquets. The coaching staff spoke with him about his presence, including how to eat in public, his wardrobe, and how to talk about people from all walks of life. Merritt had his wife give Dickey lessons on etiquette, "teaching him little things about manners that a boy isn't likely to pick up, but which they'll notice in a minute if they are looking for something to criticize him for." Merritt also added a little something extra in his training. "We know that one of these days," Merritt told a reporter, "he will have to cuss out a white boy, and he must do it in the right way." There was no class for that skill on the Tennessee State campus. That lesson came directly from Merritt. The Oakland Raiders drafted Dickey in the first round but switched him to receiver. For Black fans, that wouldn't do.

BLACK POWER AND THE BLACK QUARTERBACK

THE PUSH FOR THE BLACK QUARTERBACK CAME AT A TUMULTUOUS time in the country, coinciding with what many dubbed the "long, hot summers" in American cities. From 1964 to 1967, there were more than one hundred racial rebellions in city streets. And in 1968, after the assassination of Martin Luther King Jr., there were one hundred more. Pro football played in cities that had some of the largest rebellions. From Detroit to Los Angeles, New York to Baltimore, Black Americans pushed back against the structural inequalities in housing, the economy, education, and policing.

Throughout the late 1950s and early 1960s, Black folks let it be known that they were willing to protest a football team en masse if they felt discriminated against. Thousands boycotted and protested at games featuring the Washington Redskins until they signed a Black player, and in Houston, Black fans boycotted the Oilers until they lifted their Jim Crow seating policies. Teams were keenly aware of the power of the Black buck. When the Raiders and Jets canceled a 1963 game in Mobile after Black players refused to play in a stadium with segregated seating, one newspaper wrote that "Negroes form a solid slice of the populace where pro football flourishes. They form an even more solid slice of the crowds that have been pushing the game ever upwards in attendance as the years pass."

The white football establishment considered all these things when deciding whether to sign a Black quarterback. In 1967, when the Giants signed Hank Washington, Larry Merchant, a columnist for the *New York Post*, wrote, "There's no doubt that the players and coaches are ready for a Negro quarterback. But it's going to have to be in the right situation, where he gets the right opportunity." Merchant opined that in a wrong situation, teams would risk "alienating your Negro community, which is an important community in every pro city." He further suggested, "With the racial tensions, it has to be handled with kid gloves. The Negro community itself might not give him the chance, might put too much pressure on everyone." In 1968, that's just what happened with Eldridge Dickey and Black Oakland.

Black people wanted Black representation. In a city like
Oakland, where there was a sizable Black population, with
revolutionary-minded Black organizations like the Black Panthers, they weren't going to stand by and watch Dickey being
played like a piano. In the 1968 draft, Al Davis and the Raiders
selected Dickey with the twenty-fifth pick, but never publicly
committed to playing him at quarterback. Of course, Dickey
would have been a long shot to play that position for the Raiders that year, because the team had the reigning MVP, Daryle
Lamonica, but that did not matter to Black fans. They had been
hearing about Dickey's greatness for four years. They wanted their
man to play. During his first training camp in July 1968, when
the Raiders switched him to receiver, a "black militant" group protested the Raiders. If the Raiders were not going to give Dickey
a shot at quarterback, then Black people would not support the
team. They promised to make it difficult for others to watch too.
This could have spelled problems for the Raiders.

The Oakland Coliseum sat in a predominantly Black neighborhood, and Oakland was the home of the Black Panthers. If
the Black militants decided to protest just months after riots
ripped through the area after the assassination of Martin Luther
King Jr., the season might be finished before it started. But Davis
refused to give in. He told the protesters, "A pro football team
is not a democracy, it's a dictatorship." He let them know, "This
organization can't be pressured. We didn't draft him number one
for love and affection . . . we reserve the right to play him where
we think he can do the most good."

For his part, Dickey also helped ease tensions with a care-
fully worded public comment that displayed faith in the organization. "There is a Negro group in Oakland, I never spoke with
their leader," he told a Black reporter. "But they have had stories
in magazines since I have been out there about me not playing

quarterback. My feelings may have brought them down. I had to get them to understand that it takes time for something like this. How long they are going to wait, I don't know."

Although Dickey supported the Raiders' decision, his lack of opportunities to play his position left him mentally drained. Black players around the league tried to comfort him by telling him that this was one of the "obstacles" he had to hurdle. They wanted him to succeed just as badly as he wanted to succeed. It meant that much. Dickey saw himself as the Jackie Robinson of the NFL, and he knew he had to have patience. "I have set a goal and it may be an obstacle getting there," he told a Black writer when things were not going as planned. "But I have this goal to fulfill. Jackie Robinson had a goal, his was different from mine, but he had a goal." As Coach Merritt frequently reminded him, he had a cross to bear as the first Black quarterback, and he would have to make sacrifices for future Black quarterbacks. He just had to be patient and hope the Raiders would see the light.

For a brief time in the summer of '69, the Lord's Prayer delivered. In his first preseason game, he went 8 of 18 for 128 yards against the Cowboys. Oakland's Black fans came away from that game excited for the future. "That brother is going to be out of sight in the years to come," chirped one Black fan. On air, Bob Jones, a DJ of a local Black radio station, told his listeners, "He made a believer out of me," and played the cut, "You Made a Believer out of Me" by Ruby Andrews. Black folks in opposing cities showed their love too. When the Raiders traveled to Birmingham for a preseason game against the Chiefs, local Black fans came in droves to pay homage to the Lord's Prayer.

But unfortunately for Dickey, the Birmingham game also told a different story; it became an indictment on Dickey and the Black quarterback. Before the Birmingham game, a store owner hung a "No Nigger Quarterback in Alabama" sign on his window. On the field, things seemed bad too: Dickey had four turnovers (3 interceptions and a fumble). But despite the turnovers, Dickey put on a show, moving in and out of the pocket while looking for passing lanes. He even had a 20-yard touchdown run. After the game, Black college alumni, the Chiefs' Buck Buchanan and Ernie Ladd, who both starred at Grambling, carried him off the gridiron. Even Coach John Madden patted him on the back and told him he did a "good job." Little did Dickey know, Madden was grading on a curve.

That yo-yo style of play, with the scrambling and the freelancing, was not going to cut it for a Black quarterback in the pros. Madden wanted a classic stand-in-the-pocket passer, and after the game, he said, "We prefer our quarterbacks to drop back and throw the ball." Piling on, George Blanda took a shot at Dickey. "With a scrambler at the controls, there's no continuity in the offense, no great plays. They just don't move the ball systematically down the field. They don't search for receivers. To me it's just helter skelter high school football." Blanda wasn't done bludgeoning Dickey. He continued, "Pro football should be precision football—with all 11 men, not just one, doing their jobs to make a play work. This is the way the old Green Bay Packers used to do it. And that's the way they won." The Raiders had seen enough and soon switched him to receiver. They cut Dickey a year later, and by 1972, he was out of the league.

This was the quarterbacking world that a young Vince Evans and Doug Williams dared to dream they could be a part of. But the good news for them was that the NFL also had slowly started to open the door for the Black quarterback.

CHAPTER 5

In August 1972, twenty-five years after Jackie Robinson broke baseball's color barrier, just as Doug and Vince entered their high school senior seasons, hope stood on the horizon for Black quarterbacks. Five Black quarterbacks (James Harris, Joe Gilliam Jr., Craig Curry, Karl Douglas, and Johnnie Walton) battled for spots in the NFL. The chance for at least one breaking through seemed high enough that a *New York Daily News* columnist noted that 1972 could be pro football's Jackie Robinson moment. The column also included a sketch with the words *Another door opens* written in black on a white wall. Next to the wall stood an open door with the words *Welcome to the QB club* hanging over a pitch-black opening with one anonymous foot sticking out of the open door. While the sketch meant to show the Black quarterback had arrived and had finally been welcomed to the exclusive club, it also perfectly captured the predicament Black quarterbacks faced. The door might have been opened, but he was still treated like a day-pass guest at the YMCA rather than a full-fledged member at an exclusive club. Either way, the Black quarterback was coming through that door.

On August 4, Johnnie Walton (Rams) and Karl Douglas (Colts) made history when they started on the same preseason night. It might have only been two meaningless preseason games on two separate sides of the country, but for those who kept track of such things, this counted. As one Black writer boomed before the games, "Black America has been waiting for the day a black man would come along to set pro football on fire." To prepare for Walton's game against the Browns, a young, brash Black lawyer in Los Angeles, Johnnie Cochran, bought a section of tickets at the 50-yard line, arranged for a limousine to take clients to the game, and then planned an after-party at his night spot, Club There, to celebrate Walton after the game. Everybody who was anybody in Black Los Angeles was going to be at the club.

Unfortunately for both Walton and Douglas, the hype of their games and having the hopes of Black America resting on their shoulders was too much pressure for them to bear. Douglas went 2 of 15 passing with an interception, and Walton was 2 of 9. Douglas tried to put a positive spin on his performance, telling a reporter, "Well, it sure was the first game, wasn't it? I had the jitters right from the start. . . . But now the first game is over, and the jitters are done with," but a Black quarterback did not get second chances. Only Gilliam finished the season with his team. At the end of the preseason, the Colts and the Rams cut their Black quarterbacks. Despite their mediocre performances that night and losing their jobs, Walton and Douglas represented the race giving young Black quarterbacks like Evans and Williams hope.

THE CHANEYVILLE DRAGONS

WHEN THE SUPREME COURT PASSED THE *BROWN* DECISION IN 1954, White Louisianans went to work to ensure that integration would never come. For white parents in East Baton Rouge Parish, that meant doing everything in their power to keep Black kids from Chaneyville in Chaneyville. In 1960, a white parent in Zachary filed a lawsuit to stop integration, claiming that integration would have a "detrimental effect on white children of the community." He asserted that white parents needed to protect their children, because Black girls had illegitimate kids, Black people in general had more venereal diseases in the parish, and Black kids were not intellectually prepared for school. Their tactics worked until 1971 when the federal government forced all remaining segregated school systems to integrate via busing.

In Chaneyville, this had a minimal impact on the makeup of the student population. In what locals called the *crossover*, the district first tried to seek racial balance with teachers and staff. They sent Black teachers to white schools and white teachers to Black schools, including sending a white coach for Doug's basketball team. Teachers had no choice in any of this. They could quit or follow orders. But with students and families, that was another matter. Only four white students attended Chaneyville in that initial wave, a number so small that they are remembered in their own section of the yearbook as the first white students. Only one, Dale Lysone, played football. "The way I looked at it," Doug reflected, "you can't run all your life. If you don't want to go to school with us, that's too bad. But someday in life, you're going to have to deal with black people."

The school system spent another decade out of compliance until 1981, when they finally consolidated the all-white school of Pride and the all-Black school of Chaneyville into one school. The white families that entered the high school were so embarrassed that their white children might be affiliated with Chaneyville, they forced the school to change the name to Northeast. They also tried to destroy all records that had the name Chaneyville on them, including sports trophies and pamphlets that featured Doug Williams and his Dragon football teammates. Few records remain from that purge. That's too bad because those Dragon teams were electrifying.

Chaneyville's Black community made Doug's football dreams possible. In the mid-1950s, the fiercely independent community built their own football field. "Nobody came from town to give us a football field," remembered the school's first coach, Curtis Almond. "We built it ourselves with bulldozers and a lot of hand labor—the coaches, the teachers and the volunteers." When they finally got their field, the community continued to support the team and formed the Quarterback Club to ensure the players had proper equipment, food to eat, and travel accommodations. They had lights too but rarely turned them on. Those cost too much to operate. Within a decade, the community produced their first pro football player, Henry Dyer, who played for the Grambling Tigers before getting drafted by the Rams in 1966. In 1978, Doug Williams would be next.

From a young age, Doug believed he could play quarterback. And just like he'd done with baseball, Doug's brother Robert prepared him and forced Doug to play tackle football in the yard with his brothers. When Doug was younger, with no money for a football, the family used a Clorox jug instead. And when it came time to coach Doug at high school, Robert, who worked as an assistant football coach, insisted his brother play defense to get tougher. Doug settled on safety, but that didn't last too long. During his sophomore year against Second Ward, a small school led by a big star quarterback, Terry Robiskie, Doug tried to tackle the elusive running quarterback and got trucked. He came out of the game in pain and told his coach, "Find you another safety. I don't want any part of it." He'd rather sit and wait his turn to play quarterback than get bulldozed. Doug got his big break the next season.

During his junior year, when the Dragons' starting quarterback, Wendell Braxton, got hurt, Doug replaced him and never looked back. On a team loaded with seniors, the junior quarter-back led the Dragons to the district championship and the play-offs. According to his coach, he was a "student of the game" and the team leader who always got the team in the right sets. It was also during this successful run that he realized he could play the position long term when he saw Joe Gilliam play for the first time. He had heard about the Black quarterbacking legend, but he had to see it for himself. So he took a short trip to Southern University to see the Jaguars play the best and most electrifying Black college team in the country, Tennessee State.

In 1971, when Williams went to watch Gilliam play against Southern, the Tennessee State quarterback was the most famous Black quarterback in Black America. *Black Sport* magazine labeled him "the finest black passer ever," putting him ahead of legends like Eldridge Dickey and James Harris. His dad, Joe Sr., was the team's defensive coordinator at Tennessee State and one of the best in the business. The elder Gilliam had played quarterback in col-lege and taught his son the finer points of the game on both sides of the ball. And since Joe Sr. was a coach, Joe Jr. was always around the game. Growing up in Nashville, this meant being exposed to Eldridge Dickey and Coach John Merritt. Merritt described him as "another Joe Namath on and off the field," and noted "we couldn't call him Broadway Joe, so Jefferson Street, the name of the street which our school is located, seemed to fit." Technically, the school was not on Jefferson Street, but that small detail didn't matter. Like the street, "Jefferson Street Joe" belonged to the Black community.

Gilliam had the arm to make any throw. A beanpole at six foot two and 175 pounds, he took a long 9-to-12-yard drop, stood tall, and let it rip. He was what they called an *arm thrower*. When he threw, it looked like he had his back foot in a bucket and heaved the ball with his arm instead of having the necessary balance with his legs. He could slice up a defense with a bullet pass or deflate their hopes with a long bomb just as easily as he could loft a soft, short pass to a streaking running back. During his college career, he broke all of Dickey's passing records. In his senior season, he threw for 2,150 yards and twenty-five touchdowns. One opposing coach said, "He can throw the ball. He is almost as accurate at 50 yards as he is at 20. And he seems effortless in throwing. He gives you the impression that he throws all his passes with the same amount of effort."

Doug saw Gilliam play in late October—a game against the Jaguars in which Gilliam led Tennessee State to victory with two passing touchdowns. That game was clarifying to Williams: comparing himself to Gilliam, he knew then that he could play quarterback at the next level. "At half time," Williams recalled, "I stood down by the fence and watched him walk by. It was surprising to see how small he was. I couldn't believe this skinny guy was really Jefferson Street Joe. At that time, I was about 6-2, 180 pounds, and I thought, 'Shoot, if he can play college football, I know I can play. I'm bigger than him.'"

Coming into Doug's senior year in 1972, the local newspapers in Baton Rouge did not expect much from the Dragons. They lost twelve seniors on a team that only had thirty-four players. Moreover, like any small school, they had a lack of depth, and most of their starters played both ways. But the Dragons still had a quarterback that could get hot at any time. The kid the papers called "the Rifleman" put a lot of holes through secondaries. Headlines told the story of a young quarterback with generational arm talent: WILLIAMS SITES AIR RAID FOR SHADY GROVE and RIFLEMAN LEADS C'VILLE ON BEAR HUNT TONIGHT. Undersized and undermanned, Williams had his team primed to repeat as district champions. Coming into the final regular season game against the all-Black Southern University Laboratory School of Baton Rouge, their biggest rivals, Doug had 57 completions for 1,259 yards and thirteen touchdowns in just eight games. But the numbers don't tell the whole story. He would have more yards and touchdowns if they didn't blow out so many teams. They had wins of 46–6, 30–8, 54–0 where the big strike capability of the Dragons overwhelmed opponents, but instead of running up the score with deep passes, they chewed up the clock with their ground game.

The big play philosophy, however, didn't do much against the bigger schools who had an easier time shutting them down. In their three defeats to bigger schools, the Dragons went down 41–14, 24–18, and, in their final game against Southern Lab, they were shellacked 40–0, with the game being called after the third quarter because a massive fight broke out. Williams earned first team all-district, but only received two college offers, one from Southern and the other from Grambling. While Doug beat his opponents through the air, 860 miles away, the six-foot-two, 190-pound Vince Evans ran over the competition as a single-wing quarterback.

THE SMITH GOLDEN EAGLES

VINCE EVANS WAS A SYMBOL. FOR BLACK HIGH SCHOOL ATHletes in Greensboro, there were two phases of integration—one from 1963 to 1970, when the trickle of Black athletes slowly integrated Smith High and Page High, and another in 1971, when the federal government burst the discriminatory dam. While Greensboro was one of the last major cities to fully integrate their school system in 1971, Black athletes were at the forefront of integration eight years prior. In 1963, when the city opened two new high schools, Smith and Page, they marked those for open enrollment, while the white senior high (renamed Grimsley) and the Black high school Dudley remained racially separated. But *open enrollment* was a very loose term. The school district only allowed a few Black students to switch schools. In total, in the initial phase, Page received ten Black students, and Smith received four Black students. No white students enrolled in Dudley. Out of that small set of students who switched, a significant number were Black athletes. In many respects, integration was easier for the Black athlete when compared to their Black peers, because as star athletes, they were treated differently on campus, and in theory, as athletes, they also had a built-in system of inclusion with athletics to make the transition easier. When things got rough, they had teammates.

Black athletes left the familiar confines of Dudley and their community for various reasons. Some cited sports, others cited opportunities, and a few noted both. For example, Ray Linney, the first Black athlete to go to Smith in 1963, offered, "I wanted to go to Dudley, but my parents chose Smith because it was newer and more fully equipped for educational opportunities." Donald Crews, who went to Smith in 1965 and would go on to be the first Black athlete voted to the newly created all-city team, transferred for one simple reason: there were too many good athletes at Dudley. Bob McAdoo, a future Hall of Fame basketball star, switched to Smith because of his parents. He said, "My parents and I felt that the earlier I was placed in an integrated situation, the better off I'd be in the future." Running back Ike Oglesby, who transferred to Smith, said, "School integration offered diversity of experience, and integration on the field provided media exposure which blacks hadn't enjoyed prior to those years." Oglesby earned a scholarship to North Carolina.

To white onlookers, however, the Black players at Smith weren't barrier breakers, they were troublemakers. As soon as Smith started to win, local whites started to complain that the Black athletes at Smith were only there because they couldn't cut it in life. As one reporter said, "Smith is regarded as a haven among Greensboro's black athletes, especially those who run into difficulty elsewhere." Vince Evans was one of those kids.

By his own admission, Evans could be a bit difficult to deal with in high school. When he first entered Page High during his sophomore season, he immediately butted heads with the coach, Steve Yates. "I couldn't get along with Steve Yates," he said. "I don't think he liked me, and I guess I wasn't the easiest person to deal with back then." Evans soon quit the football team. But for Evans and other Black kids, the prejudice at Page was the problem, not them. Throughout the year, Black students held sit-ins and walkouts to protest bias on campus. They demanded Black studies classes, Black counselors, and an equitable school busing plan. Evans had the ultimate protest. He left the school and enrolled at Smith. It just so happened that his junior season at Smith coincided with forced integration and busing in Greensboro. A new school, a new team, a new system, and a new Greensboro.

Every fall, high school football offers a new season and a new school year, but fall 1971 gave an entirely new meaning to a fresh start: the federal government ordered that Greensboro had to immediately integrate their schools. Many believed that integration would go a lot smoother if their football teams were successful. With mass forced integration, however, football success would be difficult to achieve because it meant that players were coming into new school environments, with new football schemes and new coaches, all while battling the racial tensions of the city.

That fall, football would be the barometer of integration in Greensboro, as the players came to school for football camp two weeks before everyone else. The city and school board ran a Public Sunday School campaign to get parents and students ready for the new changes at the same time integrated football players were sweating in pads, tackling one another, and forming new bonds. Football also became a gauge of community acceptance.

High school football across America has a special place because
the sport forms community bonds. Generations of families show
up to games to root for the boys under the Friday night lights.
Forced integration, doubters claimed, tore up those bonds. Would
white families go to Dudley to see their boys play? Would they feel
safe? Would Black families go to Grimsley to see their boys play?
Would they feel safe? If fans stayed away, would integration fade
away? This was more than a potential social problem; this too was
an economic problem. By state law, high school football had to be
self-funded. That meant that paid attendance covered the bills. If
people stayed away because of fear of integration, then the high
school institution would crumble.

Integration also changed the player-coach relationship. It wasn't
just that students were bused in; teachers and coaches had to
switch schools as the school board imposed a 75-25 white-Black
split. Suddenly, white coaches who never had anything to do with
Black athletes were their coaches and mentors. For several Black
athletes, this new arrangement was disastrous. White coaches
believed they needed the Black athletes to win games but wanted
little else to do with them. As one local white coach put it, "Once
the white coaches discovered the black kids' abilities, steps had to
be taken to curb overzealous recruiting." Often, these Black athletes struggled when they left high school. White coaches were
accused of not caring and not being able to understand the plight
of the Black athlete. One white coach, who said that all his star
Black athletes fell off after high school, claimed it was not that he
didn't care; in fact, he argued, his problem was that he cared too
much. In his mind, caring became coddling. "My only conclusion," he said, "is that maybe I spent too much time with them
and protected them too much. Then, when they left high school,
they weren't really prepared to cope with the realities of the outside world."

The Black coaches saw it differently. Integration destroyed the familiar foundations built in the Black community. The Black players were not just athletes but part of the community. They were family. The mission of a Black coach during segregation was not only to win games but to mold men. Jonathan McKee, the head coach at Dudley who had to learn how to succeed in the era of separate and unequal, argued, "The black coach was more of a father figure for his athletes in those years. He was primarily concerned with instilling coherent values in his players and teaching them a way of life." When integration forced coaches to move to other schools, it damaged the Black community. Too many white coaches didn't care about the Black athlete beyond what he brought to the athletic field. Fortunately for Vince, he found a white coach who cared.

Even before forced integration in 1971, Smith attracted the best Black talent because their coach, Claude Manzi, had a positive reputation among Black athletes. In short, he treated them fairly. And he quickly built a dominant football program. Using the outdated single-wing offense, an offense so old that reporters called it ancient in the 1970s, Manzi wanted to use speed and toughness to run the ball down opponents' throats. Although the quarterback threw the ball, the scheme did not have what today's football fans would call *traditional receivers*. They had ends that lined up at the end of the line, like modern-day tight ends, who were also eligible to run routes. To call the signal caller a quarterback in the single wing, one must suspend what they think they know about the position. Smith ran 90 percent of the time. The quarterback made the decision to run to the strong side—the side with one end—hand off to the back, or keep it himself. To keep defenses honest, teams added deep pass plays, or flares to a wingback, but this was a running set where the quarterback was often referred to as a running back. In fact, when Vince Evans played for Manzi in 1971 and 1972, local papers selected him as an all-city running back.

With all the new players transferring, the Smith Golden Eagles were not supposed to compete for a city title in 1971, but they were helped by two things. For one, every school had the same problems. Players on every team had two weeks to learn a new offense and deal with a new racial reality. Second, they had Vince Evans. The single wing played to his strengths. He had quick feet and speed, and he could throw a deep pass when called upon. At six foot two, he was a tough and elusive runner out of the backfield with a 4.5-second 40-yard dash. One assistant coach assessed Evans as "one of the best I ever saw as far as tenacity." His combination of athleticism and intensity helped make him an all-city running back in his first year of varsity. Notably, the all-city team was racially split down the middle: eleven white players; eleven Black players.

Evans followed his junior season with an even more impressive senior season. With ten extra pounds of muscle from the previous season, he could beat teams to the outside with his speed and bulldoze defenses down the middle with his power. Before the season opener, a local paper gushed, "Evans ranks among the best backs in North Carolina, and Smith's success revolves around the 180-pounder who runs with power while being able to throw on the move. He's the key figure in the Eagles' vaunted power sweep off tackle and around end." Although he missed the first game due to injury, during the rest of the season, he starred and amassed 1,056 yards rushing and another 470 passing on the way to the city championship. He also earned the offensive player of the year for the city.

In the final regular season game, Evans had his biggest moment. As his coach recalled, "When I think of Vince, I think of the night we beat Page." Late, with the game on the line, Smith had the ball on the Page 20-yard line. "Page was expecting a pass from Vince," he recalled. "I pulled him aside and said, 'Vince, we're going off to the weak side. You're going to run the ball, and I'll let you put it in the end zone.' He did that, and we beat Page."

In high school, Evans was a runner, but when Manzi let him heave the ball, he made things happen, including several games where he threw multiple touchdowns. In all fairness, Evans was never a skilled passer—in high school, college, or the pros— because he was never taught how to be a quarterback. He was the kid who quarterbacked in street games because he was the one with the best arm and prettiest passes. He was always plagued by the same problem: they looked pretty, but they were rarely right. Part of the problem was that he was self-taught, and when learning how to throw, he became comfortable throwing without the laces. Most quarterbacks use the laces for grip and control. Without that control, those bullet passes were off target, and the ground caught a lot of strays. "He threw the ball so hard, we didn't have anybody who could catch it," Manzi recalled. "Eventually, I said to him, 'Vince, we have pretty passes, but no completions.' He had to let up on the ball." College coaches took notice.

Despite his success on the field, he only had one college offer— from North Carolina Central. The big white schools, like North Carolina, who had a run-heavy I formation, and North Carolina State, who ran a veer, stayed away. They only sent letters but no offers. There were better running backs and quarterbacks they could nab. Evans did not let that deter him. He had bigger plans. He saw himself as a leading man, and there was one perfect place for a leading man: Los Angeles, California, where the stars played.

CHAPTER 6

On November 18, 1967, Vince Evans plopped in front of his family's TV at 4:30 p.m. and flipped the knob to channel 8 to watch the national game of the week on ABC. Back in those days, before colleges and conferences signed mega TV deals, the NCAA controlled the TV contracts. To maximize viewership, and thus increase commercial fees from sponsors, the overlords of amateurism limited the number of games on TV. On this day in Greensboro, fans got one game: UCLA versus USC, number 1 versus number 4, with the Pac-8 Championship and a trip to the Rose Bowl on the line. USC mesmerized young Evans. The white horse. The fight song. O. J. Simpson. The cardinal and gold. During the game, in what would be the pivotal score and the defining moment in his college career, O. J. took a handoff from the I formation, bounced around the Bruins' defense, then darted 64 yards for a touchdown. Evans was hooked. He was only twelve, but he knew where he wanted to go to college. He knew what he wanted to do for his career. He wanted to play quarterback for USC. He wanted to be a star.

Despite being all-city and making the all-state Shrine game, where he scored a touchdown as a running back, only North

Carolina Central, one of the state's historically Black colleges and universities (HBCUs), offered him a scholarship. On what was supposed to be his signing day, his HBCU graduate parents could not have been more thrilled. Their son was going to an HBCU. NCC's coach came to the Evanses' home for Vince to sign his letter of intent, and with Robert and Rita Evans present in the living room, the coach just needed one last signature. Vince was ready to sign. The dream of Los Angeles and the cardinal and gold was all but done. Suddenly, his brother Tyrone, who had moved to Los Angeles two years prior, called an audible. He pulled Vince away from the crowd to gain a moment of clarity. "My brother and I were rapping in the back," Evans recalled. "He told me 'Don't sign with that dude, man. I'm telling you . . . you're good enough to play on the Coast. That's where the competition is at.'" Evans agreed with his brother. His best chance of making his dream come true, and eventually playing pro ball, was to head west. "I was looking at my future. Not many people get drafted [for professional teams] from the ACC." He refused to sign. Vince's dad was so upset with him for throwing away a college scholarship that he didn't talk to him for months. He thought his son had no chance of making it. But Vince Evans believed in his own abilities. His perseverance always paid off.

USC OR BUST

EVANS TOOK HIS FUTURE INTO HIS OWN HANDS. HE SENT A HIGH-light tape to USC, and as he recalled, "I wrote a letter to the athletic department, telling them who I was and why I wanted to go there." Not only was this ambitious, it was also audacious. How could he rationalize sending material to the best school, when big-time football schools in North Carolina did not show major interest in him? Fortunately, USC liked what they saw on film. But Coach John McKay rarely trusted film. Film could be sped up. Whether recruiting or scouting, it was better to see for himself. USC, however, rarely recruited players from out of state. On their 1972 championship team, thirty-seven of the best forty players were homegrown. That stay-home recruiting philosophy was helped by the fact that California had a wealth of talent, ranking second as a state in total all-Americans, and Los Angeles had more all-Americans than any region of the country. You had to be a special athlete to convince USC to bring you in from out of state.

Evans also faced another problem. He had a good tape but bad grades. Smart, but not a serious student, he coasted in high school, just doing enough to stay eligible, graduate, and satisfy his strict parents. USC had a rigid admission policy. And if that weren't enough, USC also had a stacked backfield. The Trojans were transitioning from Sam "Bam" Cunningham to Anthony Davis and Ricky Bell. At quarterback, they had golden boy Pat Haden. There was little room for an unknown kid from Greensboro. So USC took a wait-and-see approach. Perhaps if he went to a local community college, got his grades together, and performed on the field, then he could get a shot at wearing the cardinal and gold. This was also part of USC's recruiting strategy for talented kids like Evans. Instead of offering an unproven recruit a scholarship, they stashed him at a local community college, allowing Trojan coaches to keep a close eye on him and keeping him away from competitors if he blossomed. To the ire of Midwest powerhouses like Michigan, where there were few solid community colleges, West Coast schools like USC had an unfair advantage. Sure, one of USC's hidden gems could sign with UCLA or a West Coast school like Washington, but the Trojans liked their odds of competing in their own backyard. It was low risk and high reward.

With an old high school teammate already playing at Los Angeles Community College (LACC) and with a brother already living in Los Angeles, Evans liked the idea of heading west. In the summer of 1973, he packed his belongings, hopped in his car, and drove across the country. He was heading to LACC. Although he was confident in his football abilities, the kid who lived through the civil rights movement feared what awaited him in the Golden State. For Evans, it was like "going to the moon."

Los Angeles changed Vince Evans. It wasn't just the low-cut Afro he sported. Or the open shirt with the gold chain showing. Or his car with the letters *VE* painted on the door. He started blossoming into a quarterback. Under Coach Al Baldock at LACC, he finally got to throw the ball. Baldock was a coaching legend in the California community college ranks. By the time he got Evans in his program, he was one of the winningest coaches in California community college history. Most importantly for Evans, Coach Baldock believed in the pass. Three years prior to making his way to LACC in 1972, he coached the offensive line under the offensive innovator Don Coryell at San Diego State. Baldock, who already had a reputation for being forward-thinking about the pass, used his time with Coryell to pick up even more tips for his air assaults to power his veer offense. When he got the job at LACC, he took his new concepts with him.

Under Coach Baldock, Evans threw the ball frequently for the first time in his career, chucking the ball sixteen to twenty times a game. With speedy receivers to go with Evans's cannon of an arm, the offense relied on big explosive plays. They became even more potent with Evans using his elite speed as a rollout passer. As he sprinted outside the pocket, he could be a threat to run or throw. After missing the first two games with a back injury, he threw 92 of 164 for 1,270 yards and twelve touchdowns. He also darted for 358 yards on the ground and another nine scores. He led his team to the community college championship against Fresno CC, a game that ended in a 10–10 tie, with Evans winning player of the game. Soon, Willie Brown and USC came calling.

Like every Black coach on a college coaching staff at a predominantly white institution (PWI), Willie Brown was at USC for one reason: to recruit. Back then, calling a Black man at a white school an assistant coach was code word for *recruiter*. Brown had his work cut out for him. USC sat on the edge of Watts, a predominantly Black neighborhood that went up in flames in 1965 as local Black residents protested police brutality. Some parents feared dropping their kids in all that racial turmoil. Also hurting recruiting efforts was the reality that until the early 1960s, USC also had a history of being unwelcoming to Black athletes. Although the school had their first Black player as early as 1925 with Brice Taylor, the team did not have another Black player for twenty-five years after Taylor left. Things slowly started to change in the late 1950s, and when John McKay took over as head coach for the 1960 season, Willie Brown was his first major signee. McKay followed that by grabbing Ben Wilson, a six-foot-two, 230-pound fullback from Texas. Behind their Black running back and fullback, USC went undefeated in 1962. After he graduated, Brown worked to help McKay recruit Black players, and then, in 1968, McKay officially hired him as a coach. By 1972, with Brown leading the recruiting battle, half the team was Black. McKay had such a great reputation for signing Black athletes that white recruiters began trying to scare off white athletes by warning them, "Don't go to USC. It's in the middle of Watts." It didn't work. McKay got the best of both Black and white talent.

With three years of eligibility remaining, Evans jumped at the chance when Brown offered him a scholarship. As a kid who grew up in integrated Southern schools, Evans would have no problems fitting in. But there was just one caveat: John McKay wanted Vince Evans as a running back, not a quarterback. If Evans wanted to fulfill his quarterbacking dreams, he would have to bet on himself.

THE I FORMATION

Running back or quarterback? That was Vince Evans's decision in the summer of 1974. If it were up to the USC staff, that should not have been a tough choice. The invitation to try quarterback from Coach McKay was not really meant as an open tryout. Under McKay, USC recruited quarterbacks all the time with the intention of switching their positions. McKay believed that most high schools put their top athletes at the quarterback position because the best athlete would have the ball in his hands most of the time, but that did not make them true quarterbacks. Over the years, he had asked stellar high school quarterbacks, regardless of their race, to play another position. He asked white high school quarterbacks like Bobby Chandler, Rod Sherman, and Hal Bedsole to switch. Black athletes like future Hall of Famer Lynn Swann and Gene Washington were also asked to make the change. Swann switched, but Washington refused and instead signed with Stanford, where they promised him a shot at quarterback.

But Vince Evans was stubborn. The open invitation to try to play quarterback was all he needed. When he went back home in the summer of 1974 with a decision to make, his father now supported his dreams. "If I work hard enough," Evans recalled him saying, "I would get it." Robert Evans was a proud Black father who watched Black Greensboro fight for civil rights. He understood what it meant for his son to work and prove he could play quarterback. For someone who had pro aspirations, however, going to USC was not like Doug Williams going to Grambling. Unlike Eddie Robinson, McKay didn't tailor his offense to get a quarterback to the pros. He built an offense to steamroll the competition. He needed a quarterback to run the engine. This makes it even more notable that McKay became the Branch Rickey of

Black quarterbacks: a white man largely seen as responsible for letting a Black star break the color line.

Born in West Virginia in 1923, McKay used football as a vehicle out of rural poverty. His father died during the Great Depression, and young McKay had to pick up odd jobs just to support the family. An all-around athlete, he starred in high school football as a single-wing running back. An all-state running back, he accepted a scholarship to Wake Forest in 1941, but immediately returned home to care for his ailing mother. Instead of playing ball, he took a job back home as a coal mine electrician making $6.75 a day. Like all men his age, he had his life quickly changed on December 7, 1941, when the Japanese attacked Pearl Harbor. In the military, he taught calisthenics and basic training on military bases until his troop deployed to the Pacific, where he fought as a tail gunner on B-29s. At the conclusion of the war, he took his GI Bill benefits and headed to Purdue to play football.

McKay got a quick crash course in new-school football. When he graduated high school, most teams were using the single-wing offense, but now, in 1946, more than 90 percent had switched to the T formation. Like other running backs switching from the single wing to the T, McKay struggled getting the handoff from the quarterback, which slowed him down hitting the holes. He quickly learned he'd be better at defensive back.

After McKay's first year at Purdue, however, Coach Cecil Isbell left the program to lead the Baltimore Colts, so McKay headed to the University of Oregon. He redshirted his first year for the Ducks before playing halfback and defensive back on their 1948 squad that went 9–1. Unfortunately, his football career came to an end the following year when he severely injured his knee. Instead of having McKay sulk on the sidelines, Coach Jim Aiken asked him to train the running backs. Two years later, after Aiken resigned, new head coach Len Casanova kept McKay on his staff. It was a smart move.

As an assistant coach, McKay was a tinkerer and innovator. He'd draw plays while at the bar or the beach; he was always thinking about the game. His old boss at Oregon once said, "I've never known a man with more ideas on football attack than McKay. Some of the stuff he suggested was too far out for us at Oregon. We had to reject some of his plays because we would have needed motorcycles to make them work." In charge of running the T formation at Oregon, McKay used concepts from his high school single-wing days to design quarterback rollouts. This new wrinkle gave his undersized offensive line a better chance to protect the quarterback by moving the pocket instead of blocking heavier defensive tackles coming straight at them. Moreover, it gave the offense the element of surprise, because now the quarterback was more of a threat to run. His innovations caught the attention of USC, who hired him in 1959 as an assistant coach to work for Don Clark.

In McKay's first year as an assistant at USC, with Black quarterback Willie Wood leading the way, the Trojans went 8–2 in 1959. Despite a successful season, Clark resigned, leaving McKay the head job. At only thirty-six, he had big shoes to fill, and he almost failed. He went 4–6 his first season, and then he went 4–5–1 the next. Then he struck gold.

McKay liked the versatility of the T formation, but as an old running back who played the single wing, he saw some areas that needed improvement. Mostly, he didn't like that the running back was in a low crouch and couldn't see the defense over the offensive line. How did the defense shift when the offense went in motion? Were the defensive ends playing wide of the offensive tackle or on the inside? In the single wing, however, the backs were upright and could see the action in front of them. They had a better chance to run to daylight. Out of his desire to improve a running back's chances came one of the most potent running offensive schemes ever: the power I formation.

Merging concepts of the single wing, where the running backs stood up, and the T, with the quarterback under center and running backs behind him, McKay took two backs who were once horizontally lined up behind the quarterback and set them vertical, thus forming an I. He also kept one tight end on the line to block and moved the end (receiver) out farther as a split end. The key to the I formation was having the fullback and halfback several yards behind the quarterback. The distance gave the running back a running head start, the fullback gave the running back an extra blocker, being straight behind the quarterback gave him more angles to run without tipping off his direction, and standing up allowed him to see the field. Just like that, Running Back U was born.

No position benefited more from the I formation than the running back. This was a run-heavy offense, handing it off to the backs 60 percent of the time to the tune of 217 yards a game on the ground. Of course, any coach who had star athletes like Mike Garrett, O. J. Simpson, Charles White, Anthony Davis, Sam Cunningham, and Ricky Bell would run them often too. Asked if he had any depth at running back, McKay once shot back, "Simpson IS depth." When asked why he ran his backs so much, McKay mockingly responded, "Why not? It isn't very heavy. And besides, he doesn't belong to any union." Simpson averaged thirty-two carries a game on the way to breaking Mike Garrett's all-time college rushing record. Both men won the Heisman.

Since they ran 60 percent of the time and only passed to keep the defense honest, McKay did not need an all-world arm back there. According to McKay, in fact, the quarterback's arm was overrated. The position, however, required smarts and leadership.

"What he must have," McKay wrote, "are intelligence and the ability to lead. You can't be stupid and play quarterback, because you put too much of a burden on the rest of the team." He believed that "a good quarterback stands out when he walks in the huddle. Everyone knows he's there." The quarterback had to also have enough ego to believe that he could be the man, but not so much that he would force passes. McKay preferred rollout passers, who didn't need elite arm strength and could pick up yards when things broke down. The I formation was perfect for an athletic quarterback. He had his best and most significant quarterback with Jimmy Jones.

COLOR BLIND MCKAY

At USC, Jimmy Jones played Jackie Robinson to McKay's Branch Rickey. Jones was not the first Black player in his sport, but he was still a pioneer that opened doors, and in those days, that was good enough for the media. Hailing from the gritty steel mill town of Harrisburg, Pennsylvania, Jones came west to follow his dream.

McKay tabbed Jones as the starter during his sophomore year, and Jones rewarded him with a 10–0–1 record, including a victory over Michigan in the Rose Bowl. That season, the team set the school scoring record. In total, during his career, Jones had a 22–8–3 record, including a victory over Alabama in 1970, in a game many called the most important in college history. When Jones and his Black teammates, including Sam Cunningham, destroyed Alabama, many observers believe the last segregated Southern schools finally felt obliged to sign Black recruits.

In the post–civil rights era, Jones was the first Black quarterback that many Black fans saw on the national stage. He played for one of the most popular teams in the country and thus received the most attention. He was the first Black quarterback to appear on the cover of *Sports Illustrated*, on September 29, 1969. Although there had been better Black college quarterbacks before, it felt revolutionary and game-changing that USC had one, especially one that made the cover of *SI*. After McKay, by then a pro coach, drafted Doug Williams to the Bucs in 1978, Williams immediately thought of Jones. His success at USC persuaded Williams that he'd get a fair shot from the Bucs. Watching Jones succeed at USC also made the decision easier for Evans. But for some whites, it was also a problem. The FBI once had to show up to McKay's house after he received death threats for starting a Black quarterback.

It was not all easy for Jones, unfortunately. Despite his collegiate success, the pro teams didn't see him as a quarterback. He went undrafted in 1972. When he signed as a free agent with the Broncos, they tried to switch him to a defensive back. He left to play quarterback in Canada.

Two years after Jones left, in the summer of '74, Evans traveled back to Los Angeles with the confidence of a young man who finally had his father's full support. He was going to be the next Black quarterback at Running Back U. Fourth on the depth chart when he arrived in August, the kid who looked like O. J. Simpson wowed the coaches. The local Los Angeles media only gave glancing attention to the community college scene, so few folks knew what the Trojans had in Evans. All they heard was that he was fast and that he led the LACC Cubs to the state title. McKay confirmed the rumors: "He's big and he can run." Within weeks, Evans moved up the depth chart to back up Pat Haden. He impressed so much that McKay said he had "unlimited potential," and he claimed that if he were there for spring camp, USC would have an unstoppable one-two combo at quarterback, with Haden throwing and Evans keeping teams off balance with his runs. But few fans expected Evans to play. Haden was an all-American candidate. In fact, there was so little expectation that Evans would play, USC left his name off the program at the beginning of the year. The violent game of football, however, has a way of changing the script. And in Tinseltown, Vince Evans soon became the unheralded star.

In late September, the Evans family traveled up north from Greensboro to watch USC take on the University of Pittsburgh. They had no inkling Evans would play; they just wanted to see him. The game also happened to feature Pitt's star running back, Tony Dorsett. Even if the Evanses didn't get a chance to see their boy play, they would at least get to see *the man* perform. The second quarter, the Panthers' defense knocked out Pat Haden. After that, as Black writer Brad Pye put it, it was "The Vince Evans Story—Tale of a Trojan Hero." It was a story few could believe.

"As I saw Pat go down," Evans said, "I felt a shock run through me. I knew I was going in. I wasn't frightened, but I was awfully nervous." He had been with his team for less than two months, and now they expected him to win and keep their national championship hopes alive. When he wasn't handing off the ball to his all-world running back Anthony Davis, he was leaving the pocket on designed runs or rolling out for passes, with clear instructions not to throw unless somebody was wide open. He threw three passes all game. McKay did not trust his arm. He coveted his legs.

Vince could run like the wind, but he had never faced a tornado like the Panther defense. A superior athlete, he had developed bad running habits. Instead of tucking the ball tight like a running back, he held it casually like it was a loaf a bread. He lost two fumbles in the third quarter. Dejected, he thought McKay would surely take him out and never let him play again. Maybe even send him back home with his family. Instead, McKay stayed cool. He did not need a quarterback when he had the most devastating running attack in the country. As a team, they carried the ball seventy-six times, with Anthony Davis leading the way with thirty-three carries. In the fourth quarter, Evans rewarded McKay for his patience and led the team on two scoring drives, which marked USC's first offensive touchdowns of the season. Vince sealed the deal with a 13-yard scamper that pushed the score to 16–7. In total, he carried the ball twelve times for 66 yards.

Everyone finally knew his name. During the season, he rarely got to throw the ball, but he ran the ball forty-two times for 201 yards and four touchdowns as USC coasted to another Rose Bowl. With Haden graduating, Evans would have the leading role in LA for the 1975 season.

CHAPTER 7

COMING OFF A STELLAR HIGH SCHOOL SENIOR SEASON, DOUG Williams had twice as many offers as Vince Evans: two. One from Southern and one from Grambling. Both were Black schools. Wisconsin called his coach, but they never gave an offer. Besides, Doug knew that he wanted to play quarterback, so he was not going to a white school. "I always thought if I went to a big white school, they would have converted me to a tight end. I'm big, I can run, and you don't find too many black quarterbacks down South where I wanted to play," he said. If a young Black kid in the South wanted to stay home and still have a chance to make it as a pro quarterback, his best bet was to play for Eddie Robinson and his Grambling Tigers.

GRAMBLING MAN

WHILE ROBINSON TURNED GRAMBLING INTO A FOOTBALL FAC-tory, placing more than 150 players into pro football, he also made it his mission to churn out professional Black quarterbacks. This was not about his ego; rather, he did it for America. Robinson believed football was a vehicle to the betterment of his players, community, and country. "When a boy comes to Grambling," he once told a local reporter, "I want him to be a better man after having played for us. I try to tell him he's an American first, and a football player second." Robinson told his players, "A black has got to compete in America, not just with other blacks, but with all Americans. If we can prove that in sports, why can't others do it in science, mathematics, and other fields?" If America mirrored itself after the integrative qualities of sports, he thought, then the nation would be a fair and just place. In football terms, he once reasoned, "If Martin Luther King scored L.S.U.'s winning touchdown against Ole Miss he could be governor of Louisiana the next day." An assassin shot down King before Ole Miss and LSU integrated. Regardless of that racist reality, the football coach only wanted victors, not victims. He carried this philosophy with him to Grambling when he started his head coaching job in 1941 all the way to 401 wins in fifty-six years.

A high school and college quarterback from Baton Rouge, Robinson was a natural-born leader. The first moment he laid eyes on a coach, he found his life's calling. That coach was Julius Kraft. At six foot four and 190 pounds, Kraft was a dashing figure who left an indelible mark on Robinson. Kraft had played college ball at a small Black school, Bishop College, in Marshall, Texas, and came to Baton Rouge to coach at McKinley High in the early 1930s. To get the local Black community hooked on football, Kraft paraded his teams around town and at the local Black school. Robinson took the bait. He came to their games just to watch Kraft command his teams. When he finally got his chance to play for Kraft as a junior, the young quarterback led his team to two undefeated seasons. After high school, he left to quarterback for Coach Ruben Turner at Leland College, a small Black college twenty miles away.

Robinson learned from his coaches how to be a student of the game. Coach Kraft routinely cut out newspaper clippings about college football and saved the plays that he liked, especially those from Tennessee and Minnesota. Turner taught Robinson to study the game and told him that if he wanted to be a successful coach, he'd have to go to coaching clinics. When Grambling hired Robinson in 1941, he begged the administration for money to attend camps. Although resources were scarce, they always found the money in the budget. At the conclusion of his first clinic, Robinson asked Northwestern coach Pappy Waldorf for some advice. Waldorf told him to get a system. Robinson looked at him, confused. Robinson had never coached, so how could he have a system? That solution was simple. Use the plays that he liked at the clinic and that he ran during his playing days, and that was his system. Just like that, Eddie Robinson had his system. Until the 1958 season, he successfully ran a single-wing offense. He also built one of the greatest college programs in the history of the game.

As a recruiter, Robinson could sit in a boy's living room in rural Louisiana and promise him and his parents that he would make a man out of him. Not just a tough, manly man who could take the punishment dished out by other men, not just a man who would learn about the meaning of sacrifice as he sat in the sweltering summer Louisiana heat, but a man who would get a job and take care of his family in the Jim Crow South. As Sammy White, a future all-pro receiver from Monroe, Louisiana, recalled, "I could've gone to Oklahoma State, Penn State, any Big Ten and Big Eight school. What did I need to go to a little place like Grambling for? But my mother wanted me close to home. I went and talked with Eddie Robinson and he surprised me by telling me things no other coach did. He said there was no guarantee I'd make the pros, that if I came to Grambling it should be to get an education. I liked that." Along the way, Robinson taught his players manners and prepared them for the

---

(See below.)

coming day of integration when a young Black man might have to sit at a table next to white folks.

His players showed up to games in their Sunday best and took etiquette classes on dining out, which fork to use for the salad, and how to read a menu. And they never missed church. Family, faith, and football. Robinson shied away from publicly addressing civil rights talk, because he believed his players' success was the answer to racial problems. "It's hard for me to believe in Black Power," he once argued. "I believe in green power and American power. These kids are living in the finest country in the world."

While Robinson's teams worked on the finer points of their social lives, on the football field, they were his too. And that's where he truly worked his magic. By the 1950s, Grambling consistently had one of the top HBCU programs in the nation, battling yearly with the likes of Tennessee State, FAMU, Southern, Prairie View, and Jackson State. And it wasn't just that they had the top teams; they also produced the most pros. It started with Tank Younger, the first HBCU athlete to play in the NFL when he signed with the Rams in 1949. The success of Tank, an appropriately named fullback who scored bruising touchdowns as he ran over opponents, sent other teams searching for HBCU talent. And they always stopped at Grambling. By 1969, Robinson had produced seventy pro players, four of whom became Hall of Famers.

Robinson was not content with succeeding in the South; he took his Grambling show on the road. They played in New York, DC, Dallas, Houston, Los Angeles, and eventually Tokyo. His team was even the subject of a 1968 CBS documentary, and from 1971 to 1974, they were featured on a popular Sunday morning football show that aired in the South. Boys in Louisiana dreamed of being a Tiger. Like USC and Notre Dame, Grambling football was a brand.

All this success, but he still hadn't produced a pro quarterback? That was more of a challenge than a question put forth to him by legendary broadcaster Howard Cosell in 1964. On his radio show in New York, Cosell asked the coach why pro football had not had a starting Black quarterback, to which Robinson did not have the answer. To most Black observers, the answer was clear: the league did not believe a Black man was suitable to play the position. But to Robinson, it became a challenge. For this to work, he had to have the right player, and he had to have the right system. The pros were as picky as they were prejudiced. He was on a mission.

Robinson knew he could show off his players all he wanted, but nothing would leave a mark quite like having a Black quarterback in the pros. He had a strong belief that the Black athlete, specifically Grambling's athletes, had a role to play in healing America's race relations. "I didn't know if I could help lead people as a civil rights activist, but I knew that I could help to groom young black men as intelligent leaders at Grambling," he once said. At the core of this was stomping out the racial stereotypes about leadership. "The stereotype that blacks can't lead whites or that they aren't smart enough to do certain things had been trotted out so often that most whites—and sadly, some blacks—readily accepted it." With a Black quarterback in the pros, he believed he could make that change. "If we could make a big enough impact with football at Grambling," he argued, "if our plans worked and our goals were met, then the national star would provide us the opportunity to smash the stereotypes that blacks couldn't be leaders, be they athletes, civil rights activists, corporate leaders, or politicians."

Robinson looked inward for the solution. He grew tired of the so-called excuses and complaints from other Black coaches as to why there were no Black quarterbacks. "We as black coaches," he once said, "have got to create the environment—dropback, moving pocket, reading defenses, sideline passes, terminology." He argued, "A black coach has got to know about pro football." In fact, he blamed the coaches. "You can't cry about this quarterback thing until you send a boy up there who really has the skills to do the job. You can't protest in anger until you really know you have actually seen a boy deprived for a chance deserved." When he decided in 1964 that he would develop a Black quarterback for the pros, he was against all odds. But he liked those chances. Eddie Robinson was an underdog. Like the players he sought out, he was going to be a victor, not a victim.

THE WING T

EVEN BEFORE HIS QUARTERBACK MISSION, IN 1959, ROBINSON changed from the single-wing offense to the wing T to give his players a better shot at the pros. Although he won a Black college championship as late as 1956 with the single wing, in 1957, they went 4–4, and it was clear the offense had run its course. Until Robinson switched the Grambling offense, most of the football players he had placed in the pros were on the defensive side of the ball. The wing T, an offshoot of the T formation, would change that.

By the early 1960s, the wing T had become the new "it" offense in college football. Developed by Coach Dave Nelson of the University of Delaware in the early 1950s, and improved upon by Forest Evashevski at the University of Iowa, the offense shifted one of the running backs in the traditional T to a wingback. The quarterback still had two running backs behind him (one directly behind him and one to his left), but now the third running back became a wingback and was parallel to the quarterback but a few yards to his right. It also meant that he lost his flanker receiver (slot). The receiver either stayed close to the offensive line as an extra blocker, or he moved out wide for passing situations. As *Sports Illustrated* noted in 1960, "What coaches like most about the wing

T is its versatility. It permits a team to use a power offense from a tight wing T, and it also allows the team to split a back or end wide. Either variation can be employed without having to change basic blocking patterns and assignments." While the offense still emphasized running the ball, more and more colleges started to throw out of it too, because a fast wingback allowed an offense to attack a slower linebacker in space. College coaches also wanted a quarterback who could run.

When Robinson made that change to the wing T in 1959, Iowa's Wilburn Hollis was the only Black man quarterbacking the wing T to success at a big-time white school. At six foot two and 205 pounds, the Iowa quarterback had the size to be a successful pro quarterback. At one point in the 1960 season, he had the Hawkeyes ranked as the number two team in the country, one spot behind Minnesota, who had Black quarterback Sandy Stephens running their offense. Unfortunately for Hollis, the pros had no use for him at quarterback. In college, he ran more than he threw, and when he threw, like other wing T quarterbacks, he rolled out of the pocket. Although some pro teams let their quarterbacks roll out, at this point, that luxury seemed only available to white men. Hollis had to wait until the ninth round before the St. Louis Cardinals drafted him. The Cardinals switched him to flanker, but they cut him before the end of training camp. He soon signed with the Steelers, but they cut him too.

Robinson had his first pro-caliber wing T quarterback in Mike Howell. At six foot two and 180 pounds, Howell had a good arm and great speed. Rated as the best Black college quarterback in 1964, Howell led the Tigers to the Orange Blossom Classic against Florida A&M, but Howell never really popped on the pro coaches' radar. While he had a good arm—he threw for 1,032 yards and eleven touchdowns—in the wing T, Grambling was a running team, and when Howell did throw the ball, he often checked down to his backs. The pros wanted quarterbacks who could chuck it down the field.

Despite his success, Howell understood the score. He was a Black quarterback, and he realized his best shot was on the defensive side of the ball. Before his senior year, he told Robinson, "Coach, I'll play quarterback for you, but you've got to let me play defensive back for myself." In preparation, Howell used spring football practice to work on his defensive skills, especially in man-to-man coverage. He also had to learn how to tackle, since he had only played quarterback. The Cleveland Browns drafted Howell in the 1965 draft and converted him to a defensive back.

JAMES "SHACK" HARRIS

ROBINSON FINALLY FOUND HIS PERFECT QUARTERBACK CANDIDATE on the football fields of Monroe, Louisiana, about forty miles from campus. James "Shack" Harris was just a junior in high school when Robinson first saw him play, but his talent already leaped off the field. On that crisp 1964 night at Carroll High, Robinson turned to his wife and exclaimed, "Hey, look at that long, tall boy scamper." Harris was six foot four and a twig at that time, but he could run faster than most boys his size. He also threw farther. "I thought right then and there that maybe he could be the one," Robinson remembered. When Robinson saw him that night, Harris had his Carroll Bulldogs amid a thirty-nine-game winning streak and on the way to winning three Black state championships. One of those victories was a showdown against future all-star pitcher Vida Blue. Like Harris, Blue was recruited to play college football, but he was less optimistic at the chances for a Black quarterback to make it on the gridiron. Houston coach Bill Yeoman once said of Blue, "This young fellow is going to be the first big-name black quarterback. He's going to be the best lefthanded passer since Frankie Albert. That name alone will sell tickets." But

Blue opted for baseball because he believed that a Black quarterback would not get a chance. Eddie Robinson wanted a different outcome for Black boys like Vida Blue. If he could get one quarterback to the pros, then the next Vida Blue would be behind center instead of in front of a catcher.

Robinson knew that if he was going to get Harris to the pros, then he would have to modify his wing T. The offense favored the run game and a rollout passer, and Harris would have to get the ball downfield and stay in the pocket to prove to the pros he could make all the throws needed to run a professional offense. To correct this, Robinson hired Douglas Porter, who was the head coach of Mississippi Vocational College, when they upset the Tigers in 1965. While Porter was head coach at MVC in the early 1960s, his teams ranked among the top in passing for small colleges. With Robinson, Porter devised an explosive offense that led Grambling to three Black championships. Most importantly, they built an offense suited for a future pro quarterback. As Robinson told it, "We went around to the pros and said what do we have to do to train a boy to play quarterback, because it's pretty clear that whatever we've been doing hasn't been enough. We spend time with them, we learned to talk the pro terminology, to talk about seams, and reading, and screens and draws, to learn the 1-2-3 pass, the 1-2-3-4-5 pass, the 1-2-3-4-5-6-7, the short, the drop, the way to step, to drop, to throw the short, to run out."

Robinson also recruited his pro players to help. Players like Willie Davis, who played for Vince Lombardi and the Packers, came back to Grambling to install Lombardi's passing philosophies and school Harris on what Bart Starr would do. He had Tank Younger teach him about the Rams' passing attack and what Bob Waterfield would do. He got Dub Jones, a white receiver for the Cleveland Browns, who lived in nearby Ruston, to train the players in route running and teach Robinson Paul

Brown's playbook. "We wanted to have a sophisticated passing game," Robinson said, "because I always hoped we would place the first black quarterback in the NFL." Robinson was all in. "I won't kid you," he told a reporter in 1968, "it's important to me, this quarterback thing."

Robinson also made sure that Harris was mentally prepared. He gave him quarterback books like Bart Starr's *Quarterbacking*, he sent him to speech class, and he warned him never to say anything negative to the press. When Harris tried to switch positions to avoid the racial hurdles the pros would throw at him, Robinson would hear none of that. "There were times when I was at Grambling, I went to him and asked to switch positions, to a defensive back or something. At least I wanted to be prepared for the pros. He wouldn't let me. He could see farther into the future than I could." Robinson urged, "A quarterback just can't expect to play because he's black. He's got to work hard to prepare himself to play. I feel it is our responsibility as coaches to prepare him for this." It was quarterback or bust with Harris.

Harris stuffed the stat sheet while leading his team to three straight conference championships and a Black national championship. He set the state records for college quarterbacks, throwing fifty-three touchdowns in his career, with twenty-one coming in his senior season. The pros took note. A Lions scout said, "Mechanically, there isn't a better passer in the country. He can throw short and long and he's built to take the buffeting of a severe rush. He has that all important quick release and fast delivery." The Buffalo Bills scout said he was the Black Joe Namath. Before the draft, Robinson said, "I think pro football is ready for a Negro quarterback because James Harris is ready for pro football as a quarterback." The Bills selected Harris in the eighth round of the 1969 draft. "I thought if I were white," he once said, "I would have been drafted higher."

After the Bills drafted Harris, they paired him with their new coach, John Rauch. An offensive genius, Rauch had the highest winning percentage of any coach when he left the Raiders after the 1968 season. Rauch ran a very complex system. He demanded "thinking players" who were required to adjust on the fly. For his receivers, running backs, and quarterbacks, that meant that they had to be on the same page. Unlike typical offenses where receivers ran a specific route, receivers in Rauch's offense had more leeway to make their own reads and routes. Rauch wanted his receivers to have an opportunity to catch the ball and gain additional yardage. There were twenty-five different patterns incorporated in four offensive formations: a basic pro-style set, double wing, triple wing, and east, or slot, formation. Harvey Moses, the Bills' top receiver, noted, "In the new system, you may be the primary receiver on the pass play, but you also have other jobs. For instance, you might be called upon to bring as many defenders as possible with you, clearing out an area for another receiver." His running backs would have twenty flare actions out of the backfield with up to twenty different flares for each action. "It doesn't take a computer to see that it's essential to have a thinking player on the field. It no longer is enough for the receiver to know how to run a pattern and catch the football. He must know how to read a defense," Rauch said of his system. It's not that Harris wasn't capable, but until Harris came along, no NFL coach thought a Black quarterback could command an offense like that.

Despite missing an enormous amount of valuable time in training camp with an undiagnosed stomach ailment, Harris handled the complex offense well. After his first preseason game against the Lions, Rauch said Harris "displayed more than the strong arm we knew he possessed. He directed our offense with assuredness and a good choice of play calls." A few weeks later, the coach observed, "He still has a long way to go, but he has a great football mind and doesn't seem to panic or rattle when things go bad. He'll eat the ball and take a loss, yet stay in there and attempt to get the yardage back on the next play." Behind a terrible offensive line, Harris always stood tall in the pocket. He did not bail and run, like the racial myth suggested a Black quarterback would do.

Although Harris's future seemed bright, local Buffalo writers only wanted to focus on Blackness. Just weeks into training camp, local writer Larry Felser told readers that Harris was "laboring under three handicaps. 1—He is a rookie and has not played a down yet in professional football; 2—He played at a small college, Grambling; 3—He is black." Of the last note, Felser elaborated, "The third item, his race, puts the most pressure on him." The team had another rookie in O. J. Simpson, but nobody called him a *Black running back.* The Bills also had a white rookie fullback, Bill Enyart, but nobody called him a *white fullback.* They only cared about the color of the Black quarterback.

Despite the pressure, Harris worked his way to the starting lineup, and on September 14, 1969, he became the first Black quarterback to start a season opener. Publicly, Harris tried to avoid talking about race. He just wanted to play ball. "The real pressure," he said, "comes from being a rookie. 'Race' or anything else doesn't really matter a lot. I want to be judged on my ability rather than color." He elaborated, "Being the first black quarterback to start a season opener doesn't really mean that much. If I start and fail, I've accomplished nothing. My goal is to achieve something." For Robinson, the moment was so much more than a start for James Harris. It was a start for all the future Black quarterbacks. "Buffalo and (Coach) John Rauch have made an outstanding contribution to black youth," he said. "Never before had the young blacks seen a black quarterback start in the pro ranks. There's one thing about these kids. They're reluctant sometimes to go after things that are new and where you don't have many guys in the profession. But now that they have seen this kid play, there's going to be a lot of black quarterbacks." Unfortunately for Harris, he only started two more games in his three years with the Bills before they cut him in 1972. This decision had nothing to do with merit.

NEXT IN LINE

EDDIE ROBINSON COULD HAVE RESTED ON HIS LAURELS, BUT HE wanted to produce more professional Black quarterbacks for the betterment of the nation. And he had a type. They had to be tall with a big arm, because, as he said, "quarterbacks that big (6-4) and with that kind of arm turn me on." From the moment he started his special mission in 1964, all the top quarterbacks he signed fit that mold: James Harris (1964), Matthew Reed (1968), Joe Comeaux (1971), Dale Zimmerman (1972), Terry Brown (1973), and Doug Williams (1973) could all throw the ball as far as they wanted to, and they were all six foot four.

In the early 1970s, in the immediate wake of integration when formerly all-white schools started plucking Black players away from HBCUs, Robinson still had a recruiting advantage over other Black coaches: Grambling was a brand. The major media articles, interviews, and TV shows he appeared on made Grambling a household name in Black homes. From New York to DC, from Houston to Los Angeles, Black fans would circle the date for when Grambling was coming to town. And that brand got even bigger in 1971, when Robinson signed a TV deal with ABC to show Tigers games the day after they played. *Grambling's Playback* debuted that year, showing replays of Grambling's games at 10:00 a.m. on Sundays. Until the show went off the air at the conclusion of the 1974 season, all their games aired on TV. Potential recruits like Doug Williams, who watched the show every week, started dreaming about playing for Grambling and being on TV.

Robinson only had one competitor for Doug: Southern. But as good as the Jaguars were, if Doug wanted to be a pro quarterback, the school was not for him. They were bitter rivals in the same state and the same football conference, but the two schools presented Williams two entirely different paths for his football future. Coached by Charlie Bates, Southern was the only team in the SWAC that ran the wishbone. While other teams in the SWAC aired it out, Southern stuck to the ground like mud. When Bates installed the offense, he knew it would hurt his recruiting in a league dominated by passing. "We won't try to recruit a drop back passer," he said. "We'll be looking for Wishbone-type option quarterbacks." Southern had an all-state drop-back quarterback in James Johnson when Bates got there, and he promptly converted him to a wishbone quarterback. Although Williams had good speed, he fancied himself a classic quarterback. He didn't want to pitch and run.

When Eddie Robinson called the Williams house on a late November night in 1972, it was a wrap. After one phone call, Williams knew he wanted to play for the legend. Besides, despite Chaneyville's proximity to Southern, Chaneyville was a Grambling town. Folks in Chaneyville felt the Jaguars looked down on the poor, rural folks from Chaneyville when it came to football talent. In the past, Southern coaches figured they could find better players, so they rarely came looking. Their loss. Robinson and Grambling had no quarrels grabbing local Black kids. Grambling was a rural Black campus and plucked several kids out of Chaneyville, creating a sense of loyalty among the two towns.

In the early summer of 1973, Williams paid eight dollars for a one-way bus ticket to chase his dreams. He took the Continental Trailways to Alexandria and then switched to the Salt Line to Grambling. Homesick and bored, those first months before school started were miserable. One day, he and some friends just sat in front of the student union with nothing to do but watch the birds play in the dust. That was the first time he wanted to leave. There would be many others just like that.

In his first season, Williams got a rude awakening when Grambling decided to redshirt him. He could be on the team and keep his four years of eligibility, but he would not play. With Williams behind on the depth chart to Joe Comeaux (junior) and Terry Brown (freshman), two highly decorated recruits that Robinson believed could be his next NFL quarterbacks, the coach saw no point in wasting a year of eligibility on Williams. Instead, he would practice on the scout team defense and take stats during the game.

Doug watched the six-foot-four Comeaux sling passes that seemingly hit the opponents' hands more than those of his own receivers, and it just made times that much tougher. If Robinson did not think he was good enough to beat out Comeaux, Doug thought, there was no way he would ever play. Doug worried that after Comeaux graduated, Terry Brown, who was a freshman like Doug, would be next in line. Being redshirted, he would only have one year to shine.

Doug was done. In the middle of the season, he told Coach Robinson he'd rather quit than wait his turn. But Robinson saw the future. The future was Doug Williams. He just had to be patient. The legendary coach talked him back into school. "You may think you want to, but you're not going to," Robinson told his redshirt freshman. "We believe you can help us. We think you're going to be our quarterback one day." Just when he would play, that was up to Doug. Robinson never promised him anything but a chance.

Without football in the fall, Williams lost focus in the classroom. His grades fell. A 1.5 GPA almost ended his academic career. His dad gave him two choices: leave school and find a job, or buckle down and stay at Grambling. Doug chose the latter. But as the spring semester to his redshirt freshman season concluded, he still had one major test to pass: beat out the incumbent starter Comeaux and backup Brown for their head job. And the job was wide open. Comeaux threw sixteen touchdowns—but thirty interceptions—during the 1973 season. Doug failed the test. He was still behind Comeaux and Brown at the beginning of the 1974 season. He had another decision to make—fight or flight. By this time, however, this was not just about playing for Grambling. Doug had to think about his pro prospects.

In 1974, it finally looked like pro football was ready for Black quarterbacks. In the newly created World Football League (WFL), five Black quarterbacks (Matthew Reed, D. C. Nobles, Reggie Oliver, Eddie McAshan, and David Mays) either started or played significant minutes for their teams. At the start of the NFL season, three Black quarterbacks, J. J. Jones (Jets), Joe Gilliam (Steelers), and James Harris (Rams), were on NFL rosters. While Jones sat on the taxi squad with the Jets, Gilliam started the season for the Steelers over future Hall of Famer Terry Bradshaw. When he won the job, the local branch of the NAACP issued a public statement: "No National Football League team has ever opened its regular season utilizing the talents of a quarterback who just happened to be Black." They concluded, "Of course, Joe didn't back into this starting role. He earned it. His preseason accomplishments can only be termed excellent." In other words, there would be no affirmative action talk or no words about quotas. This Black man earned the most coveted spot in all of sports. Gilliam went 4–1–1 as a starter before Coach Chuck Knoll controversially benched him for Bradshaw. In Los Angeles, as Gilliam lost his gig, the Rams replaced John Hadl with James Harris, prompting prominent *Los Angeles Times* columnist Jim Murray to mock, "The industry considered the Rams were taking a miscalculated risk. It's considered all right for blacks to be U.S. senators, ambassadors to the UN, brigadier generals, rear admirals, mayors, scientists, surgeons, or spies. But not NFL quarterbacks. This was too sensitive an area. Too much was at stake. The republic would topple. The system would collapse."

With all this talent at the top level, it seemed like a seismic change had come to pro football. Writing for the *Los Angeles Times*, Black scholar Robert Chrisman observed, "In 1974 the subtle white dominance of professional football received its most significant challenge, which it has yet to meet for once and for all." He asked, "The real question is not whether the black quarterback is ready for professional football, but whether professional football and its followers are ready for the black quarterback." Chrisman understood that pro football was not just about merit, where the best player played. Instead, as he put it, "football is more than a sport. It is theater. It is one of the leading expressions of our national culture, and as such it embodies the popular culture values of the United States." As a pop culture spectacle, race fueled football. "Let's face it," he argued. "White supremacy is a concept that much of white America has yet to shake off. . . . Football, which has become a kind of national metaphor, inherited the burden of white supremacy notwithstanding its democratic demands as a sport. This has been particularly true of the quarterback." Young quarterbacks like Doug Williams and Vince Evans finally had a chance for a future in football.

CHAPTER 8

I$_N$ L$_{ATE}$ O$_{CTOBER}$ 1974, $_A$ $_{WEEK}$ $_{AFTER}$ J$_{AMES}$ H$_{ARRIS}$ $_{WON}$ $_{THE}$ Rams' starting quarterback job, Eddie Robinson rolled into Houston with his Grambling Tigers, chest puffed out and his head held high. Normally he was humble, but today was different. He had something to say about the future of the Black quarterback. His Tigers had already played games at RFK Stadium in Washington, DC, the Cotton Bowl in Dallas, and were now preparing to play Texas Southern University at the Houston Astrodome, with Shea Stadium in New York set for the following week. In three decades, Robinson built a tiny school in rural Louisiana into a brand name. He had put more than one hundred players into professional football, while teaching valuable lessons to his teams about race along the way. The Tigers coach had been selling his belief about football and racial uplift for decades, but this time, the words hit harder. They were backed up by the ultimate form of proof; he had two Black quarterbacks, Matthew Reed (WFL) and James Harris (NFL), succeeding in pro football. He also had another—redshirt freshman Doug Williams—who was going to be better than the rest.

Robinson had one bold prediction: "Within the next 10 years," he told a reporter, "over half of the quarterbacks in pro football are going to be black." At a time when only two Black quarterbacks were playing in the NFL, how could he make such a claim? For one, he believed in his formula. If a coach, especially a Black coach, wanted to put a Black quarterback into the NFL, then they would have to follow the Grambling path. Robinson installed a quarterback-friendly drop-back system, and he took advice from the pro players and coaches in how to improve their quarterback play. Once his guys made it, players like Matthew Reed and James Harris came back to Grambling to school the others. But now, he believed there was also another way for the Black quarterback, an integrated way.

On that day, as he observed the lay of the land, Robinson saw a mass of talented Black quarterbacks at white schools throughout the college landscape. The University of Tennessee had Heisman candidate Condredge Holloway, Don Gaffney ran the University of Florida's offense, Wake Forest went with Solomon Everett, the University of Tampa's Freddie Solomon passed and ran all over the opposing defense, and the University of Maryland trotted out Ben Kinard. Even LSU, the same school that made Terry Robiskie switch positions two years prior, now had Black backup Carl Otis Trimble. Up north, the Big Ten had five starting Black quarterbacks with Charlie Baggett (MSU), Tony Dungy (Minnesota), Dennis Franklin (Michigan), Cornelius Greene (Ohio State), and Willie Jones (Indiana). In the Big Eight, teams had five Black quarterbacks playing backup, and the Pac-8 had two, the University of Oregon's Herb Singleton and USC's Vince Evans.

What explains the increase in Black quarterbacks at predominantly white schools? That answer is easy. Times changed, and offenses changed. In short, integration and an evolution in offenses coincided at the same time. Coaches stopped using the

T formation that required a so-called cerebral quarterback and moved to formations that required athleticism. In place came offenses like the wishbone, veer, and triple options, where the quarterback was asked to pitch to the running back or take off on designed runs more than they were to dissect a zone defense and hit a crossing pattern. In 1974, among 127 major college teams, 54 teams ran a variation of a triple option, 36 ran the veer, 35 ran the I formation, and 15 ran the wishbone. Only 19 teams ran a pro-set system. As Joe Gilliam Sr., the defensive coordinator at Tennessee State, put it, "Today, a coach looks for the person who can fulfill the requirements of a skilled position. Before, he'd look for anyone else (besides a black) who could do it. He'd tell the black kid, 'You're gonna be a wide receiver.'" The University of Michigan's famed coach Bo Schembechler put it more bluntly. "Maybe we were all just a little too prejudiced," the Wolverine coach announced.

To be sure, the feelings about Black intelligence that had kept Black men out of the position for so long did not change; instead, colleges geared the quarterback position to athleticism. Bill Yeoman, who invented the veer at Houston and was the first white coach in the southeast to use a Black quarterback, said, "Anybody who wants to win had better get the best athlete he can find at that position. It doesn't make any difference what hue is to his skin. You'd better make sure he's a real good athlete and can function under pressure." Of course, Yeoman didn't think his Black quarterbacks were dumb. "All that other stuff," he said, "those idiotic stigmas, that's the biggest piece of tripe that's ever been known to man. I had several black kids play quarterback for me in my Veer offense, which requires extremely quick thinking in making the immediate decision while the play is being executed. And I never, never had any experience that remotely suggested those kids didn't have the intellect of any white quarterback I ever coached."

Yeoman might have seen his Black quarterbacks' quick thinking as intelligence, but NFL teams only saw them as athletes. His best, D. C. Nobles, went undrafted in the 1974. Nobles complained, "Every [NFL] scout who talked to me could not give me a reason why I was not drafted." But he knew the real reason. "I really think it was because of my color. I really feel like if I had been white, I would have been drafted in the first or second round."

Robinson saw a change in the NFL future; he just didn't think the league would continue to be shortsighted. In the mid-1970s, the NFL still had no use for the athletic Black quarterback. During the 1974 college season, the top two Black quarterbacks at these white schools, Condredge Holloway and Don Gaffney, ran the veer like Nobles, so the NFL paid them no mind. They still wanted quarterbacks who played in a pro-friendly system—like Doug Williams at Grambling.

CHAPTER 9

THE GRAMBLING TIGERS STARTED THE 1974 SEASON RANKED AS the number one Black team in the nation, an order that reflected their defense and not their offense. Unlike the past years when they were piloted by steady quarterback play, Eddie Robinson had major concerns about the passing game. He wanted to push the ball down the field, but he also wanted a quarterback who was accurate and consistent. To start the year, he gave Joe Comeaux the nod. The move made football sense. He fit Robinson's quarterback mold; big, strong, with a gatling gun for an arm. Comeaux had learned under Matthew Reed, and he had more experience than Terry Brown and Doug Williams. Because Comeaux played for Robinson, many experts also ranked him as the top quarterback prospect in Black colleges.

Despite all these accolades and potential for the big quarterback, Comeaux came up short. His inaccuracy issues from the previous season continued to plague him. His backup, Brown, was no better. The offense struggled, and the quarterbacks failed to connect with their star receivers, Sammy White and Dwight Scales. In their season-opener victory against Northwestern State, Comeaux and Brown threw four interceptions combined. Although there was an offensive coordinator change when Doug Porter headed to Howard University as their new head coach, most did not expect Grambling's offense to fall off. Robinson replaced Porter by promoting Melvin Lee, who had been his offensive line coach since 1960. At six foot six and 260 pounds, the giant was a genius. Throughout the years, it was Lee's wrinkles to the passing game that allowed Robinson to continue to use his outdated T wing offense. If it wasn't the coaches slowing down the offense, then it had to be the field generals.

Doug's frustration intensified after their second game, when the Tigers dropped a contest to Alcorn State. Comeaux threw two touchdowns in their 19–14 loss, but he also threw two interceptions and failed to convert on a fourth and goal from the 1-yard line in the closing seconds of the game. "Neither one of them is doing anything and they're still not playing me," Williams pouted. "I must not be any good." Instead of trying to compete for a job, Williams decided to quit the team. He skipped one practice. He skipped another. He was all but gone until assistant coach Fred Hobdy came to his dorm room and convinced him to come back to the team. Doug came back, but he refused to speak to anybody. The next day, the same thing happened. He was at practice, but he wanted to pout more than he wanted to play. When Friday rolled around and the team was set to leave for their game against Prairie View at the Cotton Bowl in Dallas, Doug Williams stayed back. He could hear the bus idling. They were waiting for him. Coach Hobdy came and got him again. Although Doug couldn't see it, Coach Robinson had a plan.

Robinson let Williams brood with little penalty because he was a coach that was always willing to let a young Black man work out his problems. Whereas most coaches would have their players running stairs or bear crawling up and down the field as punishment for skipping practice, Robinson welcomed Williams back with open arms. He was a teacher, and this was a lesson in life Williams had to learn. The world did not feel sorry for a Black kid who quit. As Robinson told a reporter a few weeks later, "My problem is I probably worry too much about the individual boy. When I go home each night following practice or a ball game I just want to turn over in my mind whether I have been fair to everyone. Whether I have given them the chance to play they deserve." He was fair to Doug the downer, but he was also a smart coach. He knew he would eventually need Williams. The Tigers had a stout defense and three future NFL receivers on the team. Comeaux had a big arm and the physical tools to make it as a pro quarterback, but he lacked accuracy. He still pressed for the big play more than the right play. He had more interceptions than touchdowns. Doug Williams was getting on that bus to Dallas.

Despite missing two practices, trying to skip the game, and sulking all week, when it was finally his turn, Williams was razor sharp. Early in the second half against Prairie View, Robinson finally inserted Williams into the lineup. In front of thirty thousand screaming fans in the Cotton Bowl, Williams went 6 of 8 passing and hit Sammy White for a 21-yard touchdown. Instead of letting his freshman sensation pile up more stats and get a big head, Robinson pulled him from the game. Robinson played Williams just enough to give him a taste of what it was like to sling the ball for the mighty G-Men. He also played him just enough to serve warning to Comeaux and Brown. It was a brilliant move. The Prairie View Panthers were not the dominant team of old. They were more like kittens, and Robinson knew the Tigers could play with their food. They won the game 61–0. Williams did not even get into the game until it was 47–0.

The next week, Williams got his big break. During a lackluster performance against Tennessee State, Comeaux hurt his wrist and was out for the game. Robinson turned to Brown, but Brown struggled too. Refusing to lose a game because of his quarterbacks, Robinson turned to Williams. All total, the Grambling quarterbacks went 3 of 15 for 12 yards and two interceptions. Williams did not outperform the others, but he played well enough for their dominant defense to maintain the lead. Because of that, he earned the starting job for the next week's game against Mississippi Valley State. In his first career start, he outdueled future Tampa Bay Buccaneers draft pick Parnell Dickinson, throwing for 225 yards and two touchdowns. Grambling's aerial assault was back. The job was his.

After dismantling the Delta Devils, Doug showed the quarterback intellect that would make him one of the greatest college quarterbacks ever. With Grambling taking on the Jackson State Tigers, Williams struggled in the first half, looking like a freshman on his way to a dismal 1 of 8 passing. Some of this could be chalked up to nerves, as it was his first home start, and Jackson State had the all-American running back Walter Payton—soon to be Vince Evans's teammate in Chicago—adding to the hype of the game. But Williams also showed his inexperience as he misread coverages. Knowing that they had a young quarterback in front of them, JSU head coach Robert Hill double-teamed his leading receivers, White and Scales. Without the security of being able to throw to their favorite targets, most freshman quarterbacks would break. The other quarterbacks on Grambling would have kept forcing passes, leading to turnovers.

Not Doug Williams. He found a new receiver to trust. From there, it was lights out. To close the first half, he led Grambling on an 85-yard drive, hitting tight end Rodney Singleton three times for 40 yards. The cerebral quarterback said, "They were double covering our wide receivers. So that left the tight end open." Once he started to hit Singleton, the defense had to adjust, leaving

White wide open. Doug hit him for a 14-yard touchdown. "I wish we could play all our quarterbacks," Robinson said after the game. "We've got some good ones and the ones who don't play aren't happy. Doug is moving the club now, so it's hard to change." It was time for Comeaux and Brown to get comfortable holding a clipboard.

By the end of the season, those outside of Grambling started to see what Robinson saw. With Doug in the lineup, Grambling continued to roll, running their record to 11–1, with another SWAC championship, and closing the season with a victory over South Carolina State in the Pelican Bowl, winning the National Black Football Championship. Sportswriter Jim McLain of the *Shreveport Times* led his championship game recap describing, "I don't know if anybody's thought of Dandy Doug as a nickname for Grambling quarterback Doug Williams, but that's the handle they're probably going to hang on him." Williams finished the game 13 of 18 for 207 yards, with two touchdowns in the air, and one 8-yard run into the end zone.

With Williams, the numbers never told the whole story. Robinson had so much trust in Williams that he let him call audibles at the line of scrimmage. The most successful plays in that game came from Doug's decisions. The night before the contest, he watched film and realized that throwing the bomb would not work against South Carolina State, so, as he said, "I figured we'd have to go to the curls and go under their coverage."

CHAPTER 10

Coming into Doug's 1975 sophomore season, the Grambling Tigers had great expectations. Returning thirty-seven players from a team that finished 11–1, the Tigers were ranked the number one Black college team by several polls. With offensive coordinator Melvin Lee having a whole offseason to work with Doug and the offense, the team prepared to transition into a pass-heavy attack. The wing T was designed as a run-oriented offense, but over the last decade as Robinson tried to put a quarterback into the NFL, the offense evolved into a more pass-friendly, pro-style game. They would still show run and try to commit to the running game, but it became abundantly clear that with Williams behind center, passing was more effective than running. And with three future NFL wide receivers (Sammy White, Dwight Scales, Carlos Pennywell), Williams had plenty of firepower. On occasion, they also added defensive back and kick return specialist James Hunter to the mix. Hunter was six foot three and ran a 4.3 forty, and he was nearly impossible for a linebacker to cover. With all those weapons, Grambling had the best receiver corps in the country.

THE GRAMBLING GUNNER

THE 1975 SEASON STARTED OFF WHERE GRAMBLING LEFT OFF: winning. Ever since Williams took over the starting job in their week 5 game in 1974, the Tigers were undefeated. In their opener against the formidable foe Alcorn State, a team who beat them the previous year, Williams lit up their secondary like a Christmas tree. The game, which was the first college football contest in the Louisiana Superdome, pit two of the top teams in Black college ball against each other. Unfamiliar with Williams's game, however, Alcorn State came in with the same game plan: stop the run. They stacked the line of scrimmage, but they foolishly left their secondary wide open for attack. Once it was clear that Robinson's Tigers could not run (32 yards), Williams went to the air. He noticed they were only using three defensive backs, read the defense, and let it rip. Over the summer, the "Grambling Gunner" had added eye manipulation to his passing arsenal. As his receiver Carlos Pennywell described, "He is real consistent. He can look the defense one way and then complete passes to the secondary receivers." All total, Williams went 9 of 18 for 171 yards and four touchdowns, including a 21-yarder to Pennywell. With Grambling up 27–3 in the third quarter against the Braves, Robinson pulled his prize pupil so he was sharp for their next game against Morgan State at RFK Stadium in Washington, DC.

He didn't get much work that game either, as Grambling pummeled their opponent 40–7 in front of twenty-nine thousand fans. Williams had two touchdowns and 133 yards in the first half, before Robinson decided to ride the ground game. He needed his team rested and ready for the biggest test in Grambling football history. In two weeks, they were going to face Oregon State from the Pac-8. This was what Eddie Robinson dreamed about.

The October 4, 1975, game against Oregon State was a showcase game for Robinson, or as he called it, "the biggest game of my career." This was the first time a Black college would play one of the country's top schools, and it was an opportunity for a Black David to go up against a Goliath. Grambling had played predominantly white teams before, but this was different. Those were small schools. The game would put all the noise to rest of whether one of the top Black schools could stomp with the big dogs. Robinson had heard it all before. He won a lot of games, 236 and counting, because Grambling didn't play anybody good. They just beat up on tiny Black schools that white fans hadn't heard of. Never mind that SWAC produced as much pro talent as any major football conference in America or that some people referred to Notre Dame as the "white Grambling." Until Robinson's teams played against the highest level, naysayers would always hold that against him. "We're not supposed to win," Robinson told the press. "We're just going to play our best because this game means a lot to us." This was the big time.

Robinson had always preached that America was a place of opportunity, and Black folks could not make any excuses about discrimination. "We've got to realize that we aren't the only ones who have had these problems," he'd say. "The Italians, the Chicanos, and the Jews have had to cope with the same problems." Cut from the same cloth of the early-twentieth-century Black political leader Booker T. Washington, Robinson hammered home that Black kids had to be prepared to compete against whites. He was a bootstrapper. There were no handouts in life. "They've got to realize," he would say, "that we must compete as Americans with Americans. The whole world isn't totally black. America isn't totally black." All that talk he'd given to his players about competing against whites meant that it was time to show and prove.

Oregon State might have been a Pac-8 team playing against a Black Division II foe, but Beavers coach Dee Andros had cause for concern. The Beavers would also be facing their second Black quarterback in a matter of three weeks, but the quarterbacks presented the Beavers' defense with two different styles: one that emphasized the run and another that emphasized the pass. Evans and his Trojans had recently smashed the Beavers. The Trojans ran for 319 yards, including 56 from Evans. Grambling, as Coach Andros asserted, was an even bigger team than the Trojans, averaging 240 pounds on their offensive line and a stout 260 pounds on their defensive front. "They have pro-size people with pro-size talent," Andros told the press. But unlike USC, Grambling used their bulk to protect the passer instead of steamrolling the defense. Andros, whose team started 0–3, knew what to expect: the bomb. With a backhanded compliment, he summarized, "They look for the easy route. They aren't the type to drive it down your throat." Hedging his bets heading into the game, Andros fell back on the same cozy built-in excuse Goliaths usually give: they were in a no-win situation. If Oregon State beat Grambling, no one was impressed. They were supposed to do that. But if they lost, they'd be ridiculed for losing to a Division II Black school. Either way, Doug Williams and his dynamic receivers were ready to put on a show.

In front of sixteen thousand fans, Williams showed what he could do against the big-time schools, and Robinson proved a point. In their 19–12 victory, Williams threw two touchdown passes, one to Sammy White and another in the last minute of the game to Dwight Scales that sealed the deal. Williams, who spent the offseason working on timing with his receivers, was always in sync with his crew. On the game-winning play, one Williams called the best touchdown pass of his collegiate career, Robinson pulled Williams to the side and asked him what play he wanted to run. Doug called for a corner route from Scales, his specialty. But as the play unfolded, Scales saw the safety jump that route, so in the middle of his route, Scales switched to a post. Doug hit him with a perfect strike. The two had practiced so much with each other over the summer, Williams knew what Scales would do. It was a play that put everyone on notice.

Coming off their big victory at Oregon State, the premier Black quarterback in college awaited the Tigers. Outside of the Black media circuit, few knew about Parnell Dickinson. At six foot two and 180 pounds, with a 4.5 forty time, Dickinson was a threat to score any time he touched the ball. Operating from a pro-style offense, Dickinson was named to the all-SWAC first team in his freshman and sophomore years and was named a Black college all-American his junior year in 1974. The honor put "Pay Dirt" Dickinson on the radar of NFL scouts who routinely used the list to compile their draft scouting reports. Whereas in the past, most Black quarterbacks might have been apprehensive about their chances to play quarterback in the pros, Dickinson believed that James Harris gave people like him hope. "I think the chances of a black getting a quarterback job in the NFL are a lot better now because of James Harris," said Dickinson after being named an all-American. "In the past, it was kinda hard, and I think the pros passed over a lot of good quarterbacks because they were black. But now I think that's all changed." He was right. In the 1976 draft, John McKay and Tampa Bay selected Dickinson in the seventh round. With future pro players on all three levels of Grambling's defense, Dickinson would get a taste of what awaited him in the future.

Though Grambling versus Mississippi Valley State was billed as a contest between the top gunslingers in Black college ball, the Grambling Gunner killed all hope of a Delta Devils victory before Dickinson even had a chance to draw. In the first quarter, Williams hit Sammy White for a 68-yard bomb, and then he threw a screen pass that went 64 yards for a touchdown. Adding another field goal to the mix, the Tigers were up 17–0 with Williams going

4 of 4 for 153 yards before Dickinson even completed a pass. In a 38–22 defeat, Dickinson ended the day with 162 yards. Williams, on the other hand, threw for 204 yards in the first half, before Robinson eased up on the gas pedal.

With only one hiccup all season—a 24–14 road loss to Jackson State—it seemed like nothing could go wrong for Williams and the Tigers as they headed into their showdown with Southern in the second annual Bayou Classic. In front of seventy thousand fans in the Superdome, Williams was on his way to putting on another show. In the first quarter, he hit White for a touchdown for the quarterback's twenty-third of the season, a mark that broke Terry Bradshaw's single-season record for college quarterbacks in Louisiana. Unfortunately, in the second quarter, Williams tore his knee, an injury that ended an otherwise outstanding year where he broke the state record for touchdowns and set Grambling's single-season passing record, with 1,959 yards. Despite facing a massive uphill battle to fully recover from reconstructive knee surgery, Williams had at least a silver lining—being injured at the end of the season meant he had all offseason to rehab and prepare for his junior season. The minor setback set him up for a major comeback.

COMEBACK

FOR MONTHS AFTER THE INJURY, WILLIAMS LABORED TO BECOME his old self. In the 1970s, the serious knee injury that Williams suffered could have been career ending. After surgery, the doctor put a sixty-pound cast around his leg and told him to stay off it for six weeks. Six weeks seemed like an eternity for a workaholic like Williams. After losing three offensive weapons to the NFL draft (Hunter, White, and Scales), he yearned to get on the field to get his timing back with Pennywell, receiver Edward Scott, and new tight end Mike Moore.

When the cast finally came off, Williams's leg was as stiff as a board. He worked out every day to strengthen his knee. He ran up and down the stairs, just trying to get some mobility back. All summer long, he dragged Pennywell and Scott out to the field for passing drills. Soon, Scott saw the old form returning. "The leg seems to be well," he told a reporter in August. "He's rolling left and right real well." Pennywell cautioned Doug that it was not just the physical game he had to get back, however; he had to remaster the mental aspects. Especially his toughness. Throwing to his receivers was one thing, but when the defense shot back, how would the Grambling Gunner react? Doug had to ask himself tough questions about quarterbacking. Would he be able to withstand a fierce pass rush? What was going to happen the first time he got hit? There was only one way to find out. He had to play.

In any normal situation, playing against Alcorn State's defense would be a daunting task, but battling the Braves after coming back from a knee injury would be nearly impossible. The Braves were the one team in the SWAC that had Grambling's number, and they did it with a stout defense that controlled the line of scrimmage. When the two teams battled, it was an all-out war, or as Alcorn coach Marino Casem aptly put it, "Playing Grambling is like making love to a gorilla. You can't quit without permission." Almost as big as Grambling up front, the Braves led the National Association of Intercollegiate Athletics (NAIA) in rushing defense the previous year, only allowing 16 yards a game. That meant whether Williams was ready or not, he would be tested.

Williams's knees held up, but that was about it. The Braves beat the Tigers down, holding them to 30 yards rushing and 53 yards passing. For Doug, the numbers were even worse. He was 9 of 28 passing and had four interceptions. It was the first—and only—game he failed to throw a touchdown as the Tigers fell 24–0. But not all was bad. Surviving the game meant his knee was fine. He would be back throwing touchdowns soon enough.

A week later, in Philadelphia, he threw for four touchdowns, three to Pennywell, and 258 yards in a tough loss to Temple University. Doug Williams was back. Overall, after losing eight players to the 1976 NFL draft, the Tigers did as well as one could expect. They finished the year a respectable 8–3, and with their only loss in conference play to Alcorn State, they shared the SWAC title with the Braves.

On the way to recovery, Doug continued to prove that he could play at the next level. In their tenth game of the season, Williams broke the Grambling all-time touchdown record when he connected on his third touchdown of the day against Norfolk State. The 7-yard pass to Pennywell gave Williams fifty-four touchdowns on his career, passing James Harris. Next year, he'd turn his attention to the NCAA record. With one year of eligibility left, he was now on the NFL's radar. And that meant more Black quarterback talk.

Williams's road back was made easier by his weekly phone sessions with James Harris. Even as Harris went through the turmoil with the Rams, he regularly talked to Doug about what he could expect in the pros. Although Harris soured on the NFL, he never let Doug get bitter. In fact, if Doug didn't read the press, he would never know what Harris was going through. Harris refused to bring up his situation with his mentee, because he wanted Doug to have an open mind. Eddie Robinson was the same way too. "Doug," he told him, "you've got to be a man about things. You've got to be able to handle what is thrown your way. Over the years, you'll have to cope with it. You'll have to be able to talk to the press and get your point across."

CHAPTER 11

For Vince Evans, 1975 promised to be his year. With Pat Haden gone, he'd finally be a leading man in Tinseltown. For his new role, he'd have to transform his body. The previous season, the USC fans labeled him "the Trojan Horse," but at six foot two and 220 pounds, Evans knew that if he were going to be the man, he'd have to become more like a colt. No more jokes from teammates who'd told him he'd be switched to offensive guard if he got any bigger. By working out and eating one meal a day, Evans dropped 20 pounds. He felt lighter, quicker, and ready to stampede the opposition.

Evans hoped that a new role and a new body would produce new results. The previous season, he only threw thirteen passes. As a sophomore backup, he had a great relationship with Pat Haden, who taught him how to read defenses and anticipate a defender's next move. "Some quarterbacks," Evans complimented, "wouldn't have done that. They would have been all for themselves. But not Pat." Evans also spent the offseason working on his throwing and timing with his receivers. "I know most people think of me as a runner," he told the press during the summer, "but Vince Evans in the past has always been known as a runner AND a passer." He also convinced himself, and perhaps the coaches too, that if he didn't pass the ball, "I wouldn't be exploiting my talents to the fullest."

SAVE USC FOOTBALL, SHOOT VINCE EVANS

IN TRUTH, EVANS NEEDED ALL THE PREPARATION AND PRACTICE he could get at the position. His arm was as strong as a cannon— but not much more accurate. It was nothing for him to heave the ball 60–70 yards in the air, only to see his pass drop to the turf, too far ahead of a receiver. And when he uncoiled for a 10-yard pass, the ball came in too fast, even breaking his receivers' fingers. Or as one preseason magazine simply put it, "He's a better runner than passer." For Coach John McKay, however, these were fixable problems. "I have been reading that he can't throw," McKay told reporters at the beginning of the 1975 season, "but I think he's going to be a good quarterback. He's going to be a good pro. You have to have as many passes as a pitcher has pitches in baseball, and that is what Vince has to learn." Evans had one pitch, a devastating fastball. But as a quarterback, he couldn't throw heat all the time; he'd have to learn how to take something off the ball and learn where to properly place it.

Making it harder for Evans was the reality that McKay and his 1975 staff were not the right coaches to teach Evans how to be a classic quarterback. They wanted a running quarterback. McKay said Evans was the best running quarterback he ever had, but that was all McKay saw him as. McKay was more interested in how Evans fit his system. Moreover, McKay did not believe in hiring coordinators to run his offense and defense separately. He had coaches, yes, but nobody to specifically help with the necessary details of coordinating the game or building a quarterback. As Evans recalled, "Coach (Craig) Fertig [the assistant coach] was a good coach. But we just didn't have as many meetings. Consequently, I was always undecided as to what to do."

The I formation allowed Evans to roll out, which was his strength, but McKay and the offense limited his chances of success, because in that formation, there was only one primary receiver. What happened when his one read was not open? "That was fine," Evans asserted, "for somebody like Pat Haden, who . . . ran that offense for so long," but for Evans, the lack of preparation and offensive versatility in the passing plans hurt his development. And when McKay had Evans drop back as a passer opposed to rolling out as a running threat, his troubles increased because the offense did not use running backs as outlets to relieve pressure. When he rolled out as a passer, he'd face a decision: throw to the covered receiver, or scramble. None of that helped him as a passer or as a leader.

Even though the team had lost fourteen seniors to the 1975 NFL draft, fans expected dominance from USC. Evans failed to deliver. In his first three games of the season, Evans went 2 of 10, 5 of 12, and 4 of 12 for a total of 130 yards and two interceptions. On the ground, he rushed for 133 yards and two touchdowns. In the third game, he cracked his thumb, putting him out for two weeks. When he came back against Oregon in week 6, he went 1 of 9 passing, but his only connection was a long bomb for 69 yards, a flash of his potential. The next game, in their big rivalry match against Notre Dame, Evans went 3 of 11 for 42 yards and two interceptions. Surprisingly, that putrid performance outpaced Notre Dame's Joe Montana, who was 3 of 11 for 25 yards and two interceptions. Despite poor quarterback play, the Trojans were still 7–0. But then things started to unravel, and losses started to pile. Cal, Stanford, Washington, and UCLA stomped the Trojans.

When the Trojans started to crumble, the blame came down on Evans. In their loss to Cal, he was 3 of 11 passing for 44 yards.

And then in the next week, Stanford beat the Trojans as Evans went 4 of 11 for 94 yards. McKay had finally seen enough. He benched Evans for their next game against Washington. When asked why he made the move, McKay told the press, "[Mike Stanford] is a better passer than Evans. He's not very big. He's not very fast. But he has done well in practice." As much as McKay touted Mike Stanford as a passer, he only let him throw three times, which resulted in 1 of 3 passing. Evans got his job back, but the worst was still to come.

As a passer, Evans hit his lowest point against crosstown rival UCLA. McKay and his staff believed that UCLA's defense was susceptible to the pass, and for the first time all year, USC would come out throwing the ball. Although McKay ran Ricky Bell thirty-six times, he also let Evans throw twenty-four passes, a season high. The lack of preparation all year on his mechanics, plus McKay's inability to instill confidence in Evans as a passer, hurt his field general. Evans finished the game 7 of 24 for 111 yards. Those numbers were made worse by his inability to perform when it counted most. Down 25–22 in the last quarter, he threw fourteen straight incompletions. USC lost its fourth straight game. Pouring salt into USC fans' wounds, McKay announced he was leaving to coach the new Tampa Bay Buccaneers. With a new coach coming in, alumni demanded a new quarterback. They were done with Vince Evans.

Evans ended the season having only completed 31 percent of his passes and thrown nine interceptions. Put another way, one out of twelve passes he threw went to the other team. Until that UCLA game, he'd completed no more than five passes in any game—a number he surpassed despite his disastrous overall play. These bad numbers were made worse by the national attention they garnered. After the UCLA loss, *Sports Illustrated* wrote that Evans couldn't throw the ball "into the Grand Canyon while standing at the rim."

Like that great American wonder, Vince Evans became a spectacle as folks marveled at his supposed ineptness.

This treatment would be hard for any young quarterback, but USC fans refused to see him as just another quarterback. They didn't care about the team's inexperience or the instability McKay caused as he flirted with the NFL all season before he finally ditched the Trojans for Tampa Bay. They cared about Evans's color. Bumper stickers throughout the USC campus read, SAVE USC FOOTBALL, SHOOT VINCE EVANS. Criticism is part of the quarterback's job description, but these fans didn't think to draw the line at death threats. It's even more heinous when one considers the fact that on two occasions in his senior year, he received death threats before the Stanford and UCLA games. Before the Stanford game, he received a letter that read, "Dear nigger, You better not show up to this game. If you do I will blow two holes in your back." And before the UCLA game, a fan wrote him, "Nigger, if you go out there today and play well, I'm going to shoot you at halftime." Evans had four touchdowns that game. "I had to disappoint him," Evans said. "I wasn't going to be intimidated by a crazy guy in front of my parents and myself." He tried to laugh those threats off and play his game, but the ordeal made him think about race in a new light. As one reporter stated, "But the passion that results in such hatreds and the underlying philosophy that it is the nth degree is not so easy to laugh off. Not when you are a black quarterback and determined to remain one."

Evans couldn't handle the criticism and the racism. He became depressed. "I remember those mornings last year," he told *Los Angeles Times* reporter Skip Bayless. "I didn't even want to get up. I was scared to look in the paper and see the bad things that had been written about me." He started to internalize the hate. He started to question his abilities. Inside the huddle, where he was supposed to lead, doubt crept in. "When players look at you funny in the huddle because you didn't call the play right," he reflected, "that makes you feel bad." He added, "Sometimes I'd get in a huddle and didn't know what to do and they saw it, too. They saw it in my eyes. They saw it in the way I called plays."

If the criticism were simply about his play, he could deal with it, but the prejudice hurt. "I can't understand why some people continue to mess with me," he said. "I wonder if it's the color of my skin. I know some people think that a black quarterback can't play because he can't think or lead well enough." Black quarterbacks had labels for this racism. They called it *color syndrome* or the *Black quarterback syndrome*. These were names that would assume that there was some kind of disease or condition a Black man had that kept him from succeeding at quarterback. "The color syndrome really gets to me," Evans once complained. "People sticking with the stereotype of 'He's black and he can't play quarterback' or 'He's black and he can't think.' It shouldn't have any bearing."

REDEMPTION

AFTER HIS MISERABLE JUNIOR SEASON, EVANS WALKED AROUND with his head down and "heartbroken." Looking back on the season, he said, "I didn't get much guidance . . . I was just expected to get the job done on the basis of my talent." To help with his frustration, he talked to Willie Brown, USC's only Black coach. But at the end of the 1975 season, Brown left for Tampa Bay with McKay. Few people truly understood the struggles of a Black quarterback, but Evans did not have to go too far to find someone to talk to. In Los Angeles, James Harris was dealing with the same racism. Ever since he started in 1974, the white fans had been trying to get rid of their Black quarterback. And finally midway through the 1976 season, the Rams replaced Harris with Pat Haden, despite Harris going 20–6 as a starter over three years and having the highest passer rating that season. The white fans loved Haden. He was the perfect white guy to unseat a Southern Black quarterback. Local writer Doug Krikorian once described the blond-haired, blue-eyed quarterback: "A definite Wheaties coverboy candidate, he is boyishly handsome with blond hair, rosy cheeks and blue eyes. He's polite, modest, sensitive and religious." Harris could handle a blitz, but the bigotry of losing his job to Haden was too much. "Mentally, it ruined me," Harris harped. "As a quarterback I had done all I could, more than most people could, and it still wasn't enough for the Los Angeles Rams to accept me just as a quarterback, not a black quarterback."

As Harris tried to evade the pocket of prejudice, he made sure to protect Evans. Throughout his tenure there, Harris mentored Evans on how to deal with racism. He told him two things that changed the trajectory of his career. One, he advised him to ignore the haters. The racist fans would always be there. Second, he reminded Evans he was a quarterback, and that was where he belonged. Never let a coach switch you. This mentorship changed Evans's outlook for the upcoming season.

Evans had another reason to be optimistic. USC replaced Coach McKay with John Robinson. "When I heard he was going to be the coach," said Evans, "it was like a new day." He continued, "He's the type of man who radiates motivation like no other I've ever seen." Prior to his head coaching job at USC, Robinson spent twelve years coaching at Oregon, including three years as the offensive coordinator, where his offense led by quarterback Dan Fouts and running back Bobby Moore (who later changed his name to Ahmad Rashad after converting to Islam) in 1970 and 1971 lit up scoreboards. After the 1971 season, McKay hired Robinson as an assistant, where he helped the throwing and running tandem of Pat Haden and Anthony Davis reach three straight Rose Bowls. Evans and Robinson had grown close in 1974, but in 1975, Robinson left for the pros to work with his childhood friend

John Madden as the Raiders' running backs coach. A year later, he was the head man at USC. The first question he had to answer from the media was about his quarterback position. Despite what all the doubters said about Evans, John Robinson had big plans.

For Robinson, change started with the offense. The I formation was fine for running, but he believed it lacked versatility and creativity and allowed defenders to key on the run. Sure, Ricky Bell led the nation in rushing yards in 1975 and almost broke the single-season record with 1,957 yards, but it took him 385 carries in twelve games. The Trojans needed balance. While still employing the I formation, Robinson planned to open the offense up and get the running backs to catch passes out of the backfield. "The worst thing about a one-pronged offense," he said in his first week on the job, "is that you haven't worked on anything else and you really can't convert to something new." Of course, in the minds of many fans, the worst thing about the USC offense was Vince Evans.

With Robinson talking about passing, the press wanted to know how this was possible with a guy who couldn't hit the ocean if he were standing on the Santa Monica Pier. Robinson did not waver. Evans was his guy. "Vince is an excellent athlete. Going into this past season, coach McKay thought he was going to be a successful quarterback, but there were certain things Vince didn't do well," he told reporters. Robinson had to give him time to learn and prove that he could play. "It would be foolish of me to write him off and it also would be foolish of me to be stubborn and play him," he pleaded. "Vince is in a learning situation. He's going to have to change. The type of offense we're going to run will be more strict. But I think he's going to be a hungry guy." For a quarterback hungry to learn, Robinson had a plan: a steady diet of Paul Hackett.

At twenty-nine years old, Hackett had a reputation as the best quarterback coach. In his first year as quarterback coach at Cal in 1974, he molded Steve Bartkowski into the number one pick.

In their next season, he took their community college transfer Joe Roth and quickly made him into one of the best passers in college ball, helping Cal win a share of the Pac-8 title, including a victory over USC. In 1976, he was charged with doing the unthinkable: make Vince Evans into a quarterback. Few thought he could pull off that trick. Fortunately for Evans, Hackett cared more about the finer points of the position than he did about the color of one's skin. To mold Evans, however, he needed to change his mentee's mind and mechanics.

Mechanically, Evans was a mess. He was so bad that when Hackett first watched film on him as a coach at Cal, he claimed, "We brought the film in just so we could chuckle." Holding the ball without the laces was only a small problem. He had no touch, he had no rhythm, he had no timing, he had no real experience. As Hackett observed, "Not playing quarterback as a youngster was a handicap for Vince. He has fantastic ability—he can throw the ball a mile and has quick feet—but there's actually playing the position." Because of his lack of experience, he missed the nuances of quarterbacking. Hackett talked to him about his touch and how to throw to a receiver by throwing to a spot. Evans threw high, he threw low, but he rarely threw accurately. "I've been throwing the ball too hard," Evans admitted. "Coach Hackett has taught me to throw with a lighter touch, to take something off it." No more breaking his receivers' fingers.

Hackett also went to work on Evans's mind. They talked about the "black thing." Although Hackett had never worked with a Black quarterback, he was sensitive to what Evans had to go through. On Hackett's first visit to campus, he got a stark introduction when he saw the SAVE USC FOOTBALL, SHOOT VINCE EVANS bumper stickers. He understood that Vince was motivated to be great not only because he wanted to be great but also to prove the racists wrong. Evans frequently told Hackett, "I'm going to show people I can play the position." But Hackett also believed that the race issue weighed too heavily on Vince's mind. "But you know," Hackett told journalist Skip Bayless, "sports equalizes that problem (integration) better than any other part of society. Nobody on this team could care less about it." As a white man, Hackett had some blinders on, but he saw Evans as a quarterback, and that's what counted the most. Hackett believed the best way the quarterback could get past race was to work hard. "Vince Evans's rise and fall as a quarterback just depends on how bad he wants to be great. He was a terrible quarterback last year, and he knows it. I don't care if he was pink, he was really bad." To remedy that problem, Hackett challenged Evans to study in the film room. If he didn't, Hackett warned, he would bench him or turn him into a receiver. The spark ignited a flame. Evans pestered his coach with questions and took down copious notes. He studied film so much that Hackett had to kick him out of the film room.

Evans, of course, was ready to share all of this with the media to silence the doubters. Before the season started, he told reporters, "Coach Hackett gave me a much broader perspective towards football. I know so much more now than before. He's helped me grasp what the job of quarterback includes, things like finesse in passing, audibles, knowing when to run and when not to." Hackett returned the compliment. "The most important area he's improved in is in the time and effort he's put into the job. A person has to have a yearning to learn, and Vince has put the time in the film too and in practice to become a better player." Hackett also told reporters, "He's also improved in his understanding of football, which is one of my big hangups. A quarterback should know what he's going to do at all times, how to read defenses, when to change the offense, now what type of ball to throw."

Football was not a test one took on paper. Evans had to play. Evans had to lead a team that had averaged just four completions a game the previous season. With seven returning starters on defense and eight coming back on offense, including all-American running back Ricky Bell, media, fans, and especially alumni expected big things from the Trojans, regardless of their coaching and quarterback situation. The high expectations also meant that Evans had little time to slip up. As one leading magazine put it, "The key to a truly outstanding season lies in the development of some offensive balance."

The Trojans kicked off their season against the University of Missouri. Although not a traditional powerhouse, the Tigers were a tough test for a new coach with a new offense and a remade quarterback. They were returning eight starters on defense and seven starters on offense, including their star quarterback, Steve Pisarkiewicz, who was a preseason favorite as an all-American pick. They were also capable of pulling off a big upset, as they did the previous season opener when they kicked the snot out of Alabama. Against USC, they did just that. Missouri easily handled the Trojans 46–25, giving USC their fifth straight regular season defeat going back to 1975. All eyes zoomed in on Evans, who went 10 of 18 for 154 yards.

While this was clearly his best throwing game as a quarterback, the grumblings began for Coach Robinson to replace him. Robinson refused. "He played very well," Robinson told the local press. "He missed some guys in the open. That happens. He was a 31 percent passer last year. Saturday night he was 10 for 18 and that's 55 percent. He's improved." On another occasion, he reasoned, "Some guys would say Vince threw eight incomplete passes last week. Another guy would look at the stats and say he completed 10 passes and had a good night. I'm rooting for Vince—and every other player on the team." Robinson's initial support was all Evans needed.

After blasting the University of Oregon 53–0 in a game in which Evans went 9 of 14 for 107 yards, many expected their contest against Purdue would be the true test for Evans. The Boilermak-ers had an experienced defense, and expectations were high. They planned to stack the line of scrimmage to prevent the run and dare Evans to pass. But their plan backfired. Ricky Bell set a stadium record with thirty-seven carries in a game, and Evans went 13 of 16 passing. A local writer concluded that Evans's performance was one of the best in school history. "Vince Evans, who used to do an excellent imitation of the Venus de Milo passing, did an even bet-ter job of resembling Joe Namath Saturday to let the steam out of Purdue's Boilermakers." Purdue coach Alex Agase acknowledged, "The most amazing improvement is in Evans. Their passing game gets them out of trouble now, where a year ago it didn't even pose a threat." And Coach Robinson praised his poise and patience for hitting his second and third receivers instead of bailing out when his first opening was shut off. Evans, who after three games was now 32 of 48 for 423 yards with only one interception, beamed, "I always believed I was a good passer."

By midseason, he earned national attention as one of the top quarterbacks in the nation. He was at the top of the conference in passing statistics, and most importantly, he also had the fewest interceptions of all starters. "Coming into the eighth game of the year," he reflected, "I now can look at myself as a complete quar-terback." The confident Evans elaborated, "Before I didn't under-stand all that came with the job, and that doesn't mean just being a leader and throwing passes. It includes all of the little things that go into being a quarterback and being successful." He was so confident in his ability and so focused on winning that when Stanford fans sent him hate mail and a death threat, he laughed it off. He got his revenge when he killed their defense with his best performance as a Trojan, setting the school record by throwing four touchdowns in the first half. The Trojans won 48–24. Like a true leader, however, Evans only allowed himself so much time to bask in the glory. The Trojans had a team goal to get to the Rose Bowl. To do that, they had to get by the number two ranked team in the nation: UCLA.

Once again, the 1976 contest between UCLA and USC pit two of the best teams in the nation against each other for a chance at the Rose Bowl. Even though the Bruins lost their coach from the previous season, Dick Vermeil, and had to replace their star quarterback, John Sciarra, under new coach Terry Donahue they kept rolling over opponents. Coming into the game, UCLA had a 9–0–1 record with their one tie coming against Ohio State, the team they beat in the previous Rose Bowl. In their previous two games, they scored a combined 91 points against Oregon and Oregon State. Sheer dominance. But that looked like light work compared to the Evans-led Trojans, who rolled up a combined 109 points against the two schools from Oregon. USC had the number one offense in the country. They also had a quarterback with revenge on his mind, who needed this victory to completely redeem himself.

Locked in, Evans tried to block out all the doubters and distractions one last time, even laughing off another death threat. During the game, UCLA's 3-4 defense and the pressure of the moment impacted his passing as he missed key throws and had a few bad reads, but it did not impact his leadership. His poise helped the Trojans build a 24–0 lead in the fourth quarter, which included his 36-yard running touchdown to get them to 24–0. As his coach surmised, "He played magnificently, and it was very deserving, too, after what happened to him last year." With the game over and a trip to the Rose Bowl booked, Evans lingered on the field longer than usual to soak in the moment. When he finally made his way to the locker room, he had something to get off his chest. To that *Sports Illustrated* writer who said he couldn't hit the Grand Canyon with the football, Evans retorted, "I just hope they were watching, that's all." Then he mocked, "Tell them I can throw it across the lake now." The Trojan field general then turned his sights on conquering Michigan in the Rose Bowl.

Like USC, Michigan came into the Rose Bowl with a 10–1 record. After UCLA's loss, the Wolverines had become the nation's new number two team, with an explosive running game out of the I formation that helped them score more total points during the year (426) than USC (372). Their quarterback, Rick Leach, only had 897 passing yards all year with eight interceptions and thirteen touchdowns, but despite a weak and inaccurate arm, he did not receive half the criticism pointed at Evans. Oddsmakers were so sure that the Wolverines would win, they put them as 6-point favorites. The oddsmakers did not plan on Evans to play his best college game ever. He had his passes on a rope as he dominated the Wolverines' defense for 14 of 20 passing for 181 yards on his way to leading USC to a 14–6 victory. They couldn't stop him on his runs either, including when he scored the Trojans' first touchdown on a fake halfback dive to Charles White. After the game, he was in such hot demand in the locker room that the media walked right by O. J. Simpson to talk to the player of the game. Evans coolly stated, "This was the greatest thrill of my life."

Days after the Rose Bowl, Coach Robinson saw Evans in his office and handed him a gift. It was the game film. Robinson told him, "That game film is art. You will never play a better game than that. That may be one of the great performances in the history of this game." Evans had no time to revisit his masterpiece; he had to erase the illusion that a speedy Black quarterback could not play pro ball. For as much as Evans believed in his ability to play quarterback at the next level, what happened to Harris and the Rams gave him pause. "All I could think of was 'why?'" he said. If the pros did that to a classic quarterback, what would happen to a man who could run?

CHAPTER 12

In the first week of May 1977, *TIME* magazine published a not-so-subtle article about the changing American sports landscape. Entitled "The Black Dominance," the article claimed that fans' eyes had not deceived them. The stereotypes about Black athleticism had been true. From Dr. J to O. J., the Black athlete dominated sports. And it wasn't just domination; the style and grace of their athleticism could not be matched by any white athletes. Dr. J defied gravity, and O. J. smoothly glided through defenses. The NBA was 65 percent Black, and even the great white player turned coach Jerry West admitted it was a Black league. While Major League Baseball was only 19 percent Black, since integration in 1947, Black players had dominated the sport, winning sixteen MVPs and breaking records that seemed insurmountable, like Hank Aaron did to Babe Ruth's home run mark. In the NFL, changes were also rapidly occurring. The league had grown to 42 percent Black, a high number considering a history of prejudice that persisted.

To demystify the athletic explosion, the article asked leading sports scholars, critical thinkers, and athletes to explain what had changed. Collectively, the pundits threw around the usual unscientific statements, including the popular myths that surviving slavery had made the Black athlete dominant, that whites and Blacks had different leg muscles, and they told readers that coaches, parents, and community leaders were funneling young Blacks into sports as a way out of the ghetto. Despite all this growth, the pundits claimed, Black athletes still found racial resistance, especially the quarterback. "It's very interesting," leading sport sociologist Harry Edwards posited, "that a white man can be a quarterback regardless of what his intellectual reputation is." However, he added, "a black—I don't care what his intellectual reputation is—cannot be a quarterback."

The article hit the newsstands on the second day of the 1977 NFL draft. With no Black quarterbacks selected on the first day of the draft, many started to wonder whether any would be selected at all. Throughout the 1976 college season, two Black quarterbacks at PWIs grabbed attention from the pros: Tony Dungy and Vince Evans. Dungy and Evans were not like the previous Black quarterbacks to make it in the league. They were built in the mold of the ones who were told to switch. During the draft, no team took a chance on Dungy. He eventually signed with the Steelers as a receiver before being switched to a safety. What made the slight even harder for Dungy to stomach was seeing other quarterbacks he was better than get their shot. "As I watched the guys who were playing quarterback, I saw a lot who weren't very good. It took me about a year to come to the conclusion that I could have played quarterback." If the NFL were truly going to embrace the Black quarterback, then teams would have to make room for the Black quarterbacks who could run and throw, because that's where the game was headed, even if the league did not know it yet. A decade prior, the league saw a glimpse of what that looked like when Marlin "the Magician"

Briscoe befuddled defenses with his long bombs and jetlike speed before pro football quickly grounded his act and forced him to be a receiver. Their treatment of Briscoe meant it would be much harder for guys like Vince Evans to get a chance.

THE MAGICIAN

In 1968, when Marlin Briscoe broke the starting quarterback barrier, he also opened a new conversation about quarterbacking and Black speed in professional football. With his 4.5 forty time, pro football had never seen quarterbacking speed like his before. Was there a place in the game for a dual-threat quarterback who also happened to be Black?

Briscoe was never supposed to be a barrier breaker, but sometimes one's desperation is enough to forget about one's discrimination. During his career, Broncos coach Lou Saban did not see a place for Black quarterbacks in the game, as he eventually cut four Black quarterbacks in a four-year span without giving them legit chances, but in 1968, he had no choice. His starting quarterback, Steve Tensi, broke his collarbone in the preseason. The backup quarterbacks, John McCormick, Joe DiVito, and Jim LeClair, could hardly move the offense. The Broncos cut McCormick two days after he started the first game of the season. They cut DiVito after the second game of the season. They cut LeClair after he started the third game of the season. Desperate, Saban inserted Briscoe into the game against the Boston Patriots on September 29, making Briscoe the first Black quarterback to throw a pass since 1955. The following week, the college quarterback who was drafted in the fourteenth round and then promptly switched to defensive back made history.

"Briscoe. Up. You're starting this week. Get yourself ready." He was now the starter. His mouth went dry, his body went numb. It took him the rest of the day to process what happened. He would be the first Black quarterback to start in pro football when his Broncos faced the newly minted Cincinnati Bengals on October 6, 1968. One of the most important dates in pro football history. It signaled the possibilities of the future. A Black man could lead white men. Briscoe did his best to compartmentalize the meaning of the contest. "I haven't thought too much about being the first Negro quarterback. It makes me work that much harder, knowing I have to prove myself because I am the first. It might be a stepping stone for others to get into the pros as a quarterback instead of being switched," he reflected. The Broncos had record ticket sales as fans prepared to see their Black quarterback perform. They caught the wrong act.

Briscoe was awful. To prepare for his speed, Bengals assistant coach Bill Walsh, who said before the game that the only way to stop Briscoe was on the blackboard, used a fast defensive back, Jess Phillips, as the Bengals' practice quarterback, and when the defense practiced for the Broncos plays, Walsh had Phillips run away from the defensive line when the ball was snapped while also weaving left and right as he feinted throws. The Bengals coaching staff wanted their players to get used to chasing a moving target. They also prepped their players to contain Briscoe in the middle of the field. The plan worked. He completed 4 of 11 passes for only 37 yards, and he only mustered 18 running yards. As a Cincinnati writer described it, "Briscoe looked like he had hardly been introduced to football." Saban benched Briscoe for Steve Tensi. The Broncos beat the Bengals, and Tensi won his job back. But lingering injuries forced Tensi to the bench again during several contests and eventually for the season.

When Briscoe got another turn, he showed the full range and possibilities that an athletic quarterback could bring to the league. As a backup against the Chargers, Briscoe threw 3 touchdowns, including a 60-yard pass where he rolled left and threw right. The opposing quarterback, John Hadl, marveled, "He showed a lot of poise. And he's got a strong arm. My Lord, on that one touchdown he ran to his left and threw 60 yards on the run downfield to his right." In the next game against the Dolphins, he came off the bench, and with the team down 14–0 in the third quarter, Briscoe led the Broncos to a victory that he capped off with a quarterback sneak. After pulling off that victory, the Broncos fans started to chant, "We want Marlin, we want Marlin." Caught up in the drama of the moment, a local writer added, "A magician, the dictionary says, is supposed to practice 'black magic.' And Briscoe, the only Negro quarterback in American professional football, did this to a T." That Dolphins victory earned Briscoe the AFC player of the week, but despite Briscoe's success off the bench, Saban started Tensi three more games until injuries put him out for good. Briscoe started the last four games of the season.

In his second start of his career, Briscoe threw for 335 yards and four touchdowns against the Bills. He followed that game with another three throwing touchdowns against the Chargers. Against the vaunted Raiders, who were the defending AFC champions, Briscoe passed for two touchdowns. Raiders coach John Rauch praised, "Briscoe creates a lot of problems. He can throw the ball. He could be one of the top ones in the league for a long time. We worked all week on what to do against him." After the final game of the season, Chiefs coach Hank Stram remarked that Briscoe "is the most dangerous scrambling quarterback I've seen in nine years in the AFL. He's like playing against 12 men." All told, for a guy who wasn't supposed to be there, Briscoe had a stellar year. He played in eleven games (including five starts) and threw for 1,589 yards and fourteen touchdowns. He also averaged 7.5 yards a carry and scored three times. This was enough to earn him runner-up in Rookie of the Year honors.

As a quarterback, Briscoe could beat defenders, but he could not beat stereotypes. A classic quarterback had to be tall. He had to stay in the pocket. He had to be white. Briscoe was just the opposite. He was five foot ten, 180 pounds, and blazing fast. And he was Black. As one reporter put it, "In a world inhabited by white Gullivers, Marlin Briscoe is a black Lilliputian." Naysayers argued that defenders would tip Briscoe's passes at the line of scrimmage or put their hands up to alter his throwing window. Critics also said Briscoe would never be able to see his receivers. Hall of Fame quarterback Bobby Layne argued, "He can't SEE from the pocket. Take a guy like Roman Gabriel. He can stand back there and look and see and wait. And if he gets hit, it'll be second and 15." Briscoe easily countered criticism about his size. That was the easy part. What about the big defensive linemen? "I never think of them," he coolly stated. "I can roll out and get away from them usually." What about his height? Briscoe pointed out, "I'm five ten. Bart Starr is six one. He's just that much off," while separating his fingers just a few inches apart, to show how close the two were in height. He also told reporters, "When I'm out there, I really don't feel small. And in passing it's not a question of seeing over the rushing linemen; it's a question of knowing where your man is going to be." But Briscoe could not run away from his skin or his speed.

Instead of viewing his dual-threat ability as a weapon, coaches saw his speed as a detriment. Sid Gillman of the Chargers called him a "little rascal" because defenders couldn't contain him, but when asked if Briscoe was harder to coach against than a drop-back passer, he projected, "Hell no. I'd just as soon have a good, big tall man any day." In two games against the Chargers, Briscoe lit them up for six throwing touchdowns, nearly 500 yards in the air, and 124 yards on the ground. Houston Oilers coach Wally Lemm declared, "All scramblers cause you trouble, but what happens when the chips are down? I'd rather not play against scramblers because they're so tough on your defensive line with all that running. But the only thing I've got to say about them is there's never been a scrambler that's won anything." He added, "You saw what happened out there on the field. When things got tough and we were finally able to contain him, then he wasn't able to do anything. He wasn't completing his passes." In that game, in which the Oilers won 38–17, the Broncos' starting quarterback, Tensi, went 1 of 8 for 40 yards, yet Coach Lemm wasn't concerned about that style of play, just the Black scrambler.

In truth, *scrambler* was, and is, a loaded term. Doubters could have called him a rollout passer, which Briscoe was. The rollout passer had a purpose. He would move outside of the pocket formed by the offensive line to make the most of a situation. Paul Brown started this for Otto Graham, and the football world had no issues with Graham running. The Dallas Cowboys shifted their offensive line to roll with quarterback Don Meredith to protect him and build around his style of play. But few teams were willing to do that. Instead of building around the quarterback that could run, teams would try to break them of that habit. As author Murray Olderman put it in his 1966 book, *The Pro Quarterback*, "A quarterback who runs isn't supposed to happen."

Coaches claimed the quarterback was too valuable of a position, and the running quarterback unnecessarily put himself in harm's way. "As recognition of the quarterback's vital role in the offense as a passer increased," Olderman observed, "so did his timidity as a runner." One Patriots player who saw Briscoe run against his team quipped, "Running like he did against us will make him a poor insurance risk." This talk about health sounded odd to Briscoe, who replaced a classic drop-back quarterback who got hurt.

By the 1960s, however, the experts at the pro level had convinced themselves that the scrambler had no place in football. With the advance of the passing game and timing routes, a quarterback was supposed to take a common seven-step drop and fire to an open receiver. When the quarterback took off running, he messed up his timing with his receivers. The receiver also expected the ball to come from a specific place behind the line of scrimmage, further disrupting the route. The scrambler also put the offensive line in a tizzy because those players would not know where the quarterback was. With everyone running a pro-style system, there was little place for the guy who didn't stay in place.

Briscoe tried to explain to critics that he moved with a purpose. He rolled out for passing angles, and then if his receivers were not open, he would use his 4.5 forty speed to pick up yardage. In his own way, he was being disciplined. On scrambling, Briscoe said, "I've got to learn when to scramble and when not to. If it's used when it's supposed to be, it can be a dangerous weapon. But it can also be a dangerous weapon against you, too." A teammate concurred: "Marlin scrambles all over the place. For moving around, left or right, he throws as accurately and as long as anybody. He's all over the place. He confuses the defense." Chargers defensive back Bobby Howard admitted Briscoe "changed the nature of the game." Briscoe, Howard said after facing him, "would roll out, I'd read an out (sideline pattern), but then he wouldn't throw and he'd hit the secondary receiver." Pro football was stuck in their ways. They also had blinders on.

The great Fran Tarkenton, of course, ran all the time. The undersized white quarterback used his speed and elusiveness to make plays on his way to leading the Vikings to three Super Bowls, and he retired as the game's all-time leading thrower for yards and touchdowns. His brand of play was exciting. Nobody made up excuses to keep him out of football. But Briscoe's black skin did not afford him that luxury.

Instead of celebrating Briscoe's style of play, quarterback purists denounced Briscoe's skill. Too playground. Frantic football. A local Denver reporter eviscerated his style of play, writing, "And all the screaming and yelling, all the chills and thrills and the antics—some mistake them for heroics—of our young rookie quarterback, Marlin Briscoe, cannot discuss a fundamental fact, i.e. the Broncos are still beating themselves." The writer wanted his classic drop-back passer. So did Coach Saban. The Broncos cut him in the offseason. Years later, Briscoe bemoaned, "I believed—and always will—that it was racial, that he simply wouldn't have a black quarterback." Until Vince Evans came along, pro football had no use for fast Black quarterbacks.

FROM THE ROSE BOWL TO CHICAGO

HEADING INTO THE 1977 DRAFT, EVANS KNEW EVERYTHING THE pros said about fast Black quarterbacks. He knew teams didn't see him as a field general and coveted his athleticism elsewhere on the field. But for Evans, playing quarterback in the league was a question of manhood. When asked during his senior season if he would switch positions, he answered, "That would seem like a cop-out, like I was depriving myself of my manhood." He continued, "If there's a challenge awaiting me and I'm not man enough to face it, then I don't deserve to be playing . . . football reflects what you're made of as a human being." There was no way Evans would let the league keep him from his dream. "How do you tell a young guy with a dream that he can't perfect it? I mean without giving him a real chance." He was so confident in his abilities and so set on his goals that before the draft, Evans told every team he would only play quarterback.

If he wanted to play badly enough, he could have done what others had done: run slower. To avoid the switch, some Black quarterbacks, including Warren Moon and Joe Gilliam, intentionally ran slower for scouts. Those who ran their fastest left their fates in the hands of white coaches stuck in their ways. That's exactly what happened to Grambling's Matthew Reed in 1973. Reed stood six foot four and 220 pounds, with a powerful arm and great speed. His college coach, Eddie Robinson, was so weary of the NFL's discriminatory ways, he once asked a reporter not to make a big deal of Reed's speed and size in a column because he knew NFL teams would immediately envision another position for him. When Reed went to his first training camp with the Bills, the quarterback worried he'd be switched if he was too fast, but decided to run his fastest anyway because that's what Robinson would have wanted him to do. "I got down there to run, and I knew if I ran a good time that would be it," he recalled. He ran a 4.5 forty. There went his NFL quarterback career. That summer, the Bills, Broncos, and Saints brought him into their camps to play tight end. "One of the saddest things I've ever seen was when I was playing with the Rams and Matthew Reed came up with the Denver Broncos and he was a tight end," remembered Black quarterback James Harris. Reed, who once said, "Asking me to switch positions would be like asking a person to fly an airplane when he has never been in one before," had to go to the World Football League to play quarterback.

Despite Evans winning the Rose Bowl MVP, most didn't think he had a chance at quarterback. In fact, in their pre-draft scouting report, the *Sporting News* had Evans listed as a running back and noted, "Although he made great strides in two seasons, most scouts feel Evans can't play in the pros at quarterback." Teams saw the six-foot-two, 215-pound frame with a 4.5 forty and wanted to move him to another position. General managers told him that if he switched, he would be a first- or second-round pick. After that first day, the confident Evans started to question his decision. "I understand that if I hadn't really committed myself to saying I would just play quarterback I probably would have went a lot higher. But I think with saying that, I probably would have left myself open to another position," he reasoned. "I hope it's not the black quarterback syndrome," he pleaded, "because really I like to think it doesn't matter whether you're black, white, Chinese, or purple, a guy should get credit for doing a particular job at whatever position it might be."

He had twelve rounds and two days to find out, and only two teams had shown outright interest in letting him compete for a quarterback job: the Houston Oilers and the Chicago Bears.

Finally, in the sixth round, with the first pick of the second day of the draft, the Chicago Bears nabbed Evans. Bears general manager Jim Finks couldn't believe his good fortunes. "He stuck out on that board like a sore thumb," said Finks. "You always hear the cliche, 'We couldn't believe he was still available,' but with him it was true." Finks, however, made a major mistake when he told Evans he could play another position. "That turned out to be the wrong thing to say, because he took it as a token shot," Finks noted. Vince Evans was nobody's token.

Evans bet on himself and won, but just in case, he also added his own insurance policy. He made the Bears put it in his contract that they would not switch him without his permission. This baffled Finks. He had never heard a request like that before. He had also never drafted a Black quarterback who knew the history of what happened to guys like him. Evans had two factors in his favor. First, when he participated in the rookie camp before he signed his contract, he outperformed the Bears' limited expectations. "I don't think any of us realized that he was so far advanced as a quarterback, mechanically," Finks admitted. Second, Evans had an offer from the CFL. The Saskatchewan Roughriders desperately wanted Evans. With both teams promising him a shot at quarterback, Evans said it would come down to whoever paid him the most money. The Bears ponied up for the ex-Trojan colt, and they wrote in his contract, "You will not be expected to perform any other duties than those performed by quarterback." Vince Evans just had to show and prove.

CHAPTER 13

When Vince Evans signed his unique "quarterback only" contract with the Bears in 1977, the Black writer Doc Young had a proposition for his Black readers. "Bet on this," he ordered. "Vince Evans, the USC star, will become an outstanding quarterback with the Chicago Bears, who drafted him, if they give him a full shot." That was a helluva gamble. In the three decades since pro football reintegration, only one Black quarterback (James Harris) had started for more than a season with a team. You had better odds of winning a game of three-card monte than betting on a Black quarterback to get a full shot.

FAST BLACK QUARTERBACK

Evans came to a team that had an all-time great running back but an awful passing game. Walter Payton was the offense. The Bears finished a disappointing 7–7 in 1976, even though Payton finished first in the NFC in rushing. As a team, the Bears used the combination of Payton and Roland Harper to finish sixth in the league in total rushing yards. But while their offense churned out yards on the ground, their passing game went nowhere. Led by second-year man Bob Avellini, the Bears ranked second to last in the league in passing yards. To fix their passing game, they traded for Mike Phipps, drafted Evans, and added the legendary Sid Gillman as offensive coordinator.

Gillman had a reputation as being the NFL's leading expert in the passing game. The onetime coach of the Chargers believed in using all the field, 100 yards long and 53 yards wide, to perfect the passing game. He put receivers in motion to help the quarterback read the defense, motioned his halfback to the slot receiver position, and flooded the field with deep vertical routes and crossing patterns that left a defense befuddled. His quarterbacks, like John Hadl, put up big yards and lots of points. In Chicago, Gillman was going to send his receivers out deep and turn Walter Payton into a receiving back. He must have seen something special in Vince Evans because it was Gillman who wanted Evans on the roster as quarterback, and it was Gillman who called him the steal of the draft. This was an amazing change of thinking for Gillman about the Black quarterback. A decade prior, he was the one saying a team could not win with running quarterbacks like Eldridge Dickey and Marlin Briscoe.

From the start, Evans made it known that he knew he had to sit and learn, but he also let on that he did not know how steep of a hill he had to climb. In other words, Evans was not going to play into their stereotypes about Black quarterbacks. He would not publicly complain, because that was another excuse teams used to avoid Black field generals: they said they grumbled too much about not getting their opportunities. Evans went to work.

His first description of the pro playbook was to call it a "dictionary," with so many concepts to learn, it was "mass confusion," and the practices and planning were a lot to handle. That was just the stuff above the shoulder. He still had to learn how to throw the ball properly and to improve as a drop-back passer. USC took advantage of his speed and rolled him out on the edges, but in the pros, under Gillman, that would not fly. He still wanted a quarterback who would drop back. Plus, rolling out also reduced the routes his receivers could run, and it reduced the size of the field the offense could use.

Making his first year more difficult was the fact that he could not escape the race question. He now had a responsibility. When he was in Los Angeles, James Harris had impressed upon him that he had a duty as a Black quarterback to succeed for himself and succeed for others who might follow him. He entered a rare group of players that included only four men during the 1977 season: James Harris (Chargers), Dave Mays (Browns), Johnnie Walton (Eagles), and himself. After he signed his contract, he told the press, "The color of my skin happens to be black and I'm a quarterback." He continued, "Sure, there's gonna be some pressure from that. I don't worry about it. That's what I've taken upon myself to deal with." Evans might have tried his best to concentrate on his passing more than prejudices, but the media would not let the question go. When asked during the training camp about being a Black quarterback, he acknowledged his responsibility, but Evans also responded by saying, "I wish the color of my skin didn't have a major impact upon how my performances are judged." He added, "I didn't ask to be black." He loved his Blackness; he just didn't like that it was the only way the media chose to define him. "Although I'm proud of my heritage," he stated, "I simply don't think being black should have anything to do with how people explain why things turned out the way they did on the field."

From the moment he hopped on the pro field, his physical attributes stood out. Whether he was at USC or the Chicago Bears, he was the best athlete on the team, more gifted than Ricky Bell and more talented than Walter Payton. "If I had to say anybody was the most gifted athlete on this team," Bears receiver Bo Rather claimed, "I'd say it was Vince Evans." And Vince knew it too. And that was his biggest problem. He knew he had no shot of playing quarterback his rookie year—few quarterbacks did—but he still felt the internal pressure to play. How could he waste his God-given talent holding a clipboard? he asked himself. In the past, other athletic Black quarterbacks were confronted with this same dilemma, from within and without. Coaches preyed on this. "Why sit when you can play?" they prodded their Black quarterbacks. It was never really a question of choice but always a strong suggestion to either switch or find a new job. Only in Evans's case, the Bears could not force him to switch. Still, he had an itch to play, and the Bears wanted to scratch it. They could not force him to try another position, but they did the next best thing in their interest: Coach Jack Pardee told him that he could not dress in uniform if he was not going to play. Evans had his choice, but who didn't want to dress for the game? So Vince Evans the quarterback became Vince Evans the kick returner.

"I felt the pressure of not doing anything," he sheepishly admitted. "I was naked in the world and it was time to put some clothes on." He also felt the pressure of having to prove his worth to his teammates. "The biggest thing is to gain respect from my teammates," he added. "I feel some are closer to me now. The runbacks help. I have to satisfy my mind by contributing a solid thing. Doing well helps." He also felt the constant state of worry of being Black. "The stereotype of blacks is that we're radical, impatient, that we want it all now. That's a false stereotype, and I didn't want to fall into that category. I knew my talent would manifest itself." As much as he wanted to be a signal caller, he sold himself on the move. "It goes back to my childhood days, playing in the streets and trying to outrun your partner to the goal," he told the press. "It's the same now; just playing and having fun." For a position he had never played before, he handled it quite well. In the seven games he played, he averaged 19 yards a return. Being on the field kept him energized, but he yearned to be a quarterback. And the Bears desperately needed one.

Although the 1977 Chicago Bears made the playoffs, they did so without the help of a passing game. The Sid Gillman experiment never truly worked because Coach Pardee refused to let it work. Midway through the season, with the Bears clinging to a 3–5 record, Pardee took control of the play calling. Why throw when you could run with Walter Payton? This was a question made a lot easier to answer because starter Bob Avellini was turnover prone, throwing eighteen interceptions. In the end, the Bears ranked twenty-fifth out of twenty-eight teams in passing attempts, but fourth in rushing attempts and first in rushing yards, with Payton leading the way with 1,852 yards. In their last six games with Pardee calling the plays, they leaned heavily on Payton to win all six contests. As for Evans, he said if he had to endure another situation like he did his rookie year, he'd be searching for a new team.

Riding Payton's legs, the Bears made the playoffs for the first time in fourteen years, but after a first-round loss to Dallas, instead of getting ready for the next season to rebuild, the Bears coaching staff called it quits. Frustrated over being handcuffed, Gillman quit. Soon, Pardee left for Washington to coach the Redskins. And then everyone else was gone. To replace them, the Bears brought in defensive-minded Neill Armstrong as the head coach. They hired Buddy Ryan to run the defense and Ken Meyer to run the offense. Evans had to start all over.

INVISIBLE VINCE

FOR EVANS, THE COACHING CHANGE MEANT A WHOLE NEW SYStem to learn, but a brand-new opportunity. "This is a break for me, having new coaches," he told a reporter. "I'm really excited about it. I just want to be judged on my ability to perform—nothing else. And if I show more than somebody else I should be moved up." He needed a clean slate and a fair shot in the worst way, because the language in his contract only guaranteed him a shot at quarterback for one year. At this point, the Bears were off the hook if he did not pan out.

Vince had every reason to feel optimistic. While head coach Neill Armstrong was defensive minded, when he was the defensive coordinator at Minnesota, he got an up-close look at a running quarterback in Fran Tarkenton. Armstrong knew the advantages of having a mobile quarterback. Moreover, offensive coordinator Ken Meyer, who was the offensive coordinator for James Harris at the Rams, was one of a handful of coaches who had experience with having a Black quarterback. In this regard, Vince would be fine. But a quarterback needed more than fair-minded coaches; he also had to have an offense that suited him.

Meyer came to camp promising a more balanced run/pass attack, and that did not bode well for Evans. When Meyer looked at tape from the 1977 Bears season, he surmised that their problem was that they tried too many deep patterns. To fix that, he added more medium and short passes. Evans could throw a beautiful deep pass, but he was still years away from mastering the intermediate passing game. Moreover, Meyer did not want his quarterbacks rolling out to pass.

A year into his career, Evans was still unpolished. He showed signs of improvement, like not sticking with one primary receiver in passing situations, but his arm was wild. "He hasn't tamed that howitzer arm of his enough to avoid giving receivers an occasional how-it-hurts pass," one local writer observed. And his teammates felt that way too, as Evans's passes stung their hands. Receiver Bo Rather critiqued, "Experience is knowing when do I drill the ball and when do I lay it up and let the receiver run for it?" With

Evans's ball, a defender would have less time to react, but that also made it harder on the receiver. When Evans was not hurting his receivers' hands, he was still wildly inaccurate with his passes, often sailing them over receivers' heads. Coming into the pros, he knew it would take time, but he was also short on patience. All great athletes are.

A quarter through the 1978 season, the frustration of not playing got to him. The best he could do was scout-team quarterback. But playing as the other team's quarterback didn't prepare him for playing with his team. He wasn't working on timing and routes with his receivers. "If I'm not playing, there's no way I can get better," he would say. In his mind, he was being robbed of his chance. "I know without a doubt that I can play. It's frustrating to see—I don't care who it is—somebody with talent whose athletic skills are going down because he isn't able to use them." Evans was so bummed by his lack of playing time, when not on the field or in the facility, he would just stare off into space. At times, he could not even have a regular conversation with his girlfriend because all he could think about was that he was being robbed of his gifts. "God has given me the ability to do whatever I want to do in athletics," he reflected. "I praise Him all the time for that. Sometimes I'll be going down the street and tears just start going down my face because I'm not able to exploit it."

God may have given him his abilities, but the coach had to give him his playing time. Coach Armstrong refused to budge. "Vince Evans does have good ability and I think he has a bright future in this league," Armstrong asserted, "but this is not the time to give people playing experience to see what they can do. We need to win ball games." Deep down, even though he knew Evans wasn't ready for the big time, he also knew what would happen if he played the brilliantly talented Evans: he'd have a quarterback controversy. Very few fans could resist the temptation of an electrifying quarterback, especially when the starter was bad. By midseason with the Bears floundering, it was too late to worry about those things. Coach Armstrong already had a quarterback controversy.

Although the team started out with a 3–0 record, the Bears soon started to drop with seemingly no bottom in sight. One loss turned into another, and when they looked up, they were on an eight-game losing streak. During the seventh loss, a match against the Seahawks, Armstrong finally benched Avellini for Mike Phipps. The fans went wild, showering Phipps with cheers. But soon the shine was off Phipps too.

In their twelfth game of the season, facing the Atlanta Falcons, with forty-eight seconds remaining in the first half, a Falcons defender drilled Phipps as he completed a pass, putting him on the ground and out of the game. Thinking he was the next man up, Avellini started to warm up on the sidelines to a loud chorus of boos. Then to the fans' delight, Evans came darting onto the field. The crowd gave him a long standing ovation. In just forty-eight seconds, Evans, on three straight-designed rollout runs, led the Bears to a field goal for their first points all game. Cool as a late-summer Lake Michigan breeze, Evans said, "When I went out there, I knew I was the man." Although he only played those forty-eight seconds, after the game, the Black quarterback was the talk of the town.

While the fans clamored for more Evans, Coach Armstrong refused to give in to their demands. The press started calling Evans "invisible Vince" to note the fact that Armstrong refused to play him. Every reporter flocked to Armstrong with the same question: "When will the exciting young quarterback play?" To that question, he reminded them that Evans would not start but that he looked forward to incorporating him into the game plan. And what about the boos for his other quarterbacks? Coach Armstrong claimed he ignored the boos and also added, "We want the people to enjoy the game but we have to win. We showed we had confidence in Evans by sending him in when we did." But no matter what he said, as long as Vince was on the sidelines, the boos kept coming.

For any fan unconvinced by Armstrong's insistence on not giving Evans significant playing time, they just had to watch the Monday Night Football contest on December 4 against the Chargers. Actually, it wasn't a contest; it was the kind of bludgeoning awaiting the cows at the old stockyards. The Bears were down 10–0 before they even ran a play and 17–0 before Walter Payton even touched the ball. The underwhelming Avellini finished the game 2 of 12 before being pulled for Phipps. Phipps was not much better. At the end of the game, with forty-nine seconds left, Armstrong finally let Evans play. He went 1 of 2 for 38 yards and an interception. The Chargers beat the Bears 40–7.

Hidden in the massacre was a milestone. In the fourth quarter, the Chargers inserted James Harris into the game. Harris went 3 of 5 for 63 yards and a touchdown. With Harris and Evans on the field, it marked the first time that two modern Black quarterbacks played in the same game.

At this point, Black fans didn't care about small tokens. They wanted legitimate chances. Vince's lack of playing time was a sign. Local Black fans bombarded sports talk shows with calls about why Armstrong did Vince wrong. Why not play Evans earlier if Coach Armstrong thought he had a chance to be the quarterback of the Bears' future? As one writer coldly put it, "That means, plainly, that Bear executives and coaches have decided Evans isn't their quarterback of the future." He closed by selecting an old stereotype: "I wonder how he'd do at cornerback?"

CHAPTER 14

"How long have you been a Black quarterback?" When folks thought they heard reporter Butch John ask Doug Williams that infamous question as Williams prepared for the 1988 Super Bowl, many mocked and ridiculed the reporter. The question seemed both simple and ridiculous at the same time. Doug Williams was Black and played quarterback, thus he had always been a Black quarterback. But that was not the question. That's just what everyone heard. Instead, John noted the obvious—that Williams was indeed a Black quarterback, and then he asked him for how long that fact had mattered. That's a smart question. Because Doug Williams, who grew up in an all-Black community and went to a Black college, had only ever been a quarterback. Plain and simple. There was never a need for anyone to label him as a *Black quarterback*, because his presence only existed in an all-Black context. In that world, all the Black quarterbacks were just quarterbacks. And that's all he knew. As Williams said a decade prior to that infamous Super Bowl question, "In high school, you're called a quarterback. In college, you're called a quarterback. But as soon as you go to the pros, you're a black quarterback. Call me a quarterback, period."

A *quarterback* became a *Black quarterback* when he entered white space. For some, like Vince Evans, that moment came early. Evans had been a Black quarterback when he was bused to a predominantly white high school. But for others, like Williams, that moment took longer. They did not become Black quarterbacks until the white media discovered them and decided they had a chance to become pros. Doug Williams became a full-fledged Black quarterback in 1977, when the senior rewrote the NCAA record books. He also became a Black hope. More than just a pioneer, Williams was looked to as a symbol. Could he become the first player from a small school—a small Black school at that—to win the Heisman? Could he become the first player from a Black school to be an all-American? Could he become the first great Black professional quarterback? Along the way, Grambling and Eddie Robinson did all they could to keep Williams in the national spotlight. With Williams, Robinson could show other Black kids in America that anything was truly possible. No Black college player before him had ever received this much attention. This is when Doug Williams, born and raised in a rural Black Louisiana community, finally became a Black quarterback.

The summer of '77 went on like any other summer in the all-Black community of Chaneyville, with kids and adults playing sports in the muggy heat. If anybody needed to find Doug, they'd have to look outside. Whether he was playing softball, baseball, basketball, or tossing the pigskin, Williams was carefree, hanging with his people as he prepared for his last year of college ball. Then one day, he heard a call from around the way. "Hey, Mr. Heisman!" What did folks know about a Heisman in tiny Chaneyville? he thought. Must have been some kids playing around. He smiled and laughed. But it was true. Someone saw it on television. Doug Williams, the kid from a community that was so small one needed a microscope to find it on a map, had his face splattered across televisions all over America. He couldn't believe it. When he finally got home from the softball field, his mom told him she saw it too. He could be a Heisman winner. Not only that, but he could also be the first player from a Black school to win the Heisman. Walter Payton, the record-setting running back from Jackson State, the one who was now the best back in the NFL, barely registered a token honorable mention in 1974. Doug had a real chance. That summer changed everything. Whether in his community, in his classroom, or on the football field, he lived in a fishbowl. Everybody had their faces pressed against the glass, watching for his next move.

How did this even happen? Why would the college football world even think that his numbers could match the big boys at Pitt, Oklahoma, Texas, or USC? If one had been around Grambling long enough, figuring out that answer was easy. That was Collie Nicholson, the man with the magic pen. Over the years, as Grambling's sports information director (SID), Nicholson hyped his players like no SID ever had or ever would. If a guy was six foot one, he'd be six foot three. If a player ran a 4.6 forty, it would be 4.3 in the press. Offensive linemen who weighed 230 pounds were 250. And it worked. He helped put 160 players in the pros before Doug Williams threw his first pass for Grambling. True, the players had skills, but Nicholson was the one who put them in the spotlight. He wrote the articles and the headlines. He was the one who told the football world that James Harris would be first, that Matthew Reed would be next, and that Doug Williams would be the best. And during Doug's senior season, Nicholson went to work like never before. He and Eddie Robinson had a new mission; they wanted a Heisman just like those big white schools. They wanted to prove to all the Black players at the Black schools that America was a fair place. No more thinking small of yourself because you went to a tiny Black school. Doug would be that vehicle to push hope through Black boys' veins. Nicholson sent out film and press clippings and told media outlets across the country to come to Grambling. It all seemed shameless, but he had to. That's how Heismans were won. It was a popularity contest.

And 1977 just happened to be the perfect time to make a move. Coming into the year, there were no clear-cut favorites. Running backs Terry Miller of Oklahoma State and Earl Campbell of the University of Texas had not set themselves apart from the field. Neither had quarterbacks like Stanford's Guy Benjamin or Pitt's Matt Cavanaugh. So why not the record-breaking quarterback from a tiny Black school? Even Doug got into the act. "I don't want to brag, but I don't know of too many quarterbacks who can match those stats," he said before the season. This all seemed like a long shot, because unlike the players from the big schools, Grambling had no national TV games scheduled. They only appeared in regional TV games, if they appeared at all. And he would more than likely only be on TVs at Black homes. For Robinson and Nicholson, it was worth a shot. They expected big numbers from Williams.

Williams lived up to the hype. In their first game against Alcorn State, the same team that beat the brakes off them the previous season, the Grambling Gunner was brilliant. He hit Carlos Pennywell for bombs of 91 and 81 yards on his way to 362 yards in the air and five touchdowns, breaking James Harris's single-game record. In the previous years, Robinson would have pulled Doug early in the game, but not this time. He wanted a Heisman. He was going to run up the score and put the ball in the air. Throughout the year, Williams averaged thirty-one passes per game. Next up, Morgan State Bears under the bright lights in the big city.

Since 1968, Robinson had taken his Tigers on the road to play in New York as part showcase and part charity. Named the Whitney Young Classic to honor the civil rights leader who headed the

Urban League, Robinson helped create the game to raise money for the Urban League's adult education initiative to help economically struggling adults earn their GEDs. He also saw it as an opportunity to raise Black college football's brand. What was once just a concept became a reality after the assassination of Martin Luther King Jr. as businesses across the country were looking for ways to calm Black Americans by showing that they cared about their economic plight. Knowing the game needed a home, the Yankees immediately stepped in to offer Yankee Stadium for the cause. The first game in 1968 went better than anyone expected and brought in sixty thousand fans to see the best of Black college ball battle. After that success, organizers—with the prodding from Robinson and his media friend Howard Cosell—decided to have Grambling in the game every year while rotating in other Black colleges. Robinson and his Tigers were the big draw, and in the fall of 1977, they came rambling into the stadium with the biggest star.

The 1977 game became a Heisman showcase for Doug in the epicenter of America's media. All game long, Morgan State was at his mercy. The Bears tried to blitz him up the middle. That didn't work. They tried to triple-team Pennywell. That didn't work. Whatever they tried to do, Williams audibled into the right play. All told, he bombed the Bears' defense with 21 of 36 passing for 370 yards and four touchdowns. "I guess that's what it means when I say we turn him loose," Robinson told the press after the game. "You can tell when we let him go because he really likes to bomb away."

Those were gaudy stats, and sportswriters from the Big Apple ate it up. The *New York Times*, *Newsday*, and the *New York Daily News* fawned over the new Black sensation. Larry Carmody of *Newsday* wrote, "The overall physical size and strength are more than adequate for his position. The right arm throws the ball with accurate precision. But Douglas Williams is more than a wind-it-up quarterback automaton. He's an independent thinker in the huddle and Grambling coach Eddie Robinson wouldn't have it any other way." Norm Miller of the *Daily News* added, Williams had a "cool drop-back style" and a "quick release like Joe Namath." Being compared to Namath was fine with Doug. Namath was one of his idols.

The awesome combination of Nicholson, New York, and Doug's magic arm worked. The hype train took off. Each touchdown Doug threw was like a fishing line luring reporters back to Grambling to tell stories about the big fish in the small pond. *Sports Illustrated, Sport, Newsweek, Sporting News, Gridweek, Black Sports, Jet, Chicago Defender, Los Angeles Times, Los Angeles Sentinel, Chicago Sun-Times, New York Times, Houston Chronicle, Washington Post, Washington Star,* and the *New Orleans Times-Picayune* wrote stories about the "Black Hope." Even the television stations got in on the act, including luminary personalities like Cosell and Bob Hope. The *Shreveport Journal* one-upped everyone when they came to campus in late September and chronicled his whole day, from sunup to sundown. Reporter Jeff Rude followed Doug from the dorm room he shared with his younger brother, Mike, a quarterback just like Doug, to his first 8:00 a.m. class, Education 307, until he returned home from practice at 9:00 p.m., then a visit to his girlfriend, Janice, then hanging out with his teammates, and finally back home at midnight. Along the way, everyone from teachers to students talked about his Heisman chances.

His four years at Grambling had prepared him well for this moment. His whole life was shaped by Jim Crow, yet to listen to Doug, one would have thought he was not bitter. A bit cautious about his future, yes, but for the most part, he played his role as the grateful rural Black kid well. He fed reporters stories about what it was like growing up rural, how he was always overlooked, and how moving to tiny Grambling meant he went from "candle lights to the bright lights." With all that attention and the history of knowing what happened to guys who looked like he did, only one thing still nagged him: being a Black quarterback.

He loved his Blackness, his Black community, and his Black college, but he understood others would never see him outside of his Blackness. He just wanted to be judged as Doug Williams, quarterback. Being a Black quarterback came with too much pressure and prejudice. "I wouldn't mind just being a quarterback," he told *Jet*. "Being a Black quarterback, you have to be extra special. Cause this is not supposed to happen. By being a Black quarterback, there'll be so many eyes watching what I do, trying to find out what I do wrong, but not what I do good." But like it or not, he was a Black quarterback.

Where others might have burst, all the pressure made Doug into a diamond. A black diamond. There were four touchdowns against Alcorn State, five against Morgan State, and seven against overmatched Langston University. After that Langston game, the Associated Press named him national player of the week, the first time a player from a Black college ever received that award. And the records kept falling. He broke James Harris's Grambling record for passing yardage. He lapped Terry Bradshaw's state record for most passing yards. When he threw three touchdowns against Southern in the Bayou Classic in front of seventy thousand fans, giving him eighty-nine on his career, he owned the college career mark for touchdowns. He threw so many touchdowns that they failed to excite him anymore. "It's got to where when I throw one," he said, "I just walk off the field and say, 'There goes another one.'" After the Southern game, all that was left for him was the single-season touchdown record of thirty-nine set by Dennis Shaw. He'd get his chance in the last game of the season, a bowl game against Temple in Tokyo.

He could have broken that record too, but Doug Williams put winning ahead of records. Heading into the final drive, with the

Tigers down 32–28, and Doug with four touchdowns in the game, bringing him one away from tying Shaw's thirty-nine touchdowns, he drove his team all the way down to the 8-yard line while calling all the plays himself. It was classic Doug. From Temple's 8-yard line, with less than a minute to go, he called time-out to discuss the final play with Robinson. Coach wanted him to throw the ball, win the game, and break the record. But knowing Temple was only rushing two players and dropping back nine in coverage, the star quarterback decided that a run would be their best option. He told Robinson to give him a running play: 37 sweep. Running back Floyd Womack went untouched for the score. Wins over records.

For Doug, winning his final game was bittersweet. Earlier that week, he learned that Earl Campbell won the Heisman Award. All fall, as the media speculated about his chances, Doug stayed humble. He gave himself twenty-to-one odds to win. While some Black media outlets like the *New York Amsterdam News* questioned if the NCAA's race bias would prevent Doug from winning, he did his best to ignore any talks about discrimination. Well schooled by Eddie Robinson, Williams said that his role was to pave the way for others. Just as James Harris had for him. "I guess I'm a pioneer," he told the *Washington Post*. "Someone has to pave the way for the future. There will be someone else, I'm sure." With his college career complete, it was time to prepare for the 1978 NFL draft. Not as a quarterback but a Black quarterback. The issue weighed on his mind like an Alcorn State pass rush. To make it, he'd have to figure out how to get teams to focus more on his passing than his pigment.

CHAPTER 15

DOUG WILLIAMS WAS THE ONLY BLACK QUARTERBACK IN THE 1978 draft. The other collegiate standout that year, Warren Moon, grew tired of teams slighting his talents. Despite winning the Rose Bowl MVP and earning the Pac-8 co-player of the year along with Stanford's Guy Benjamin, a quarterback who was eventually picked in the second round, few teams would even talk to Moon. General managers said he would be picked late in the draft or he might not get picked at all. Some pundits did not even rate Moon as one of the top twenty-seven quarterbacks in the draft. The few teams that he visited asked him to switch positions. Teams claimed it was his skills and not his skin that they scouted, but Moon knew the real reason: racism. "Right now, the situation of a black quarterback in the NFL is not where I'd like it to be. It's better than it was, but it's not where I'd like it." He took his talents to the CFL. To reserve an opportunity to come back to the league on his own terms, Moon and his agent, Leigh Steinberg, asked teams not to draft him. If a team drafted Moon, they would still own his rights, even if he went to Canada. That would limit his ability to come back to the States to play, because one team would still control his fate.

Luckily for him, teams listened. After dominating the CFL for five seasons, Moon was ready to return to the NFL in 1984. In what was the first case of true free agency in the league, Moon signed with the Houston Oilers and became the highest-paid player in the league.

Like Moon, Williams hoped his Blackness did not eclipse his future. Most believed that despite Williams's skin color, he would still get a chance that others did not. He was too good for a quarterback-desperate team to pass up. As Eddie Robinson said during Williams's record-setting senior season, "Doug Williams walks the earth holding the distinction of having thrown more touchdowns in four years than any man in organized football." Gil Brandt, the Cowboys' lead scout, noted that Williams had the intangibles as he was "an exceptionally fine person" and was "articulate, poised, has good leadership qualities and a lot of desire." For his tangibles, he was nonpareil. "He's got a big league arm, enormous hands and a good delivery," Brandt observed. But like most quarterbacks with a big arm, Williams took big chances. He tended to think his arm could get him out of any situation. He forced the ball, Brandt said, but that was "correctable." Up to that point, he was the best Black quarterback to come out of college. But that didn't mean he did not have to worry. He was still Black.

Like clockwork, the football stereotype machine went into overdrive. Did he have the mental capacity to play the position? One scout, who obviously knew the racial territory he was treading in when he critiqued Williams, observed, "He throws in crowds a lot and makes a lot of mental mistakes and that has nothing to do with race." Well schooled by Robinson, Williams had a plan of attack. Rather than ignore the jabs, Williams hit back. "They say Bradshaw isn't too smart, don't they," Williams countered. It was a smooth remark that let people know that Terry Bradshaw had a reputation of being unintelligent, yet he won multiple Super Bowls.

Heading into the draft, it was clear that the Tampa Bay Buccaneers would be the team most likely to draft Doug. On paper, the pairing worked. As a new franchise, they lost their first twenty-six games in their first two years and desperately needed a quarterback. Guys like Steve Spurrier, Parnell Dickinson, Gary Huff, and Mike Boryla had failed to move the team in the right direction. While other teams showed interest in Williams—the Giants told him they would select him as the tenth pick—out of all the teams that needed a quarterback, only the Bucs had the coach who was prepared to handle a Black quarterback. Any coach who had a Black quarterback had to be ready for a media blitz about Blackness as equally as they would be to face the Steelers' defense. Both would be relentless. John McKay fit the bill. He had already coached three Black quarterbacks.

Slated to have the number one draft pick, the Bucs had to do their homework. To test Williams, McKay sent offensive assistant coach Joe Gibbs to Grambling for the special assignment. During their skull sessions, Williams passed with flying colors as he quickly dispelled those pesky innuendos that all Black quarterbacks had faced. "We discounted the rumors about his intelligence," McKay told the press. McKay also reprimanded anyone who would make such accusations. "I believe there were once rumors about the intelligence of Terry Bradshaw, who happens to be white. I don't seem to hear them much anymore." McKay had Williams's back, but it also helped that he loved Williams's arm. "I wasn't a bit concerned about drafting a black quarterback," he stated. "We had them at Southern Cal, and they won championships for us. All we wanted was a quarterback with a good arm and the intelligence to play."

Williams fit McKay's offensive philosophy. His old "student body right" plays were still a staple of the Bucs' offense, but he also believed that in the pros, a team had to have big, explosive plays to score. The only way to do that, he thought, was to throw the ball deep. A deep passing game would also back the defense up, making life easier on his bruising running backs. Only one quarterback in the draft could do that. "Doug Williams has the strongest arm in football," said the coach. "He can rifle the ball with people crawling all over him, just with his arm strength alone."

As the draft inched closer, McKay took a calculated gamble. He knew that other teams were blinded by Doug's Blackness, thus the Bucs' number one pick became even more valuable. "It was a strange thing," McKay recalled. "All the scouting reports were extremely positive, and yet there were the rumors. We couldn't find anybody on any other club who would talk about him. Normally you'll hear somebody say, 'Well, if this guy is still here when our turn comes, we'll take him.' But we never heard that anybody was after Williams." Sensing teams were wary about drafting a Black quarterback, McKay traded their number one pick to the Oilers, who used the pick to nab Heisman winner Earl Campbell. In exchange, the Buccaneers dropped down to the number seventeen pick and also received tight end Jimmie Giles, a player who would be instrumental in Doug's development.

McKay's premonition about prejudice turned out to be right. Quarterback-desperate teams passed on Williams. The quarterback-starved Giants, who told Williams that they would take him tenth if he were available, took a tackle instead. The Bucs selected him seventeenth. "If anybody passed him over because he was black," McKay mentioned, "then there is something wrong with our society. I'd have taken him if he was Chinese." He could have waited until the second round. The other teams, as McKay would later say, didn't have the guts to take

Doug. In the first round, he sent a signal to the rest of the league that they could lower their guards and let the Black quarterback in the league.

For Eddie Robinson, this historic occasion gave him another opportunity to sell his version of America, one where a Black man was simply an American. "Doug is apple pie," he told a writer. "In Doug Williams, you have the typical American boy. He goes to church. He has humility. He comes from a large family. He courted the same girl the whole time he has been here . . ." Robinson had spent nearly four decades preaching the normalcy of Blackness, trying to get his players to believe that they were no different from white people, despite all the racism they faced, and through his players, he would teach white America the same things. Finally, with his quarterback picked in the first round, he had his proof.

Doug bought into his mentor's vision. From the moment the Bucs drafted him, he spent his career trying to sell the idea that he was just a quarterback. After the draft, he told Norm Miller of the *Daily News*, "I think of myself as a quarterback. I've got to do what the rest of the quarterbacks do, what the white quarterbacks have to do and the black quarterbacks have to do. I've got to produce." Williams also believed that his key to success in the league would be to play for his teammates before he played for his race. "Do you know what my burdens would be, how many passes I would have had intercepted if I said to myself, 'I have to go out there and [perform] for the Blacks'?" he asked *Ebony*. There was no answer to that. The pressure of prejudice could be heavy, the burden of Blackness just as overbearing.

Deep down, Doug Williams always knew his success was bigger than he was. When he was at Grambling, the opposing Black quarterbacks would say to him, "Man, go up there and pave the way for us." Williams understood their hope. Reflecting on his new position, he said, "James Harris was the pioneer who opened the door for black quarterbacks. Now it's up to me to be a success." One of the young pro quarterbacks that took a close note of Williams was Vince Evans, who proudly observed, "It's a great thing to see another brother quarterbacking at the helm of an NFL team."

CHAPTER 16

Mɪᴄʜᴀᴇʟ A. Hᴀʟʟ ʜᴀᴅ ʙᴇᴇɴ ᴀ Bᴜᴄѕ ꜰᴀɴ ꜰʀᴏᴍ ᴛʜᴇ ʙᴇɢɪɴɴɪɴɢ. For two years, he went to the stadium for every Sunday home game to cheer for his losing team. When the Buccaneers started 0–26, he didn't jump ship. And when they drafted Doug Williams in 1978, as a Black man, Hall was ready to captain the Doug Williams fan club. When Doug played his first preseason game, Hall was there too. With his first pass, the rookie uncorked one of his customary bombs for a touchdown. The crowd went wild. The Bucs finally had a quarterback. Then, as things settled down, Hall heard a man tell his wife, "That nigger can throw!" That perked his ears to what had been going on around him. He was in a sea of whiteness. As the only Black fan in his section, all season long, he had to sit there and listen to the racism. Nigger. Monkey. Black SOB. He heard it all. It got so bad that season, Hall gave up his season tickets to find another section. But no matter where he sat, he could not escape the racist vitriol. No matter how well Doug played, there were some fans who could not get over the fact that he was Black.

The great Black sportswriter Ralph Wiley once wrote that Doug Williams was the first Black quarterback. Of course, Wiley knew about all the others who preceded Williams, but because Williams was the first Black quarterback where his team would be nothing without him, "in that sense," Wiley reasoned, "Doug Williams is the first black quarterback in the NFL." To Wiley, Williams was "more symbol than man," because he was the most important person in a franchise. And during his rookie year, Williams would learn what it truly felt like to be a Black quarterback. His senior year at Grambling gave him just a taste. No matter what happened at Grambling, he was shielded by a loving Black institution. Now he was on his own, another pioneer discovering the difficult terrain of the life of a Black quarterback.

BUILDING THE BUCS

WHEN JOHN MCKAY SIGNED ON AS COACH AND GENERAL MANager to steer the Buccaneers in the right direction, he promised that he had a five-year plan. Those five years just happened to coincide with the length of his contract. Taking over a franchise that had no chance of winning, he would have sold the fans anything to keep them off his back. As a new franchise, they started building their team with other teams' scraps, plus what shiny new objects they could find from the draft. They lost their first twenty-six games and finished 2–26 in the first two years. Along the way, McKay and the Bucs became the laughingstock of American sports. Fans chanted "Throw McKay in the Bay," and late-night comedian Johnny Carson joked, "The answer to the question is the Tampa Bay Bucs and the sinking of the *Titanic*; the question is, 'What two disasters were accompanied by band music?'" Whatever plan McKay had at the time, most onlookers thought he was sinking the Buccaneers' ship. But the man had a plan.

McKay figured the best way to build an NFL franchise was to shape them in the mold of his conquering Trojans, with talent, speed, and beef up front. First, he started with the defense. In his first draft in 1976, he nabbed six-foot-three, 255-pound all-American defensive lineman Lee Roy Selmon from the University of Oklahoma. Then, with his third pick, he grabbed his brother Dewey, six foot one and 242 pounds, who he eventually moved to middle linebacker. With the brilliant Dewey, who was also working on his PhD in ancient philosophy, calling the defense and Lee Roy wreaking havoc on teams' offense, the Bucs employed a 3-4 defense and went from the twenty-fourth-ranked defensive unit in 1976 to the fourth-ranked squad by the end of 1978. Hard hitting and fast, the Bucs' defense made games miserable for elite runners like Walter Payton, who labeled them the best in the league.

Until Doug Williams came aboard, however, the Buccaneers' offense struggled. McKay's biggest problem was that he could not keep a healthy quarterback, because he could not protect his quarterback. Their offensive line provided as much protection as a screen door in a Tampa hurricane. But during the first three seasons, through the draft, trades, and switching Charley Hannah from a defensive end to an offensive guard, McKay built a sturdy line. By the end of the decade, they had one of the league's best lines. In 1979, Williams set an NFL record by only getting sacked seven times.

To emulate his "student body right" running philosophy, in the 1977 draft, McKay took his former running back at USC, Ricky Bell, over Heisman winner Tony Dorsett. The following draft, he left the fans scratching their heads even more when he traded out of the number one pick, letting Heisman winner Earl Campbell go to the Oilers, and dropping down to seventeen to put the future in the hands of a Black quarterback. But that was all part of his plan.

BLACK ROOKIE

TIME MUST WAIT FOR THE FUTURE. SO MUST OWNERS, COACHES, and fans, especially when the future is a quarterback who knows his worth and the owner is cheap. In this case, Bucs owner Hugh Culverhouse undervalued Doug. After they drafted Williams, team leadership immediately tried to lowball him. The Bucs' front office argued that even though Williams was the first quarterback picked, he was not the number one pick—a fact made convenient because they traded their number one pick—and therefore did not deserve as much as the top players. They also tried to get Williams on a reduced contract, reasoning that since he probably would not play in his first three years, because quarterbacks had to sit and learn, Doug should not get as much money as other top picks who would play immediately. Williams scoffed at their original offer of five years for $350,000 and concluded, "I think they wanted a slave, to be a quarterback."

After watching their dismal quarterbacks throw in camp the first week, the Bucs finally gave Williams a five-year package worth $565,000, which included his signing bonus. To put this in perspective, Earl Campbell, the number one pick, signed for a total of $1.38 million. Williams's salary seemed so low when compared to other top picks, many of Doug's teammates laughed at him. They were right. His contract was a joke. By 1982, he was the fifty-fourth highest-paid quarterback. He and his agent figured the Bucs shortchanged him because he was Black. His agent complained, "It seems there might have been someone taking advantage of this poor little black boy. They tell him he's not going to play for three to five years, and all of a sudden he starts the first year. It's a shame that one of the finest young athletes ever to play in the NFL may be one of the lowest-paid. If that's because he's black, then it's a frightening shame."

Any rookie holding out would have a problem selling his position to paying fans, but a Black quarterback holding out exacerbated the issue. Fans grew impatient with Williams, and instead of looking at him as a savior, they saw him as spoiled. How could this guy who had never played demand more money? they complained. Some went as far as suggesting the Bucs should not sign him and instead make him sit out for a year. When he finally got to training camp, he addressed the situation. To him, the fans' animosity boiled down to race. "Really," he observed, "the criticism is because I'm the first black quarterback drafted this high."

From day one, Williams decided to take the issue of race head-on. As he said early in his career, "It [the race question] won't end as long as I am living." Even though there were three other Black quarterbacks in the league (James Harris, Vince Evans, and Johnnie Walton), Williams was still a novelty, as he was the first one playing in the Deep South. He tried to drive home the point that he was just another quarterback, but that part never stuck. He also wanted to address Black fans' expectations. "I know a lot of people in this community and in the country will be looking to see how I do," he acknowledged. "But, hey," he added, "I've got nothing to prove." He reiterated that if he worried about race or tried "to prove something to the world just because I'm a black quarterback," he would fail. It would be easier, he assumed, if he told everyone, "I'm a quarterback."

In truth, he didn't have time to worry about race. His holdout left him a week behind, and it showed. He had a steep learning curve going from college to the pros, where the playbooks were larger and the defenses were more intricate. In college, most teams played vanilla defenses. In the pros, the linebackers tried to fool the quarterback on every play. Were they blitzing? Were they dropping back into coverage? Everything was a disguise, and Doug did not know how to see through it all. "When I stepped out on the field the first time," he reflected, "it was like I was in Tokyo. I was lost. I didn't speak the language and I didn't know the customs." During training camp, he missed his receivers long and short, he threw tons of interceptions, and he messed up play calls. In the huddle, he could not get more than one play out at a time, leaving himself no contingencies if the defense did something unexpected. But he also showed potential, and for a team that was 2–26, the good outweighed the bad.

Anyone who saw Williams throw said he had the best arm they had ever seen. Tight end Jimmie Giles figured Doug could throw the ball 90 yards. Teammate Wally Chambers, who had played with the Bears the previous year, claimed that the only quarterback that had an arm as strong as Doug's was Vince Evans. Receiver Morris Owens, who spent the first year complaining that Doug threw the ball too hard, also surmised, "Doug throws the ball like Bert Jones. Sometimes you're open for a split second and if the ball's not there, don't worry, Doug gets it there." He threw his passes with ease and with a quick release. Even the great Johnny Unitas observed, "Williams has the arm and quickness to be a great one and his tremendous wrist action makes him hard to sack."

Still, some were never impressed. As one reporter once observed, "Williams can throw the ball through a stone wall, but he can't move. Guys like him are a dime a dozen." But Williams did not need to move like other quarterbacks, because he had a quick release that all great gunslingers are blessed with. Guys moved out of the pocket to avoid the sack; Williams's quick wrist was as good as anyone's legs. Of course, Doug's belief in his release always got him in trouble, as he tried to force too many passes. But his arm also made it hard for McKay to keep him off the field. So confident in his gunslinger, McKay named him his week 1 starter. Upon hearing the news, Doug joked, "As far as being the first black quarterback to start, I'll just try and not be the first black quarterback to mess up."

"Eighty-four weak side!" That was the play he was supposed to run. But Williams heard, "Ninety-four strong side!" On the second throw of Doug's professional career, he read the wrong side of the field, and he threw to the wrong receiver. Giants defensive back Terry Jackson feasted on Doug's mistake. Jackson had prepared for the moment all week, studying Doug's tendencies and learning what to look for. "Watching Doug Williams on films," Jackson explained after the game, "I saw he eyes the ball to his receivers. He stares at his receivers. That's where he throws the ball. He was definitely looking my way. I knew it was coming." Interception. Touchdown Giants.

Things got worse that game. A few minutes later, while getting ready to take what would be his sixth snap from center, he fell backward. Fear momentarily ran through the stadium and the sidelines. Did somebody shoot the Black quarterback? Nope. On the previous play, linebacker Gary Jeter crushed Williams out-of-bounds. Williams thought he was fine. He thought he could shake it off. But soon the pain was so bad that he could no longer stand. That was the end of his game: 1 of 5 passing for 9 yards. Not exactly what folks expected out of a pioneer. But Doug Williams was resilient. He had to be. He grew up in the rural Jim Crow South. Two games later, when he finally came back, he beat the Minnesota Vikings. He was only 5 of 19 for 63 yards, but his one touchdown made all the difference in their 16–10 victory.

As the season progressed, he became one of the most popular players in the league. "This may be weird to say at this fledgling state of his NFL life, but Williams may be equal to almost anybody in drawing power in his home stadium. Even to O.J. Simpson or Bert Jones," a local writer opined. Local fans appreciated him so much that one section hung a huge banner that read DOUG's KREWE. Week by week, newspapers like the *Chicago Tribune, Chicago Sun-Times*, and *Detroit Free Press* wrote spreads about the new quarterback sensation. Fans were tantalized by his big arm. With McKay calling the plays, he often let Doug unleash a couple of long bombs every game. This meant Doug had a lower completion percentage than most quarterbacks, but McKay thought that was a meaningless stat anyway, so he had him sling away. As one writer put it, "With his arm, you can't turn your back." Even opposing players were mesmerized by his cannon. Chuck Foreman of the Vikings came up to him after one game and told him, "Just keep cockin', because every time you cock your arm it scares me to death." With his fireball arm and big-strike capability, some started to compare him to baseball players, like home run hitter Dave Kingman, who, like Doug, went from the long bomb but also missed a lot, and they said he was like strikeout artist Nolan Ryan, who often overpowered hitters but missed big too, leading to tons of strikeouts and walks.

It also helped that he was winning. By the ninth game of the season, he had the Bucs at 4–4 and ready to make the playoffs. Then, in week 10, Fred Dryer of the Rams—that same Fred Dryer who would later play the TV character Hunter—broke Doug's jaw on a vicious hit. Doug completed the pass, but he was out for six weeks. There went the Bucs' chances of making the playoffs. Although the Bucs were out of the playoff hunt, Doug endeared himself to his teammates when he came back to play in the season finale against the Saints. In the game, he stared down a blitz from the Saints' linebackers, stood in the pocket, and delivered a strike to Jimmie Giles. "Right then and there," running back Ricky Bell said, "if anyone still had any doubts about Doug Williams' courage, it had to be dispelled."

Despite his growing popularity and the team's improvement, there were still fans and writers who would never be satisfied. Doug Williams could not handle that criticism. It wasn't that he was a prima donna, but the truth was, he had never seen the caliber of racist attacks that Vince Evans had. But now he was a franchise player, and as it had for all Black quarterbacks, the vitriol came for Doug. He did not know how to respond. He had torn up small-town Louisiana teams with ease, then spent four years shredding opposing defenses from tiny schools. If there were flaws in his game, they were hidden by the gaudy stats. But the pros exposed him, and the critics came for him. They said he threw too hard, stared down his receivers too much, forced too many passes, and could not get to his second read. Then there were the locals who poked fun at his mishaps. A common joke said, "Williams tried to commit suicide, but somebody intercepted the bullet." Another chided, "We should send Doug Williams to Iran, because he's the only one that can overthrow the Ayatollah." But Doug had a comeback for that one. "It wouldn't do me any good," he rifled back, "because they've already sent all the black people back on a plane." It was the perfect clapback that strategically hit home his point that criticism and his color were intertwined. Besides, numbers lie.

In his ten games as a rookie, he only completed 37.6 percent of his passes and only had a 53.5 efficiency rating, but those numbers provided zero context. Those long bombs were low-percentage throws that his coach ordered. And unlike other quarterbacks, his completion percentage was lower because he did not take sacks. Instead of giving up seven yards on a sack and keeping a high completion percentage, he often threw the ball away. Plus, his receivers dropped too many passes. And to those teammates who complained he threw too hard, Doug replied that in college, his guys caught the passes. Even opposing players like Vikings receiver

Ahmad Rashad noticed his receivers let him down. "Every time I watched Tampa Bay play early in the season," he observed, "his ball would be right on the money, but a lot of times they couldn't hold on to it. That doesn't reflect in the statistics."

Fortunately for Doug, he was not alone in his fight. He had "Color Blind" McKay. "If he believes a black athlete is the best man for that position," journalist Doc Young said of McKay, "the black athlete plays that position. Nobody intimidates John McKay, a West Virginia–born white man who says his parents taught him as a child that racial prejudice was wrong." Maybe the pioneering path for Doug would not have been so difficult if the previous Black quarterbacks had had a coach like McKay. He not only stood by his Black quarterback, he also stood up for him. Every criticism that people had of Doug, McKay was there for a rebuttal. He took the blame for Doug's inaccuracy, and he told the press those stats did not matter. When the receivers kept dropping the ball, he publicly admonished them for their drops. He eventually cut the ones who could not catch Williams's fastballs. When the criticism did not stop, he called it out by name. It was plain and simple racism. McKay's persistent protection of Williams earned him the nickname of "Color Blind." Williams was the first Black quarterback who truly had white support. And that made all the difference.

If Doug were being honest with himself, however, he'd have to admit that some of the criticism was warranted. Williams did force too many passes. Who wouldn't with an arm like that? And he did have accuracy issues. Those years at Chaneyville and Grambling throwing deep to receivers did not help him refine his short game. Coming into his first training camp, one coach noted his short-yardage accuracy was the biggest flaw he needed to fix. He missed the easy checkdown to the running back out of the backfield. For Doug, however, too often these critiques seemed like more than just an assessment of his skills. There was animosity in them that went beyond the football field. When his critics punctuated their words suggesting he was a "spoiled brat" or a "black quarterback from Grambling," Doug felt they crossed the line. "That's personal," Doug complained. All the junk about him not being able to read the defense or saying he could not get to his second or third option came from the fact that too many people were still stuck in their old, racist ways of thinking. "They think we're all just plain dumb," he shot back. They could not get over the fact that he was Black.

A package came to his house in a big box. The fact that it had no return address told him all he needed to know. This was going to be another racist letter. This one stunk too. When he opened it, he found a rotten watermelon with a note that read, "Try throwing this to your niggers. Maybe they can catch this." It was a stark reminder that no matter how far he could throw the ball, he could not distance himself from the racism. When the racism didn't come by mail, it came through the air. Every so often, he would hear the vitriol from the stands: "Hey, McKay, why don't you go back to Southern Cal and take your niggers with you." Each time, Doug seethed with anger. But what could he do? The racism made Joe Gilliam turn to drugs. The racism made James Harris angry and isolated. To get by, Doug Williams decided to keep chucking.

CHAPTER 17

Coming into their historic matchup on September 30, 1979, with the Bears, the Bucs were 4–0 and the hottest team in the NFL for two main reasons: Doug Williams and defense. By 1979, as Doug entered his second season in the league, the Buccaneers had one of the top defensive teams. In the NFC, they were first in total yards allowed, first in rushing yards allowed, second in points allowed, and led the conference in sacks, with seventeen. Those sack numbers were even more impressive because they rarely blitzed. Led by the Selmon brothers, five of their last ten sacks heading into the game came with only a three-man front. For the last two years, coaches around the league had worried about the day when the offense caught up with the defense.

McKay built the offense around his Black quarterback. Even though Williams had a quick release that kept him from being sacked, McKay knew he had to address his offensive line. During Doug's first year, players and the press knocked him for locking onto one receiver, but with a weak offensive line, he did not have time to scan the field. He usually got one read. McKay was bent on changing that. In the 1978 draft, he traded his 1979 first-round pick to the Bears for their underperforming defensive end Wally Chambers. This move improved the defense, but it also allowed McKay to convert defensive end Charley Hannah to right tackle. Hannah was big and fast, and McKay wanted his speed up front for protection, but also to move the running game. Then in 1979, he drafted the best offensive lineman in college, Greg Roberts, which gave him more speed and power up front.

For years, doubters wondered if a Black man could lead Southern whites. The Buccaneers answered those questions. Of those five starters, four were from the South. Doug and the Bucs' big bodies up front proved all along that the racial myth about Black leadership was all pure hogwash. During their 4–0 start, they did not allow a sack. Williams was free to bomb away.

To take more pressure off Doug, McKay also added depth to the running game. In 1979, he drafted Arkansas's running back Jerry Eckwood, a player who was often hurt during his college career but when healthy was as good as Ricky Bell. The Bucs also upgraded Doug's receiving pool and used their second-round pick on Gordon Jones, a speedy receiver from Pitt, and they promoted the sure-handed Isaac Hagins as a starter. With a newly built line, a better running attack, and better receivers, coming into the Bears game, the Bucs led the league in rushing—the Bears and Walter Payton were second—and they led the NFC in total points with 102. That was a miraculous number considering they only scored 103 points in all the 1977 season. The Bucs' offense's success would not have been possible without Williams steering the ship.

His rookie season humbled Williams and made him hungry to learn. He was often unprepared for what to "expect" and struggled with the coverages and tricks a defense would play on his eyes. Reflecting on his rookie year, he said, "I learned to have patience.

I learned to adjust myself to the mental game. The National Football League is more of a mental game than college." He started to understand coverages and realized that as the field general, he had to "keep the defense wondering what he's going to do." After intensely studying his playbook and the long skull sessions with offensive coordinator Joe Gibbs, Williams came into the 1979 season in command of the offense.

With his confidence and a rebuilt offense, Williams began the season on a tear. Heading into the Bears game, although his passing completion percentage was still near the bottom of the league, he had already thrown for seven touchdowns, tying his mark from his rookie year. Players from across the league took note. After they beat the Rams, their great defensive end Jack Youngblood said, "Doug Williams is really maturing. He has come a long way in one year. He's going to be a fine, fine, fine quarterback. Maybe, I should say he is a fine, fine quarterback." In less than two seasons after drafting Doug, the Bucs went from worst to first. With the Bears up next, they intended to keep things that way. The game pitted the two best running teams in the league, led by two of the hottest quarterbacks in the league. They both happened to be Black. It just took Vince Evans a little longer to get there.

INVINCEABLE

When the Bears' first minicamp rolled around in April 1979, Evans let everyone know his intentions. "I want so badly to be the first-string quarterback," he proclaimed. "I've got so many things to prove to so many people. No. 1, I have to prove I'm good enough to play in this league. No. 2, I have to prove myself to the fans of Chicago. They're so hungry for a winner." Words and emotions were great, but he had to back it up with improved play. Despite showing some improvement during camp, the Bears still signed a rookie free agent, Pete Kraker, to compete with Evans for the third quarterback spot.

When training camp opened in July, it was judgment time for Evans. He was either going to be a quarterback, be switched, or be on a bus to Canada. "There's no question that I can play," he told a Black reporter at the start of training camp. "I feel I'm going to get the opportunity to prove myself, and I'm hoping it's right here on this field." His confidence came from his newfound belief in God. On Easter 1979, he had a major breakdown that led to a religious experience. As he watched Robert Schuller, a California TV evangelist, a sunbeam hit his face on a cloudy Chicago day. To Evans, it was a sign from God. He called his family and teammate Dan Jiggetts crying, to let them know what happened. From that moment on, Evans dedicated his life to God. Before then, he'd never cared what anyone thought of him. As he put it, he was a millionaire athlete and walked around carefree—parties, limousines, and everything that came with that status. On Easter, it all stopped. When he came back to the team, he became a leader. On a team that was known as being "religious," Evans led Bible study. He brought his faith with him to meetings, to practice, and on the field. Before Tim Tebow would become known for "Tebowing" after a touchdown, it was Vince Evans who struck a praying pose after he scored. If you asked his teammates, they'd say his new faith in God changed him into an NFL quarterback. He just had to wait for his coaches to see the light.

For the first time in his career, Evans looked like a pro quarterback. Everyone took note. As Jiggetts put it, "Vince has been turning a lot of heads in practice." Coach Neill Armstrong noted that Evans had "more confidence in himself" than in previous years. The quarterback had always been a cool customer on the sidelines, but when it was his turn to perform, he would get jitters, and the plays would stumble out of his mouth. Now they were coming out crisp and clear as a May Chicago day. Evans, who said, "I used to be proud of how hard I could throw," would still play a game with Walter Payton on the sidelines, seeing how hard they could throw the ball at each other's hands, which made the coaches cringe, but in practice, the blazing-hot passes that ripped right through the receivers' hands now came in with precise touch.

The Bears badly needed a quarterback. They finished twenty-sixth in the league in passing, and they only accumulated seven throwing touchdowns, tied for worst in the league. With a weak passing game, defenses would stack the line of scrimmage, giving Payton very little room to maneuver. Even with the odds against him on every play, he was still the best in the league. But as good as Payton was, he'd be even better with a passing game. Coach Armstrong summed up this need to pass: "That's [running] the bread and butter. The passing is frosting on the cake. But the way I see it, you've got to have the frosting to win a divisional championship."

Desperate for a real field general, teammates started to talk. Which quarterback was better? At this point, it was clear to the Bears players that Bob Avellini was out of the running. He had been the quarterback for statistically one of the worst teams in the league. He and his seven touchdowns were not coming back from that. Between Mike Phipps and Evans, Phipps had more command of the offense and could read a defense better, but everything else about Evans jumped out. He had the better arm and was the better athlete, a much-needed attribute since the offensive line was not good at pass protecting. To hear it from Vince, he had it all too. "I'm more of a mobile-type quarterback. I'm a pocket passer too, but my ability to throw on the run allows me to make things happen outside the pocket as well."

Evans also had an intangible factor that teammates latched onto. Everyone recognized him as the leader. Offensive guard

Noah Jackson observed, "I think the guys respond to him for some reason. I'm not saying the other guys don't have ability. But Vince has something, a kind of charisma." Despite all this, his lack of experience made it hard for the coaches to trust him. Making it even harder for Evans to earn his start, Phipps had just signed a new contract. To start the preseason, Coach Armstrong went with Phipps.

No quarterback beat the odds like Vince Evans. In the first preseason game against the Jets, Evans took flight. During the second quarter, in what was his only quarter of play, he went 9 of 12 for 165 yards and three touchdowns, including a ball he lofted into a receiver's hands, displaying the touch few believed he had. Coach Armstrong said he was impressed by Evans but still wanted to see more. Everyone else, however, knew at that moment that Evans had the goods. Teammates praised him, and local white journalists salivated over him. One writer wrote, "Evans has everything but experience; a fine arm, keen football intellect, reasonable poise under pressure, and scrambling ability. So why isn't he the quarterback? He will be, for certain, barring injury. But when?" Even Sonny Jurgensen, one of the greatest quarterbacks ever, saw it too. During the game, the Hall of Famer turned football broadcaster said, "I'm really impressed with young Evans. He handles himself pretty well out there and adds a new dimension to the Bears' offense. I think he can play." Vince moved the offense, and he moved the crowd. It was just a matter of time before coaches moved him into the starting lineup.

By now, Evans moved Black Chicago too. It took a while, but Evans began to see there was some upside to being known as a Black quarterback too. "Even whites look up to other white quarterbacks," he reasoned. Locally, Black reporters stepped over the white quarterbacks just to get a quote from Vince or have him say something on their radio shows. And with two major Black newspapers in town, the *Chicago Defender* and *Chicago Metro News*, Evans got a lot of ink. He was in articles and ads, and he even had a TV spot. Evans believed that his success would inspire others, and in return, he would give back to his people, especially Black kids. "I wish some days that I could do well and just go into the ghettoes, talking to kids, setting an example for kids who are into drugs and drinking and stand on the streets waiting for trouble. Sometimes I get in my car and ride through the ghetto and it's frightening," he said. Eventually, he did just that. When he was not on the field, he could be found at the Cabrini-Green projects talking to kids about their futures. But first, he had to convince his white coach he could play.

ARMSTRONG IS A RACIST, the headline blasted from the *Chicago Metro News*. "Racism," the writer asserted, "is instilled within his attitude." The writer pointed out that while everyone was praising Evans for his performance against the Jets, Armstrong was being a "low-key racist" when he remarked, "one game doesn't change the fact that Evans is still the third string quarterback." The writer further complained that in the exhibition game, Armstrong played Evans with backup offensive linemen so that he wouldn't have a chance to compete fairly. Armstrong ignored the charges of racism and went with Phipps as the opening-day starter. But Phipps might as well have been the winter solstice because his days as Neill Armstrong's quarterback were short.

Armstrong finally landed on Vince Evans on September 9, 1979, in the second quarter of the second game of the season. Although the Bears were 1–0 heading into that game against the Vikings, they did not score a touchdown against the Packers in their opener. In the Vikings contest, Phipps continued to struggle, going 5 of 12 for 35 yards and one interception to start the game. Walter Payton couldn't get it going either; the Vikings kept crowding the line of scrimmage. Trailing 7–3, with 5:15 in the second quarter, Armstrong inserted Evans into the lineup. Evans jogged in, looked at remnants of a once-dominant defense that was dubbed the "Purple People Eaters," licked his fingers, and was ready to feast. In one play, he hit a 56-yard bomb to receiver James Scott. The Bears went up 10–7 and never looked back. With Evans in the lineup, the Vikings could no longer key on Payton. Linebacker Scott Studwell admitted, "In the first half, Payton didn't get outside us at all. The support on the corners was so good he didn't have any place to run." After that, the corners were confused on where to go—key on Payton or watch the receiver? Worrying about Evans, they let Payton loose for 182 yards. Evans finished the game 4 of 7 for 88 yards and a touchdown, but most importantly, he finally earned a starting job. His offensive coordinator just had one piece of advice for his new starter. "There's an old axiom, don't ever forget it," he warned his new star quarterback. "The axiom says, 'Don't overload your rear with your mouth.'" To that, Evans smiled, turned to the press, and said, "He's the man."

When Evans made his first start the following week against Roger Staubach and the defending champion Dallas Cowboys, he became the first Black quarterback who was known as a runner to earn a starting job. As others would point out, Marlin Briscoe fell into the job. Six years prior to this start, Evans was essentially a running back—or, as a scout might say today, AN ATHLETE PLAYING QUARTERBACK. His success could have opened the doors for so many more quarterbacks, as the league would see the advantage of having a dual-threat general in the pocket. He and the Bears showed that teams could have patience and turn an athlete into a quarterback.

In his first start against the Cowboys, Evans exhibited the full possibilities of what a dual-threat quarterback could be. And this was no easy task. Dallas had a dominating defense and was led by one of the most innovative defensive coaches in the history of the game, Tom Landry. Landry devised schemes to defend every type of offense and made quarterbacks shudder at what he might throw at them. Evans wasn't worried. "That's not a bad way to go," Evans said as he looked ahead to the matchup. "Sometimes it's best to take the toughest things first in line." Although he was confident, his nerves got the best of him during the game. He missed most of his short passes and only threw 5 of 16. But when he did connect, he hit big. He bombed the Cowboys for a 52-yard and then a 64-yard touchdown. The passes showed off his arm and his mind. On each throw, he stayed in the pocket against a fierce Cowboys blitz, displaying that, indeed, the Black quarterback could read defenses. Asked about his bombs, he replied, "What's so complicated? If the other guys are in a flex or if they're double covering, you just have to adjust." The dual-threat quarterback also ran in a score.

The Bears lost the game, dropping them to 2–1, but with Evans at the helm, it finally allowed the Bears to walk around with their chins up. The threat of his speed and powerful arm made them dangerous. "Any time you get into a fight with the town bully and you do pretty good against him," Armstrong proudly said, "it makes you want to pop your buttons a little bit, even though your nose is a little bloody." Of course, Evans would need a lot more work, as was displayed in the following week's game in Miami, when the Dolphins backed their defense up and protected against the long bomb and made him hit the intermediate passes. But all new quarterbacks had to learn that part of the game. His next game would be one of the biggest milestones in NFL history, when the Bucs battled the Bears, pitting two starting Black quarterbacks against each other for the first time.

THE GAME

I<small>T WAS A PERFECT DAY FOR FOOTBALL AT</small> C<small>HICAGO'S</small> S<small>OLDIER</small> Field. Sunny, seventy-five degrees, and winds were swirling at 20 mph. Fans could hear small planes fly over the stadium and see sailboats in Lake Michigan, and on the field, there were two Black bombers.

In football terms, the Bucs-Bears battle on September 30, 1979, was a big game. The Bucs entered the contest undefeated but still had something to prove. The experts had discounted their 4–0 record as fool's gold. They had the worst record in the league the previous season, so they had the easiest schedule in 1979. Those early victories against the Lions, Colts, and Packers did not mean much. Those three teams were marginal at best. And what about the Rams? That was pure luck, they claimed. But no matter what the pundits said, a win in Chicago would be huge. The Bucs would still have the easiest schedule in the league, and they only had to face one more team that made the playoffs the previous year. If they beat the Bears, even if it was early in the season, only a massive meltdown would keep them from winning the NFC Central Division.

The Bears, on the other hand, came in the game with a 2–2 record and a tougher schedule moving forward. Facing their third straight undefeated team, if they dropped another game, that would place them a full three games behind the Bucs in the playoff race. Not an impossible hole to climb out of but one that would need some serious digging if they lost. And one that could get a coach fired if they failed to make the playoffs. This was as pivotal of a week 5 game as there could be.

Then there was an extra element adding to the hype of this game. It pitted McKay against his old quarterback Evans. The previous week, McKay had dismantled the Rams' Pat Haden even before the game got rolling, when he told the press he knew how to beat his ex-USC quarterback. It was the type of gamesmanship designed to get into the quarterback's head, make him question every throw, and it worked. Haden went 13 of 27 for 64 yards, and the Rams' offense failed to score. Unlike Haden, Evans was not going to let McKay get into his noggin. Instead, he struck first. McKay might have been his coach for two years, Evans said, but he hardly knew that man. "I wasn't close to Coach McKay at all," he chided. "He never talked to his players in college, and I thought that was strange. I guess I was seeking some kind of father image from him, but I didn't get it. At USC, it was like Coach McKay was on a pedestal, looking down at the rest of us." He seemed bitter because he was. McKay never gave Evans the attention he gave Haden. In truth, Evans was more worried about his impending date with ex-USC linebackers Richard "Batman" Wood and Dave Lewis, who were intent to rip his head off. When the two teams played the previous year—Williams was hurt, and Evans only played a few snaps—Evans took the field and told Lewis, "Get ready, I'm coming outside at you." To that, Lewis laid down the law, saying, "Hey, man, don't bring that mess out here today." The Bucs had the most aggressive linebackers in the league, who looked to knock out opposing players with every blow delivered. Evans had his hands full. And that was just the on-field stuff.

This game was bigger than football because this game meant something for Black Americans. In fact, it should have been a bigger deal. Sure, there was the *Los Angeles Times, Los Angeles Sentinel, Chicago Sun-Times,* and *Tampa Bay Times,* but other than that, most major papers let the moment slip by. Were they tired of talking about race? Did they hope that by not pointing out the fact that two Black quarterbacks started meant that somehow America was ready to move beyond race? Big deals are only big deals if people make a big deal out of them. And those who commented on the game did not quite know what to say. Just how big was the game? After all, while two Black quarterbacks were starting against each other for the first time in the modern NFL, there were only four in the league. If that was progress, it was limited progress. Should they eviscerate the NFL for all its past prejudices or applaud the league for this barrier-breaking moment? In the end, these writers chose to mark the moment but did not want to go beyond that. The headlines said it all: BLACK QB RULE NO BIG DEAL; BLACK QUARTERBACKS MAKING NFL HISTORY; EVANS, WILLIAMS FINALLY TREATED AS "JUST PLAIN QUARTERBACKS"; UNHERALDED BUT HISTORIC HAPPENING IN CHICAGO.

The quarterbacks took the same tactic. They had already spent too much time in their careers talking about what it was like to be a Black quarterback. They just wanted to move on and play. Both believed that continuously talking about race would be a hindrance to their careers. As Doug declared, "I don't put color into the situation. If people never write about us as being black quarterbacks, it wouldn't be such a big deal, there'd be nothing to say. I consider myself as a quarterback period. I know what color I am. I see it every day." In other words, talking about their race separated them from their peers instead of putting them on the same plane. They were Black and thus different, and they would always be judged like that. But what about being heroes to the Black community? "That's not fair," Williams observed. "Bradshaw and Namath, they're heroes of all people. When I was small, I pretended I was Joe Namath, and I was black." Still, after all that, Williams had a message for Evans: "Tell him to keep it in the league, add some more to it. There's only a few of us."

Billed as the "Battle of the Bombers" by CBS, the Bucs-Bears game was like a heavyweight fight. An apt comparison considering Doug Williams wore a Muhammad Ali T-shirt to the contest that had the words I'M THE GREATEST on the front. With quarterbacks who could throw haymakers with their deep passes, each team could score quickly, so the defenses stayed deep, trying to prevent big bombs. While each team had one explosive score—the Bucs' Jerry Eckwood had a 61-yard touchdown run in the second quarter, and Walter Payton took a screen pass to the house in the fourth quarter for 65 yards—both quarterbacks missed on their downfield throws. Each threw passes that smoothly sailed in the air more than 60 yards, only for their receivers to drop that ball. Without big plays, the game boiled down to the two exciting quarterbacks having to be patient as their offenses picked and prodded the defense, trying to get what they could.

With the two best running attacks in the NFC, both teams tried to establish the run early, control the line of scrimmage, and prove their physical toughness. For Payton, however, having an inexperienced Evans was a blessing and a curse. In theory, defenses had to respect Evans's running ability, so it opened some running lanes for Payton as the opposing linebackers in their 3-4 defense spread out, as they had to worry about Vince running. But with Vince in the game, the linebackers also changed how they manned the field. Understanding that Vince was more of a threat to roll out and run on the outside, defenses started to funnel everything toward the middle, which meant they also keyed in on shutting down Payton's outside lanes.

When the ground game ran into resistance, Coach Armstrong grew impatient and looked to Vince to get the offense rolling. For Vince, who was confident in his own abilities, and proclaimed before the game, "Coach McKay knows I can run the ball and throw the ball, and you can't really set any defenses for a quarterback who operates outside of the pocket," that was fine by him. He thought he could shred any defense. And why wouldn't he? He could throw the ball through a tornado. But by shutting down Payton and forcing the Bears to be a passing team, they played right into McKay's hands. McKay spent two years with Evans at

USC, but he knew Evans's weakness—his inaccuracy on intermediate passes. On the ground, they limited Evans to 17 yards on four attempts. This forced Evans to be a passer.

The Bucs' defense was difficult for any team to throw on, but for someone with little experience, it became nearly impossible. To prevent the long pass, the linebackers took deep drops, which forced Evans to throw shallow passes. He hit Payton and his tight ends on short completions, but that's what the Bucs wanted. While he beat the linebackers a few times with his arm and hit the occasional 15-yard completion, he missed too often on the long passes to be effective. Throughout the game when he had to make the crucial throw, Evans sailed his passes too high.

But Evans was not in the game for his ability to methodically break down a defense. He was there to be electrifying. And in the fourth quarter with the Bears trailing 10–6, he caught lightning. Evans ran a play-action screen pass to perfection and hit Payton with a precise pass that he took for a 65-yard touchdown.

Up to that point in the fourth quarter, statistically, Williams did not have a great game. But he displayed the leadership that explained why the undefeated Bucs had one of the best turnarounds in league history. The scouting report on Doug read like this: take away the deep ball and wait for him to force an intermediate pass. But Doug had worked all season long on his soft, short passes and the patience he needed to work through his progressions on the field when the defense took away his deep target. Throughout the game, he hit short passes to their running backs or quick outs to their receivers. Although McKay still had him rifle the ball downfield—he let loose two passes that flew over 60 yards—hitting the short passes kept the chains moving and the Bears offense off the field. His ability to hit the quick swings to Eckwood and outs to his receivers, Hagins and Jones, also improved on his passing percentage. He finished the game 14 of

31 for 168 yards, a mark that upped his 34.8 percentage. Williams's numbers would have been much higher if his receivers did not drop eight passes, including two that should have been deep touchdowns.

The book on the Black quarterback said that he could not think, and when the going got tough, he would mentally fold. Down 13–10 in the fourth quarter, Williams quickly dispelled that notion. On a day when the Bucs struggled to sustain a drive, Williams was at his best when his best was needed. Starting their drive from their 45 after Chicago tried to squib the kickoff to avoid a kick return, the Bucs called five straight runs before they put the ball in Williams's hand. On third and 5, at the Bears' 35, from a pro-style split back set, Williams sent a dart to the right side to rookie Gordon Jones on a 10-yard out. First down. Then after two more runs, facing third and 2 from the Bears' 8-yard line, with the Bears expecting McKay to call a conservative run, Williams took the snap from a split back set, rolled back, and pumped right to receiver Isaac Hagins, who was running a slant. The fake fooled the defensive back Mike Spivey, who turned inside to jump a slant, and then Hagins ran outside to the corner of the end zone, where Williams lofted him an easy touchdown. "Doug Williams shows his enormous poise," an announcer said after the score. While the play design called for Hagins to run that route, it was Doug's pump that got him open. It was also the pump that got Doug yelled at by the receivers coach, who was mad at him for hotdogging. He thought that fake was careless. But that's how Grambling football players played—with swag.

Now, it was Evans's turn. During the game, the Bucs held Payton to only 46 yards on the ground. With Payton unable to spit out yards against the Bucs, the Bears had to tap the well that was Vince Evans. Unfortunately, he came up empty. Evans threw two interceptions in the Bears' last two drives.

But Evans's inability to get going was not all his fault. The play calling was too bland. One Bears player complained, "Our offense runs the same plays, drops the ball, and in the end the defense gets blamed." Too often, the predictable pass plays called for play-action (faking a run and pivoting to a pass). That might work if Payton had it rolling in the running game, but he did not. Although they attempted a few deep passes, what they really needed were out patterns. The Bucs played "900 yards" off the Bears' receivers, daring them to throw short outs, but Armstrong and offensive coordinator Ken Meyer refused to call any short out passes. Making matters worse, they only called one pass play to their top receiver, Golden Richards, to which Richards complained, "One token pass." An irate defender chimed in, "We got out and make the trade of the century to get Golden Richards and he only gets one dinky pass thrown to him." The Bears traded a fifth (1979) and a third (1980) pick to the Cowboys for Richards in 1978. Hardly the "trade of the century," but a big-enough haul to upset a Bears defender who thought Richards should have received more targets.

Compounding the poor pass calls with more bad decisions, Armstrong also should have taken advantage of Vince being a dual-threat quarterback. The offense needed more rollouts and fewer drop-backs. Of the twenty-three passes he threw, only four of them were designed rollouts. A dual-threat quarterback with only one threat is hardly intimidating. Armstrong had a missile at quarterback, but instead decided to use Evans as a stationary cannon.

BIGGER THAN A GAME

DESPITE EVANS'S OVERALL INEFFECTIVENESS AND ARMSTRONG'S lack of imagination, anybody rewatching the game will see a flash of the future of football. Although NFL insiders did not quite see it at that time, the era of the plodding quarterback was coming to an end. Defenses were catching up to the pass-happy offenses by employing more speedy linebackers who could cover receivers and go after the quarterback. As defenses increased how often they blitzed, having a mobile quarterback would be a near necessity. During the game, Evans escaped several sacks, saving his team field position. On one amazing play, which shows up in the books as a reception for Walter Payton for 2 yards, the Bucs' defense quickly met Evans in the backfield as he rolled to his left; Lee Roy Selmon even had him in his grasp, but Evans quickly escaped and rolled back 25 yards to avoid the sack, set his feet, then uncoiled a rocket to Payton back to the line of scrimmage, where Payton was tackled after gaining 2 yards. On another play, he rolled left, then threw a perfect pass that traveled 55 yards to a receiver, who dropped the ball. On his longest run, he avoided a sack and then quickly scampered 14 yards. For his touchdown pass to Payton, he rolled back 10 yards on a screen pass as the defense barreled down on him; he hit Payton, who then took the ball 65 yards for a touchdown. As the announcers mentioned during the game, Evans added "another dimension" to the offense with his speed.

Armstrong, however, could not see Evans as the future proto-type. After the first few offensive series, the coach contemplated benching Evans. He would not say why, just that he did not think Evans was the right quarterback for the Bears. Maybe he wanted to avoid the backlash of benching a Black quarterback? After all, a local Black paper called him racist for not starting Evans just three weeks prior. Whatever was the case, he stuck with Evans during the game, but Armstrong had no plans beyond that contest to cement Evans as the future quarterback, and he told the press that by Friday, he'd announce a new starter. After three games, Evans lost his starting job, but the worst was yet to come.

If one asked Vince Evans, he'd tell them the devil put him in the hospital. In reality, a deep cut he sustained on his left arm against the Dolphins on September 23 and a blind side blitz from Bucs safety Mark Cotney a week later nearly snatched his soul. The Bears' staff neither properly cleaned nor stitched up the cut against the Dolphins. The exchange of sweat and other bodily fluids from football led to an undetected staph infection, which seeks weak areas in the body to flourish. That jarring third-quarter hit from Cotney weakened the tissue and sent a signal to the infection to spread. Evans felt fine throughout the game and even during the next day's practice.

The thought of losing his starting job had his mind elsewhere. But by the next night, the pain had become unbearable. All hell had broken loose in his body. Called to Evans's house to help, the team doctor and trainer could not even move Evans to get him to a hospital. When he finally reached the hospital by ambulance, he was in screeching pain with a temperature of 103. The temperature kept increasing with no signs of slowing. With a temperature now at 105 degrees, a twenty-four-year-old man in shape like Evans could survive that type of heat for about three hours. If his body continued to deteriorate, Evans would be deceased. The doctors did all they could to get his temperature down; they flooded him with ice packs and put a cold mattress under his body. The remedy gave him chills, but within thirty minutes, he was down to 104. "He had a very stormy night. Thank God he was a young, healthy kid," the doctor said. But he was not in the clear. The doctors pumped him with antibiotics, hoping they would not have to operate on him. As they waited for the drugs to work, Evans lay in pain, unable to roll on his side or stomach without the help of assistance. Evans prayed that he'd survive. "Satan put me here," he observed. "This is a test of faith and courage." Some questioned if he would ever play again. "I felt like I was going to die," he later said.

By the grace of God, Vince survived his staph infection. But he needed another miracle if he were ever going to play again. The doctors doubted he would. Just walking would be his first step. He left the hospital assisted by a walker. Then, when he tried to throw a football, he could not get it to the other side of the room. When the Bears had their first mini training camp in April 1980, he was in good spirits but in bad condition. He could hardly jog. But few players in the NFL were as determined as Vince Evans. If anyone could climb out from the depths of hell, it was the born-again Christian.

CHAPTER 18

THE BEARS' 1980 SEASON STARTED LIKE THE PREVIOUS FIVE YEARS: awfully. Once again, the starting quarterback—this time, it was Mike Phipps—could not get the offense moving. Of course, it was not entirely the quarterback's fault. As play callers, Neill Armstrong and Ken Meyer were as conservative as Reagan and Bush. The plays were basic and predictable, and the receivers ran bland routes. With a marginal quarterback like Phipps running the show, the offense sputtered. Luckily for the Bears, they had a spark plug. After another lackluster performance in their week 3 game against the Vikings, Armstrong inserted Evans into the lineup. Although they lost the game, Evans gave them the flash they needed. He went 14 of 34 for 204 yards, including an 89-yard bomb to receiver Rickey Watts. Evans also added a rushing touchdown. It was just a matter of time before he got his job back. Four games later, with the Bears sitting at 2–4 and the offense continuing to struggle, Armstrong finally tabbed Evans as the starter. He'd hold that job until the end of the 1981 season.

A SECOND CHANCE

WHEN ARMSTRONG WENT WITH EVANS IN 1979, THE MOVE
seemed desperate, but when Armstrong came back to Evans in
1980, the move seemed deliberate. He was ready to do what no
other coach had done: hand the keys to a speedy Black quarterback. For most in the league, this still seemed unthinkable. As
one reporter explained, "There have been numerous raps leveled at
Vince Evans. They said he had itchy feet and an itchy trigger fin-
ger. They said he could throw the ball through brick walls, except
that brick walls don't run post patterns. They said he could read
playbooks in his leisure, but not defenses under pressure. They
said, ever so politely, that the sum of his parts didn't equal a very
impressive IQ." Those were the same remarks pundits would continue to use to degrade Black quarterbacks, but Coach Armstrong
believed there could be an upgrade. Instead of bottling him up,
he finally concluded that it was better to let him bubble a bit. He
wanted Evans to use his athleticism, but in the right way. Instead of
jetting out of the pocket when he first felt pressure or fleeing backward when the defense barreled down on him, he asked him to
step up in the pocket to create more time for his receivers and then
take off when things broke down. To date, nobody had tried that
with an athletic Black quarterback. They gave up early, thinking
they could never convert him. "The new-wave stuff," one reporter
wrote about Evans as a dual-threat quarterback, "goes against the
grain of everything they [his coaches] hold sacred, makes them
think they are catering a graffiti party in a cathedral."

Evans broke the mold of what a fast quarterback should and
could be. He was the future of football. During the last ten games
of the 1980 season, Armstrong and Evans showed a maturation
in thinking as coach and athletic quarterback. In his first start
against Detroit, Evans demonstrated the menace of a dual-threat
quarterback. Coming into the game, the Lions worried about his

threat to run. "He'll take off and go if you don't contain him," Coach Monte Clark warned. "Whoever has the outside (on the pass rush) has got to be conscious of containing him." The Lions kept Evans from scrambling, but their single-mindedness got them beat at the end. In the fourth quarter, with the Lions trailing 17–7, Evans, who was 4 of 7 passing for 108 yards and had a rushing touchdown up to that point, caught the Lions napping and hit them with a 64-yard bomb to James Scott. "They weren't showing much respect for our passing game," he said. "Their safeties were coming up and so I thought the pass might keep them honest." The scouting report was a lie. Vince Evans could beat you with his mind. Although they lost their next two games, Evans continued to blossom, including two passing touchdowns and a rushing touchdown against the Browns. And against Washington in week 10, he threw three first-half touchdowns, including a 40-yard shot to Scott and a 54-yarder to Walter Payton. But it was a run by Payton in the first quarter that showed the full growth of Evans. The Bears had called an off-tackle play to Payton, but seeing that Washington had shifted their front four with plans to stop that play, Evans audibled to a trap play up the gut with the right guard pulling and the center blocking a tackle. Payton took it to the house for 50 yards.

Three games later, on Thanksgiving, with all the country watching, Evans had his finest moment as a pro. The previous Thanksgiving, he was unable to walk, but on this day, he walked all over the defense. With 3:37 left in the game and trailing by 7 points, Evans took the Bears on a 14-play, 94-yard drive. *Chicago Tribune* sportswriter David Israel, who titled his postgame piece, "It Was the Making of Vince Evans, QB," praised, "Vince Evans, at the age of 25 and in his fourth season as a professional, seemed to become a quarterback: the whole, the sum of the parts." During that last drive, he was simply brilliant. He patiently stayed in the pocket looking for receivers and hit Scott four times for 66 yards. He ran only when he had to, and he stepped up in the pocket to avoid the rush instead of backpedaling. To end the drive, he scored on a 4-yard run with no time remaining. The Bears won the game in overtime with a 95-yard kick return to start the overtime. A pumped Coach Armstrong exclaimed, "I can't wait until next game to see him play again." The following game, they beat the Packers 61–7 with Evans going 18 of 22 for 316 yards and three touchdowns. Evans threw 4 interceptions a week after he beat the Packers, and the Bears finished their season 7–9 and missed the playoffs, but for the first time since Sid Luckman quarterbacked the Bears, Chicago finally felt they had a field general.

Until Vince Evans's 1980 explosion, no fan base had felt so sure that their future was Black. James Harris led the Rams to the NFC Championship game three times, and the organization and fan base spent three years trying to get rid of him. Doug Williams had just led the Bucs to the NFC Championship, and the fan base wanted to throw him in the bay. But Evans momentarily elicited something different. The Black fans always had his back, but now it was the blue-collar white fans, the same ones who would protest if a Black family moved into their neighborhood, that celebrated their Black football future. It drove them mad that he was not the starter all season long. One headline read, BEARS "CON-VINCE-D"—EVANS IS FOR REAL, while another blasted, EVANS MAKES "WAIT 'TIL NEXT YEAR" SOUND ALMOST GOOD. One *Tribune* writer summed up the new giddy feeling when he wrote, "Win, lose, tie, or disband, however, the Bears must commit their immediate future to Vince Evans. They owe it to themselves, and they owe it to Vince Evans."

Evans played so well in those ten starts—his eight rushing touchdowns led the team and all quarterbacks in the NFL—that it seemed as if Evans would be the first Black quarterback to move past the stereotypes. After the season, when asked about all the stereotypes he faced as a Black quarterback, he seemed optimistic. "Yeah stigmas. Part of it is because I'm black, and because blacks aren't supposed to be NFL quarterbacks. I would hope that people still don't think that shallow, but there will always be some. I can't worry about fans, though. I have to worry about the confidence my teammates have in me." At the end of the year, offensive coordinator Ken Meyer stepped down, and the Bears hired passing-game specialist Ted Marchibroda with the understanding that Vince Evans was his quarterback.

THE EXPERIMENT

TED MARCHIBRODA HAD ONE CHARGE: GET THE MEANDERING offense moving. In 1980, the Bears were twenty-fourth in the league in total offense and last in passing. Although Payton's rushing numbers were down from the previous season, he was still second in the league behind Earl Campbell. Not bad for an offense that was "three rushes by Payton and a cloud of Astro Turf." But cranking up the offense didn't mean finding new ways to run the ball with Walter Payton. As great as Sweetness was, the game was moving away from ground-control offense as more coaches got a taste of what they dubbed "throw ball." Pro football had started to trend toward throw ball in the 1978 season, when changes to blocking rules for offensive linemen allowed more time for the quarterbacks to throw, and rule changes that impacted a defensive back's ability to manhandle the receiver led to more wideouts getting free. Passing numbers took off. In 1977, there were only five games with 300 or more passing yards, but in 1980, there were fifty-four such games. By 1980, touchdown passes accounted for nearly 55 percent of all touchdowns. Speedy wideouts and tight ends were going downfield looking for big chunk plays, and teams were sending sure-handed running backs out of the backfield to catch more passes instead of having them ground and pound.

Marchibroda came with all the offensive credentials. As a coordinator with the Rams in the 1960s, he turned Roman Gabriel into an all-pro quarterback. In 1975, his first season as the head coach of the Baltimore Colts, he brought the team from worst to first in the AFC East on his way to winning three straight AFC East titles. Along the way, he turned Bert Jones into an all-league quarterback. The Colts also had the top offense in 1975 and 1976. His top receiver, Roger Carr, led the league in yards and average, and his running back, Lydell Mitchell, was always among the league leaders in total receptions, including winning the receptions title in 1977. In Chicago, Marchibroda promised to throw the ball deep to his receivers and also utilize Payton as a pass catcher coming out of the backfield. That kind of talk got the fans excited. Most important for the fan base, Marchibroda had a philosophy.

In those days, *philosophy* was a sophisticated term for "offensive system." More than just the plays a team ran, a philosophy was about how the team ran them and why they chose those plays. Under Armstrong's regime, the Bears had no philosophy. "I looked at last year's playbook and couldn't believe it. No system. I could have kicked myself for not looking at it before," owner George Halas remarked. All throughout the offseason, everyone talked about their new philosophy. As one writer explained, Marchibroda "feels that when you return from Las Vegas, either be broke or loaded. To break even is to waste breaking a sweat." In other words, high risk, high reward. Get to a manageable second-down situation and, as he said, "make the defense play defense." Then strike. He believed that no matter if it was first down or third down, the offense had to counter the defense. "He drills it into us—take what the defense gives you," wideout Brian Baschnagel said. This put everything on the quarterback's shoulders because he empowered the quarterback to call the plays. "Quarterbacks should call their own plays as much to get out of a bad play as to get into a good one," Marchibroda believed.

Was Vince Evans up to the task? Marchibroda admitted, "I do know that he seems to have all the attributes—strong arm, good athlete—to be an excellent quarterback," but as he said after he got hired, "I don't know whether he has a philosophy." Right from the beginning, Marchibroda was not sure that Evans could make all the right reads or throws. He was not sure if he could carry out the game plan all on his own, he questioned if Evans could read the defense, and he worried that Evans did not have consistency as a passer, and he expected him to have a "scatter-arm." It was stereotypical stuff one would say about a Black quarterback. Once again, Evans had to show and prove.

Evans went to work. He practically lived at the Bears' training facility at Lake Forest, studying film to the point where the coaches had to send him home to get rest. When he was not studying, he worked out with his receivers practicing on timing routes in their new system. It seemed to work. He had command of the offense. He had control of the team. He dominated the preseason. In his first preseason game, he hit on ten straight passes against the Bengals. In the next game, he nailed thirteen of his first fourteen tosses. Calling all the plays, Evans rarely ran Payton, making the all-time great quip, "They don't need me anymore."

Along the way, Evans was the toast of the town. There was Vince Evans Day at Malcolm X College, and local papers started to write more pieces about Evans and his maturation, with headlines like VINCE EVANS "PRIMED TO SUCCEED" and VINCE EVANS: PRECISELY ON TARGET. The *Chicago Tribune* did a seven-page feature article on him, and *Pro Football* magazine printed their own feature. *Mahogany*, a local Black magazine, also did a spread. Fans and folks in the organization started to talk Super Bowl. It was clear, if everything went right, Vince Evans was the future of football. There was only one thing left to do: play the regular season.

Within a month, fans were calling Evans the dumbest quarterback in the league, and by the end of the year, fans were cheering when he got hurt. Evans threw twenty interceptions, and the team went 6–10. What happened? Two words: *pressure* and *philosophy*. The pressure to perform overwhelmed Evans. The pressure to win was no longer about just improving on the previous season but also saving jobs. It was clear from the beginning that if the offense did not turn around, Armstrong and Marchibroda would be gone. As Marchibroda said at the beginning of the season, "Vince Evans is on the spot. But how many people wouldn't want to be Vince Evans?" Behind a shaky offensive line? Nobody wanted to be Vince Evans with so little protection from all those hulking defensemen. All season, the Bears' offensive line failed to protect Evans. There was no time for him to scan the field and read the defense. And his receiving corps was subpar. If everyone were being honest with themselves, they would have known since July that things would not go as planned for the offense. Marchibroda's offense called for a deep ball threat, but during the offseason, the Bears' speedy home run threat, James Scott, jetted to Canada for more money. Sensing an opportunity to upgrade his own contract, their second receiver, Rickey Watts, "retired," until he got a new contract. He returned out of football shape, and he got hurt early in the season. The other two receivers, Brian Baschnagel and rookie Ken Margerum, were route runners, not burners.

The offense was out of whack from the beginning. Evans made the offense look good in the preseason playing against vanilla defenses, with no pressure to win, but in the regular season, things quickly changed. The defenses flew at him, and he was not ready.

And that's where Evans's limited time at quarterback came back to haunt him. The fact that he did not hold the laces created accuracy issues. In short, he threw too high, especially in the first quarter. In his words, it took him a while to "get cranking," but the trouble was, he and the offense did not have time to wait. And this gets to the second problem: philosophy.

Because the new philosophy emphasized the pass more, if the Bears threw early on first and second downs, and Evans was off, they'd face third and long. In the first six games, the Bears failed to score in the first quarter. Making things harder was the fact that Marchibroda had Evans calling plays. Inexperienced, he passed when he should have run, and other times, he ran when he should have thrown. In retrospect, Marchibroda admitted, he should have called the plays at the beginning of the season while Vince was still learning the offense. Adding to Evans's troubles, he let the philosophy get to his head. Armstrong and Marchibroda appreciated his athleticism, but they also asked him to stay in the pocket longer and wait for his receivers to clear the field. And they asked him not to take too many chances. Trying to please his coaches, Vince stopped being himself. He did not look to throw the bomb, and he rarely ran. He was a Corvette that stayed parked in the garage.

It was clear to all—the coaches, his teammates, the media, and the fans—that Evans was not the same. As one nameless teammate said in early December, "He has lost all his confidence, and I have lost my confidence in him." By that time, the season was done. There would be no improvement, there would be no play-offs, and for the coaches, there would be no jobs. George Halas fired Armstrong. Marchibroda left on his own. To replace Armstrong, Halas hired Mike Ditka, a former Bears legend who had been working as an offensive coordinator for the Dallas Cowboys. Nobody knew when, but everybody knew it was just a matter of time when Evans's days would be done in Chicago.

DONE WITH DITKA

WITH CURLY HAIR, DEEP-SET EYES, AND A TENACIOUS, NO-nonsense personality, Ditka arrived in 1982 promising changes in players' attitudes and the offense. The ex-Bears great came back to town with a reputation as an offensive coach, but as a tough and intimidating disciplinarian, Ditka wound up being more of a master motivator than a mastermind. He was going to run the "Dallas system" of offense, with multiple formations that relied on passing more than running. Although Ditka never gets much credit for the Cowboys' innovative offense of the late 1970s and early 1980s, they were lethal. Using multiple formations, like the shotgun, split back, I formation, double wing, and their version of the spread offense, they could quick-strike a team at any time. And they especially loved going deep off a play-action pass. That's what Ditka planned to bring to Chicago, and he all but guaranteed he'd get the offense going in the right direction.

For that, however, he needed a quarterback, which meant he needed his own quarterback. Although his offensive coordinator, Ed Hughes, told the press that they would play to Evans's strengths and use him as a rollout quarterback, Ditka really wanted nothing to do with Vince Evans. He would tolerate Evans as long as he needed to, but the coach made that clear from the beginning when he publicly pondered about bringing in veterans Bert Jones or Archie Manning if the price was right. And when he realized he'd have to pay too much for them, he turned his attention to the draft. Then, for the first time since 1951, the Bears used their first-round pick on a quarterback when they selected BYU all-American Jim McMahon with the fifth pick. For Evans, it was just a matter of time.

If it were up to Jim McMahon, he would have been the starter from day one when the Bears drafted him in 1982. In his first interview, he told the press, "I feel that I can come in and start on this team. They need a consistent quarterback. Vince Evans was great one day, not so good the next." McMahon also believed the job was his because he was a classic quarterback. "I feel I have an advantage coming from a school like BYU where the formations are basically the same as in the press."

For his part, Evans remained calm. During training camp in July, he coolly stated, "I think Jim McMahon will be a valuable attribute to this team, as long as he is playing behind me." Evans did what he did the previous year; he went to work. He mastered the play-book, and for the first time in his career, he even started throwing with the laces, per Ditka's suggestion. Frequently asked about the quarterback competition, he gave a stock answer. "What battle?" he asked. "I'm simply trying to be the best quarterback I can be. My life isn't built around being the Bears No. 1 quarterback. My main purpose in life is to glorify God and use the skills and talents he blessed me with." It helped that Ditka named him the starter at the beginning of training camp, telling the media, "Right now, Vince is my No. 1 quarterback and will be there as the No. 1 man when the season begins unless someone shows that he is head-and-shoulders better than Vince." Of course, the two men emphasized two different parts of Ditka's words. Evans heard that the job was his, but Ditka put the weight on "right now." And Ditka was not going to wait that long.

For the week 1 game, Ditka gave Bob Avellini the nod. An upset Evans told the press, "Anytime you have to give up a job you can't be too happy. I guess I wasn't doing something as efficient as I should have. I'll keep fighting until I get it back. I'm not saying I played my way out of it, because I didn't think I did. But he must have seen some things Bob did differently." In a pure football sense, starting Avellini was a curious decision, because the Bears had an awful offensive line, and Avellini was a statue waiting to be torn down by an aggressive defense. An elusive quarterback like

Evans would be much better, but when asked the obvious question about using Evans to avoid the rush, Ditka declared, "You don't design an offense thinking it's not going to work." Ditka should have worried about those details.

The offensive line was a disaster, and the quarterbacks suffered. In their first game against the Lions, the defense momentarily knocked Avellini out of the game in the third series after he suffered a nasty hit to the head that resulted in several chipped teeth and a gash that required twenty-three stitches to close. Evans finished the first half and led the team to their only touchdown drive. After the half, Ditka inserted Avellini back in the lineup. The Bears did not score again, and he finished the game a miserable 5 of 11 for 51 yards and was sacked four times.

Despite that showing, Ditka named Avellini the week 2 starter. In their next game against the Saints, Avellini went 3 of 9 for 33 yards before Ditka replaced him with Evans at the end of the second quarter. Ditka was done with Evans in just nine plays. On a third down, with the Bears in field-goal range, Evans missed a blitz and got sacked for 12 yards, taking them out of field goal range. When he came back to the bench, Ditka chewed him out. In the next two series, Evans threw two interceptions. At halftime, Ditka had seen enough. McMahon was going to be his starter moving forward. A frustrated Evans complained, "I really don't understand why he (Ditka) didn't use me in the second half. I was moving the team right before the first half ended. Ditka did get on me for missing that blitz call, but I'm gonna make mistakes. Everybody does." He further vented, "I really don't understand why he took me out, 'cause I was expecting to start the second half."

The following Monday, Evans went to meet with Ditka about his future with the team. From the beginning, Ditka let his players know that his office was always open to them, but when Evans went to see him, Ditka blew him off and said he was too tired to talk. Evans was incensed. In an exclusive interview with the *Chicago Defender*, the mild-mannered Evans lashed out. "The unfairness of the situation hurts more than anything. I'm tired over having to prove myself every year that I can play in the NFL. Each year I go into a new season hoping things will get better, but this year has been especially tough because I haven't been getting the time. No team can go into a season playing musical chairs with the quarterbacks." Evans wanted to know where he stood with Ditka. Was he part of the plans or not? "I don't want to sit around and just collect a paycheck . . . I want to play," he protested. He said he was going to march back to Ditka's office the next day and demand a meeting. Evans would not get that conversation with Ditka on Tuesday. He'd have to wait for nearly two months to see if he'd ever get a legitimate shot at starting, because after the second game of the season, the NFL players went on strike. When the players came back, Vince Evans hardly played. He wanted out of Chicago, but the team refused to trade him. He was stuck on the bench.

CHAPTER 19

As Doug drove his big brother Robert to the airport on Monday morning, October 15, 1979, the gravity of the situation finally hit the quarterback. "Come on, Doug," Robert told him, "You're better than that." At that moment, Doug knew he had messed up. He'd overstepped the bounds of acceptable behavior of a Black quarterback. The next day, the headlines read, "I'm sorry," but in the heat of the moment after Sunday's game, it sure felt good.

The Bucs started that 1979 season 5–0, but then they dropped their next two games. First, they lost to the previously winless New York Giants and their rookie quarterback, Phil Simms, then in a home game on October 14, the New Orleans Saints marched all over them. What started as a 7–0 Bucs lead in the third quarter ended in a 42–14 defeat. Williams was off the mark, throwing 10 of 28 for 142 yards and two interceptions. That wasn't the problem. For the first time since he'd broken through as a star in the NFL, the fans turned on him. They cheered when the Saints scored their final two touchdowns, they sang "When the Saints Go Marching In" throughout the onslaught, and they showered Williams with a cascade of boos that increased in ferocity with each mistake. Finally, Coach John McKay had no choice but to bench him. While Williams brooded on the bench, the fans booed him even more. He understood the benching, but the boos hit him harder than Jack Tatum.

In the moment, Williams fumed. "We've got some good fans and we've got some who aren't worth a damn. The fans are not taking care of me. The hell with them," he told reporters. "Does it bother me?" he asked. "No, I'm going to the bank tomorrow." Deep down, he knew those boos came from another place. As he often reminded his teammates, "You can't go no farther south than Florida." The fans weren't just booing any quarterback; they were booing a Black quarterback. In the South. This outburst was Williams's Sidney Poitier *In the Heat of the Night* moment. Williams's metaphoric slap to the white fans might have felt just as good and felt just as empowering as it did for Poitier's character, Virgil Tibbs, but in sports, no one could ever tell that to fans, especially a Black quarterback.

By the next day, Williams backpedaled quicker than Deion Sanders. "I said it and I'm sorry," Doug declared. "It was a thing I just blabbed off at the moment. You know the frustration. I had a bad day, we lost, and the booing and then the questions. You just haul off and try to equalize things." It was a typical apology. One that he had to make. But he was right. The fans had treated him differently because he was Black. That would never change.

After their week 7 loss to the Saints, the Bucs continued to play inconsistent ball. They won four of their next five games, but they lost three out of their last four. Along the way, Williams kept missing receivers, McKay kept supporting his quarterback, and the fans kept demanding better play. But when the team needed him the most, Williams rose to the occasion. In the last game of the regular season, sitting at 9–6 and facing elimination from the playoffs, Williams, who was a horrid 5 of 13 passing for 51 yards and two interceptions on a rainy day, kept a thirteen-play drive alive with two third-down completions to his tight end Jimmie Giles that led to a game-winning field goal to beat the Chiefs and win a playoff berth. After defeating the Eagles in the first round, the Bucs had a date with the Rams with the Super Bowl on the line.

Williams sat there in front of reporters, dressed like the star he was. Sporting a black leather jacket, a white Buccaneers T-shirt, blue jeans, tan loafers with no socks, and a $500 gold watch, he fielded questions as smoothly as Ozzie Smith fielded ground balls. By now, Williams was used to it. As a Black quarterback, he was the center of a lot of conversations. As the only starting Black quarterback in the league, he became a barometer of how to measure bigotry. The reporters swarmed him, trying to get a sound bite on what it was like being a Black quarterback. They came back with headlines like WILLIAMS MUST CONQUER PLANTATION THINKING and pondered about prejudice, writing, "The social barriers of pro football have taken until 1980 to come tumbling down thanks to a remarkable young man named Douglas Williams." The six-foot-four Williams took it all in stride. "I'm sure the average black family in America was for Tampa Bay last Saturday—because of who I am. But there should have been a lot of black quarterbacks before me. I was the one who got the opportunity to play," he told one reporter. And what about the meaning of this NFC Championship game? Was he making a statement? "I'm not trying to prove anything," he claimed. "I'm just trying to set an example for everybody, black and white." What about the Super Bowl? Was he ready for what that meant? "If kids say, 'I'm Doug Williams,' I think that'd be great."

He'd get to the big game one day, but 1980 would not be the year Doug Williams took a team to the Super Bowl. Through the first three quarters of play, he was a pathetic 2 of 13 passing. Making matters worse, on his thirteenth pass, a Rams defender's helmet smashed into his bicep, tearing a muscle in his throwing arm. He was done for the game. There went the Bucs' hope. Without their star quarterback, the Bucs fell to the Rams, 9–0.

Despite the loss, the Bucs had their quarterback of the future, and with the top young quarterback in the league, they should have been the team of the future. Everything seemed to be heading in the right direction. But very quickly, Williams would fall ill to the Black quarterback syndrome.

1980: EVERYBODY TALKS

The boos could never be separated from Doug's Blackness. It was a symptom of the Black quarterback syndrome. Reporters tried to diagnose the cause, anything to say it wasn't race, but no matter how hard they pried, the racist reality of the prejudice always stuck. No matter how well a Black person did, the syndrome said it would never be good enough. Doug thought winning would cure the Black quarterback syndrome, but after he took the Bucs to the NFC Championship in 1979, the fans expected more from the team. They started to question if a Black quarterback could steer the Bucs' championship aspirations. "Hey, I see where you forecast the Bucs to have a 10–6 record," a fan wrote a local reporter. "I hope you're right, but I don't see them going even 8–8 with that chimpanzee at quarterback." And when Doug didn't deliver, the fans were relentless in letting him know their disappointment. For fifty-eight minutes in their week 2 home game against the Rams, seventy-two thousand fans let him hear it every time he missed a pass, as he went 10 of 23 passing for 97 yards. Making matters worse, this was a Thursday-night prime-time game live on ABC for the whole nation to witness. The first prime-time game in franchise history. Broadcasters Howard Cosell and Fran Tarkenton were like a tag team, piledriving insults on top of Doug's head. But few quarterbacks could persevere and cut through the bull like Doug Williams. Down 9–3 in the final minutes of the game, Doug silenced the critics with his legs. During the drive, he ran for an important first down, then he plowed in the end zone for the victory. Most important, as one paper put it, his victory prevented a "lynching." Anybody reading that word in the South knew what that writer meant.

Doug had heard it all before. He was inaccurate. He threw too hard. He was too dumb to read defenses. His white teammates could not understand his Black Southern dialect. Doug let it roll off his back. "EVERYBODY TALKS about what Williams CAN'T do instead of what Williams can do," he said after the game. "I've been listening to it for three years and it don't bother me none." That was Doug's attitude. But Color Blind McKay was different. He was going to fire back at the critics.

McKay's breaking point came in week 3 after a tough loss to Dallas. Statistically, Doug had his best game to date as a pro, throwing for 258 yards and running for 77 yards. But after standing in the ninety-degree heat and watching Cowboys quarterback Danny White torch his defense, McKay was angry. In his press conference, he offered all his usual coach-speak about the game—the defense could have been better, the receivers dropped the ball, the running game didn't get it going—but then he scorched the local reporters. For three seasons as Doug's coach, he had watched every week as newspapers from the opposing team's city descended on Doug to talk about him being a Black quarterback. McKay had grown tired of it. Not because it distracted Doug from his duties but because the questions isolated Doug as something different. They weren't treating him as any other player. They were treating him as a Black quarterback.

This time, in Dallas, it wasn't just his playing style but his Southern dialect. In his pregame write-up before the game, Dallas reporter Skip Bayless noted that fans and pundits saw Doug as "dumb." In trying to defend Doug, Bayless brought up Doug's grammar. Nobody else had. "Yet, neither in Zachary nor Grambling was he exposed to grammar and diction critics expect," he wrote. "This is no knock on Williams' education," he parsed. "He was an honor student who probably learned more about life than many do. Several studies have shown regional black cultures have almost developed languages of their own. Williams communicates quite well." Still after all that, Bayless thought it was appropriate to quote Williams's speech. "Yet, he says 'aks' instead of 'ask.' He says 'less'n' and 'sicheashun' and used 'ain't' a lot." Bayless tried to point out that Southern white men like Bum Phillips and Terry Bradshaw spoke with their own white Southern slang, but the damage had already been done. Bayless had painted Doug as a slow, dim-witted Black Southerner. When word got back to Doug, he said, "I know there are guys out there who are going to try and make me look bad, and I know they can do it if they want to. Maybe they think I'm dumb because my grammar isn't perfect. But I think I talk okay. I mean, people can understand what I'm trying to say. I think the content of what I say makes sense, and that's what's most important." Doug took the high road. "It won't end as long as I am living. But I'm not saying that some people won't change their minds later," he told a reporter. McKay took the racists right on.

The articles, the letters, and phone calls the coach received from fans saying to get rid of his Black quarterback had become too much. McKay sensed Doug was feeling it too. Fed up, McKay called the reporters out. "[Doug] had quite a few drops, so that gives you sports writers another chance to say what a poor quarterback and passer he is. It'll just give another racist a chance to say that Doug's not a good quarterback and I'm getting sick and tired of it." He wasn't done. The next day, when reporters pushed him to elaborate more, McKay gave them an earful. "Just judge him as a quarterback. He's our quarterback," McKay shot back. "I get tired of hearing 'black quarterback.' All that is is inferring that he's dumb." McKay had diagnosed the Black quarterback syndrome. To be a Black quarterback automatically meant that the quarterback was incapable of playing the position. A Black man could not lead. It was up to the Black quarterback to prove otherwise. But every time they made a mistake, the supposed symptoms of being a Black quarterback came to the surface. To be a Black quarterback was an incurable curse.

Instead of looking at themselves as part of the symptoms, the reporters dug in. They called McKay's words an "uncalled-for outburst," and one wrote, "All right, John, just for you, Williams is a poor quarterback and passer, and he's not a good quarterback. Not much else needs to be said. Unless John McKay wants to take a few more minutes to remind us that Doug Williams is a black quarterback." Hubert Mizell, the same sports editor of the *St. Petersburg Times* who had just recently received a letter calling Williams a chimpanzee, asked McKay and Williams to ignore the racism. "It would be better," he said, "if John McKay would do that. And Williams and all others." Mizell mused that if Williams continued to play well, "Any racism would be bowled over." The racism never stopped.

Even though the team underperformed in 1980 and finished 5–10–1, Doug had his best statistical season as a pro. He completed 48.8 percent of his passes for 3,396 yards and twenty touchdowns. He had four games with more than 300 yards passing, including his best of his career in a shoot-out with the Vikings on November 16 after McKay let him loose. After fifty-five passes, Doug ended the game with 486 yards and four touchdowns. Those 486 yards were the fourth-highest yardage to date in league history and the best game in the last twelve years. Vikings head coach Bud Grant admitted, "Now is there any question about his being a top quarterback?"

Despite that monster game against the Vikings, the experts still underrated Williams. In fact, ex-coach George Allen did not even rate him. Coming into the 1981 season, Allen left Williams off his top ten list, and he omitted Williams from his list for emerging quarterbacks even though only two quarterbacks in NFL history had as much early success in their careers as Williams. Doug had another solid season, throwing for 3,563 yards, nineteen touchdowns on 50.5 percent passing, and led the Bucs to a 9–7 season and first place in the NFC Central, before the Cowboys ended their season in the playoffs.

1982 STRIKE

DURING THE LATE 1970S AND EARLY 1980S, AS PRO FOOTBALL continued to grow in popularity and rake in more revenue from TV contracts, the players demanded more of an equitable cut. In 1982, after the NFL signed a new five-year TV deal that gave teams $2 billion, a 100 percent increase over their previous contract, the players wanted a fair share. The NFL had revenue sharing among teams and split 97 percent of that money evenly. While this allowed for parity, the players argued that it suppressed salaries, because outside of winning a championship, teams had no real incentives to attract free agents. To counter that, the NFLPA wanted a 55 percent revenue split for player salaries, a wage scale that increased based on service in the league, and salary incentives like making the Pro Bowl. Calling the union's plan socialist, the NFL owners refused to meet their demands. When those negotiations broke down, the NFLPA went on strike.

Doug Williams, however, went to bat for Doug Williams. Unlike Black athletes of the past like Curt Flood (MLB) and Oscar Robertson (NBA), who became the faces of the fight for free agency in their respective leagues, Williams became the face of management. He was, as the Black writer Doc Young put it, "a company man." Simply put, Williams wanted nothing to do with the NFLPA's proposal and was the most vocal player about it. But he had his reasons.

For Doug, the issue was simple: he wanted the dollars and did not want to share the dividends. As someone who was grossly underpaid from his first contract and was set to be a free agent at the end of the season, the wage scale worked against him. He was going into his fifth year and had been the starting quarterback of a playoff-contending team. Why should a reserve linebacker get paid as much as he was simply because they had played the same number of years? Williams was a Black man from the Jim Crow South, and he knew what economic unfairness looked like, even if it was in professional sports, where the players made more in one game than a sharecropper could make in a lifetime. As Williams stated, "I was taught by my hard-working parents that you work for what you get. . . . I do not believe it's right that someone else with the same service only should make exactly the same no matter what." Williams's willingness to weigh in against the union did not make him popular among his teammates.

During the preseason as both sides negotiated, Williams made it clear where he stood. As part of a sign of solidarity, the players around the league agreed to shake hands before each preseason game. But Williams wanted no part of this. Before a game against the Falcons, while all the players went to the middle of the field and shook hands to a chorus of boos, Williams remained on the sidelines, talking to his coaches. When asked about that action, he simply stated, "It is time for something more than a handshake." Just what, he never really stated. Lee Roy Selmon, the Bucs' player rep, said that "there will be no ramifications" for Williams, but to onlookers, Doug eventually paid the price. In their week 2 regular season game against the Washington Redskins, he had four fumbles after the center snapped the ball. While it's plausible that the rain made the ball slick, which led to the fumbles, most onlookers suspected something nefarious. The other quarterback did not fumble the ball. As one local writer put it, "Many wondered aloud and in print if Williams was purposely abandoned by his appointed blockers because of his no-strike stand." No player ever admitted to tanking to hurt Doug, but the damage was done. After week 2 wrapped, the players went on strike. Doug headed to Chaneyville to work as a substitute teacher.

As the strike neared its fiftieth day, the union changed its demands from asking for a 55 percent split to asking for $1.6 billion over four years for all salaries, but Doug Williams continued to side with himself. "Let me negotiate my own contract," he stated. "They want me to give up my negotiation rights to help somebody else. This is my time now. . . . How many quarterbacks would have survived the abuse I have taken?" Abuse? He was talking about racism from the fans. He wanted his reparations for what they put him through.

When the players ended the strike on November 16, settling for a $1.6 billion pot for salaries over the next five years with no wage scale, everyone in Tampa Bay watched for one thing: Would the offensive linemen protect Doug Williams? In their first game back against the Cowboys, the line only gave up one sack, a sign that everything was fine. Although they lost that contest, the Bucs won five of their last six regular season games, including a season-ending win over the Bears, who by then had benched Vince Evans. Against Chicago, Doug went 25 of 49 for 367 yards and threw two touchdowns, pushing the Bucs to a 5–4 mark and the playoffs. Overall, Williams placed sixth in passing yards, and his fullback, James Wilder, was third in the league in receptions—a clear sign that Doug had improved as a quarterback, because he checked the ball to his backs. "I knew then that Dougie was on his way," McKay reflected. Next up, a rematch with the Dallas Cowboys in the NFC wild card game.

In the previous year's playoffs, the Cowboys and their famed flex defense corralled Williams and the Bucs to the tune of 38–0, holding Doug to a dreary 187 yards passing and 4 interceptions. Despite that disappointing showing, Williams believed that familiarity with the Cowboys would lead to a Bucs victory. He was wrong. Hobbling on an injured hamstring and a bad knee that would require surgery after the season, Doug was a dismal 8 of 28 for 113 yards, with one touchdown and three interceptions. Unfortunately, things went from bad to worse.

NEGOTIATING WITH A RACIST

JUST FIVE DAYS AFTER LOSING THE WILD CARD GAME TO THE Cowboys, on January 14, 1983, Doug and his wife Janice welcomed their first child into the world. That was not the bad part. Baby Ashley Monique was a blessing that made Doug momentarily forget about the business of football. Then the horrors of life crept in. Ever since his sophomore year in 1974 when Doug met Janice, the two had been inseparable. The beautiful country girl from Gainesville, Georgia, who could light up the Grambling library with her smile was always there to brighten Doug's moods. When Coach Robinson got on him, when he tore his ACL, when the Black quarterback stuff had become too much for him, she held him up. All their friends at Grambling and their families back home in Louisiana and Georgia knew that one day they would get married. But Doug never thought to rush. He knew she would always be his and he would always be hers. They got married on April 17, 1982.

During the 1982 strike, Janice started to get alarming headaches. She thought they came with the pregnancy, but after Ashley came into the world, the problem persisted. Finally in March 1983, the headaches became too much to bear. A CAT scan revealed awful news. She had a grapefruit-size brain tumor that at any time could burst and kill her. She needed immediate surgery. The surgery seemed like a success, and a week later, she enjoyed a day of having regular conversations with friends and family. But later that night, the pain in her brain came back. Doug screamed for help. By the time the doctors arrived, fluid in her body had overwhelmed her lungs. On April 6, 1983, Janice Williams died. Little Ashley Monique was just eleven weeks old.

Doug spent the next days in a daze, but he had little time to mourn. He still needed to sign his new contract. He was going to make the Bucs pay for everything he went through the last five years. "You know I fought a lot of odds when I came in here. The team was 2–26. I was a black quarterback. Eyes were focused on me, and I was fighting the critics," he explained when detailing his contract demands.

He hated the owner, Hugh Culverhouse, whom he saw as a racist redneck from Alabama who, according to Doug, approached their relationship as if to remind Doug that he was never more than a poor, rural Black man from Louisiana. How could he negotiate fairly with a man like that? Doug thought the owner took his title literally and tried to negotiate with him like he was a slave. For their first negotiation talks before the 1982 season, Culverhouse didn't offer Doug a salary; he offered him a shady opportunity. He wanted Doug to take out a $250,000 line of credit to go into a real estate deal with him. Doug had grown up in the segregated South, where white men had trapped Black men into debt their whole lives. He knew exploitation when he saw it. Signing a $250,000 line of credit would put Doug in instant debt. Doug refused. "Culverhouse thought I was a good ol' black boy who never had nothin' and would go along with whatever Mr. Culverhouse wanted. He paid me like a slave, but I wasn't that much of a slave to sign that deal." Smart move. The real estate deal went bust.

Williams knew his worth. And he knew being the fifty-fourth highest-paid quarterback was not it. He made $120,000 in 1982, but the league average for quarterbacks was $131,206. And the numbers kept increasing. Veteran Dan Fouts and rookie John Elway had just signed deals that would earn them $1 million a year. The $600,000 a year Doug was asking for was a bargain. The Bucs stayed at $400,000.

In July, the negotiation talks hovered around the city, thicker than the humid air. From the beginning, the local Black community always supported Doug, so when the Bucs tried to buck him, they pushed back. Some showed up to the Bucs' headquarters and protested with signs that read, DOUG DESERVES MORE and DOUG WILLIAMS HAS PAID HIS DUES, NOW LET'S PAY DOUG WILLIAMS. When asked why she was there, protester Lucille Franklin pleaded, "Had he not been black, they would have given him what he deserved." The Bucs were not moved. The *Tampa Bay Times* asked their readers, "If you owned the Bucs, would you pay him an annual salary of $600,000 per year, or would you refuse to sign him at such an amount?" Out of the 2,389 votes, 52 percent of the readers said that Williams was not worth $600,000. The Bucs saw the writing on the wall. They could get away with offering less money, they thought, because the people—white fans—backed them. They did not budge from their $400,000 mark.

Freedom of mobility is a basic right of citizenship, and Doug Williams, the poor kid from Jim Crow Chaneyville, exercised that right. In August, instead of allowing the Bucs to short him money, he signed with the Oklahoma Outlaws of the USFL for five years and $3 million. "Tampa Bay let the black folks down," he opined.

"Most places I go, the first thing people tell me is they're glad I made the move, because it looks like to black folks that a black player was able to tell an organization that he had another place to go. If I had gone back for what the Buccaneers had offered, it would look like they did what they did 200 years ago—forcing blacks into things they didn't want to do. I didn't succumb to the pressure." He put his move in terms of race and class that many Black folks could understand.

A good portion of those fans who stayed away were Black fans who thought the Bucs did Williams wrong. In her article, "To Many Blacks, the Bucs Got the Season They Deserve," Peggy Peterman asserted that Black fans believed that had Doug been white, this would have never happened. One preacher noted that several season ticket holders in his congregation stopped going to the games. But it was more than just local fans that they lost; the Bucs lost Black America. Doug Williams was a hero. "As long as Doug was quarterback of the Tampa Bay Buccaneers," a fan claimed, "20-million black Americans regarded the Tampa Bay Buccaneers as their team and that was lost when they let him go." Doug Williams was the victim of the Black quarterback syndrome. And soon, Vince Evans would be gone too.

DOWN AND OUT IN CHICAGO

LEADING INTO THE 1983 SEASON, AS WILLIAMS BATTLED WITH the Bucs for more money, Evans battled with Ditka and the Bears for his dignity. And the Black community had his back. In his nationally syndicated column, Doc Young blasted, "If Vince Evans were a Caucasian American, he certainly would now be entering the superstar years of his professional football career. But since the melaninic content of his skin clearly distinguishes him as an Afro-American, his present status is that of a back-up quarterback with the Chicago Bears, and his future is more difficult to predict." According to Young, Evans was the perfect candidate to be a leading face of the league and his race. "Vince Evans is well-spoken, gentlemanly, religious, happily married, interested in public welfare. In other words, he is both a fine citizen and a fine athlete. He is a credit to his family, to his race, to his country, to his sport," he praised. Evans, however, was the wrong color for the NFL. Young called the NFL "un-American" and pointed out, "When it comes to the quarterback position, there is no such thing as affirmative action or fair employment practices in the National Football League."

At the *Chicago Metro News*, Ferman Mentrell Beckless charged the Bears and Ditka with being a racist organization and fumed, "The Black community feels that Ditka is using racist tactics in deciding who plays." He lamented, "If Ditka, Chicago Bears Head Coach, hasn't thought for once about how he insulted the Black community, he should really give thought now to what he says for publication." At issue for Beckless was Ditka's remarks after the Bears' week 3 loss, in which he said he replaced McMahon with Evans because he did not want his young quarterback killed behind the Bears' bad offensive line. Why would Ditka want Evans to get killed? they asked. To a Black community weary of how Evans had been treated for the previous six years, that reeked of racism. In retaliation for being called racist, the Bears revoked the *Chicago Metro News*'s press pass for the rest of the season.

The Blacks fans' and Evans's frustrations continued to grow during the first quarter of the season. To them, it was clear that Evans was outplaying McMahon. That's how the Black quarter-back syndrome went. Even when you were twice as good as the white guy, it would never be enough. In their first four games of the 1983 season, Evans played three quarters to McMahon's thirteen, but the Bears had scored 40 points with Evans in the game compared to 37 with McMahon. In their week 4 game, Evans came off the bench and rallied the team to force overtime, and in the process, he scored a rushing touchdown and had a 57-yard bomb to Olympic sprinter Willie Gault. Ditka stuck with McMahon. When Evans replaced McMahon the following week, he promptly threw a 72-yard strike to Gault. After McMahon went 4 of 11 for 35 yards with two interceptions against the Vikings, Ditka named Evans the starter for their week 7 game against the Lions.

Ditka's decision to start Evans was about teaching his white quarterback a lesson, not giving a Black man a chance. He thought his young white quarterback was too cocky and careless with the ball, and he used his Black quarterback as a warning. If Vince did not see this context when Ditka named him a starter, he learned it right before the game, when a reporter told Ditka that Evans asked for more patience this time, and Ditka shot back, "I frankly don't care what he says about my patience. It doesn't interest me one bit." Behind an awful offensive line, for a quarterback who was not getting starter's reps in practice, Evans played commendably, including going 28 of 45 for 336 yards and two touchdowns in his first start against the Lions, and throwing a touchdown the following week in their 7–6 victory over the Eagles. But it was never going to be good enough. Ditka was just waiting for the right time to bench him permanently. In his third start, and their second game against the Lions, Evans threw two interceptions, and Ditka inserted McMahon back in the lineup. After the game, he announced, "Jim McMahon is the best quarterback. He's the quarterback of the future. He's the starting quarterback and will not come out unless he's injured. If the Bears are going to win, Jim McMahon will be the catalyst."

The proud Black quarterback wanted out from the Bears. Luckily for him, there was the USFL. Even better, they had a local team, the Chicago Blitz. Evans started negotiating a contract in the middle of the Bears' season. There was no point in sticking around if he was not going to play. He was a starter, not a backup. Just weeks after being benched, Evans signed with the Blitz. As Evans's wife, Chyla, explained, "He had wanted to make contributions as a black quarterback in the NFL. He wanted to go to the Super Bowl and he had doubts about the viability of the USFL, but the Bears were so hard to deal with. Ditka likes people who are totally dedicated to him. Once he found out Vince had talked to other teams, he cut him out immediately. He didn't think Vince had loyalty." Understanding Evans's drawing power in the city of Chicago, the Blitz offered him a four-year deal for $5 million. He was making more than any quarterback in the NFL. Owner Dr. James Hoffman said, "Vince Evans was my choice. He's one of the best athletes in the NFL. He's extremely intelligent, impeccable character. A perfect leader." Vince Evans was now the face of a franchise.

Although happy for Vince, the Black community fumed at the Bears. For them, it was more than just a Black quarterback losing a job: the Bears' sacking of Evans was symbolic to other Black people in leadership. *Chicago Tribune* columnist Leanita McClain wrote a piece entitled "The Black Quarterback Syndrome" to lament her and other Black folks' frustrations. She started, "The defection of quarterback Vince Evans from the Chicago Bears provides an ideal introduction for the fable of the black everyman and his drive to life's greater goals." As she put it, "To a great many black Chicagoans, Evans is the literal embodiment of 'the quarterback syndrome,' this society's pathological unwillingness to accept blacks in leadership roles. His predicament is representative of black life in sports, in politics, in business, or whatever."

The Black quarterback meant something to Black Americans beyond just pure fandom. Black folks saw their own predicaments and potentials in how the Black quarterback was treated. Having a starting Black quarterback that a team was willing to invest in meant more than just wins and losses for Black Americans. It meant they too would have a chance to cross the moat white folks had built to protect their privilege, in business, law, education, medicine, and everyday life. McClain closed her article with one last proclamation: "The more black quarterbacks there are—trained adequately, competing equitably, trusted unquestioningly—the fairer life will be." That's what Doug Williams represented. That's what Vince Evans represented. Hope. And the Bucs and the Bears tried to take it away. But growing up Black in the South made Doug and Vince resilient. They'd be back.

CHAPTER 20

THE USFL GAVE DOUG WILLIAMS MORE MONEY, BUT THAT WAS about it. He had the drive to succeed but was not surrounded by talent to get him there. During his time with the Oklahoma Outlaws, the team spent most of their money on Williams and aging veteran Mel Gray, meaning the rest of the team was put together on the cheap with guys just trying to hang on to their pro careers. For Williams, that meant he was playing behind an awful offensive line. Like a straw house in a Tulsa tornado, he had little time and no protection. Making it worse for him, he was taking a beating, and few people cared. In Tulsa, they never received a crowd larger than fifteen thousand people. The city was not ready for pro football.

The next year was even worse for Doug when the team moved to Phoenix. At least Tulsa had Black people. As he recalled, Arizona was "Barry Goldwater country," and "no Blacks want to live in Barry Goldwater's state." For Doug, who grew up in the Jim Crow South, he hated that white folks in Phoenix tried to hide their racism. He wanted to know where he stood at all times. "It's really better for blacks in the South. At least you know who you're dealing with in the South," he observed. "You know who are the bigots. In Arizona, it's not as obvious. They're more secretive about it." And that meant that they did not want a Black quarterback. "I got to be perfect a majority of the time," he told a reporter. "This town is built for Rick Johnson [the blond backup] to be quarterback. Doug Williams has got to be 22 for 21, not the other way around." Despite all of that, Williams had his finest passing season as a pro in spring 1985, throwing for 3,673 yards and twenty-one touchdowns.

When the USFL imploded, those numbers should have jumped on the NFL's radar, but no team wanted to bring Williams into their building. Teams quickly signed white USFL quarterbacks like Jim Kelly, Steve Young, Bobby Hebert, and Doug's old backup in Tampa Bay, Chuck Fusina. The Fusina signing really got to Doug. *Why would any team pick Chuck ahead of me?* he asked himself. The answer was all too obvious. Once again, Doug found himself in a familiar position with the NFL. If he was going to get a chance to play, a white coach with the guts to sign a Black quarterback would have to step up. And once again, that man was Joe Gibbs. Gibbs, who was Doug's first offensive coordinator down at Tampa and vouched for him when all the other teams questioned his intelligence before the 1978 draft, was now the head man for the Washington Redskins, and with a young starting quarterback in Jay Schroeder leading a Super Bowl–contending squad, Gibbs wanted a capable backup he could trust. It was a hard pill to swallow for a guy who had always been an NFL starter, but at the age of thirty-one, Doug just wanted back in the league.

Playing for Gibbs made football sense for a big-arm quarterback like Williams. With Washington, Gibbs, who revolutionized the use of a blocking H-back and relished playing with two tight ends to dominate the ground game, also liked to run the ball to set up the deep pass off a play-action fake. Few players could hum the ball down the field like Williams. If he ever got a real shot, he'd certainly be able to take advantage of the situation.

Plus, there was one more caveat that made Washington work for Williams. Being in a town that was nearly 75 percent Black, one that Black folks called "Chocolate City" made his new reality even sweeter. As Doug said, "If there's a city made for Doug Williams, it has to be Washington, D.C. I think that's where I belonged all along."

CHOCOLATE CITY

DURING THE 1986 SEASON, DOUG ONLY PLAYED IN ONE GAME, A blowout victory versus Dallas. The contest also pitted him against another Black backup, Reggie Collier. When both men played that game, the Black fans in the stands and the stadium erupted in cheers. Each team's Black fan base bragged to the other that their Black quarterback was better. Life was coming full circle for Doug. Collier idolized Doug Williams. Doug saw something special in Collier too. When Collier was in college, Doug sent him a letter telling him to never switch. Despite pro football's best effort to make him a receiver, Collier stuck to his guns. This meant fewer opportunities, but at least he kept his dignity.

For the 1987 season, Doug promised himself things would be different. He was going to be a starter again. For what team, he wasn't sure; he just knew he had to start. He liked Coach Gibbs, but figured with a young quarterback in Schroeder who'd just made the Pro Bowl and then signed a huge contract, he would never play. He wanted a trade. A deal was in place with the Raiders, until the last minute when Washington pulled out. They thought too much of Doug as a backup to let him go. It was a smart decision. An injury to Schroeder in week 1 against the Eagles pushed Doug into the lineup. Black fans cheered—not for the Schroeder injury but because their guy finally got a chance.

In his first significant NFL playing time since the 1982 season, he outdueled Randall Cunningham to take Washington to a victory. At six foot four, running a 4.5 forty, and with a bazooka for an arm, Cunningham was on his way to being the next sensation in the NFL. Two years later, Cunningham would be the Michael Jordan of football, but on this day, Doug Williams proved he still had the magic.

And in the Chocolate City, Black fans took note. Black writer Courtland Milloy of the *Washington Post* tried to capture the meaning of Williams, but the right words eluded him. "It is difficult to explain how much this gentleman's demonstration of talent and determination meant to the city's young black people, who are virtually surrounded by examples of black political leadership that leave much to be desired." Milloy concluded, "There is no question that in a city that is about 70 percent black, the good vibes from the Redskins win were amplified because Williams, too, is black— and even if some white fans don't understand this, Williams does." Milloy was correct. Williams knew the Black fans appreciated his presence. "There are lots of fans in this area looking forward to seeing Doug Williams play," he said in the third person.

With Schroeder still injured heading into their week 2 contest against the Falcons, Coach Gibbs tabbed Doug as his starter. In his first start in the NFL since 1982, Williams threw for three touchdowns in a narrow 21–20 defeat to the Falcons. But win or lose, it was not going to be enough to keep his job, because Coach Gibbs had a policy that an injured starting quarterback got their job back when they healed. When the NFL went on strike following week 2 on the 1987 season, Schroeder was ready to play by the time the players came back for week 6. Doug sat on the bench until the second quarter of week 10, when Gibbs tabbed him to replace the lackluster Schroeder against the Lions. Gibbs had never benched a quarterback mid-game. A shocked Williams said, "I had to look around and see if he was talking to someone else. My heart jumped out of my chest." His heart might have been racing, but Williams had ice water in his veins. He promptly threw two second-quarter touchdowns. Washington got the win, and Coach Gibbs tabbed Williams as the starter for their upcoming Monday Night Football game against the Los Angeles Rams.

Black fans in Chocolate City could not have been more pleased. As one *Washington Post* headline aptly put it, FANS' DREAMS FULFILLED BY WILLIAMS' START. *Post* writer Patrice Gaines-Carter commented, "For black fans, particularly, last night was a time for enchantment, a night that began so sweetly it defied description." Black fans saw themselves in Williams's career. He persevered over prejudice. He showed them a way. As one fan noted, "Having Doug Williams as a quarterback sets the tone for this city and lets everyone know how far we've come." When a reporter asked Doug if he understood what he meant to the Black community, he simply answered, "Most definitely." In another interview, he further elaborated, "It's the same as Jesse Jackson running for President. There's not too many blacks running for President and there's not too many blacks playing quarterback." At that time, in fact, there was only one Black man running for president and three starting Black quarterbacks. Either way one looked at it, it was a big deal. His start against the Rams also marked the first time in league history a team started a Black center, Raleigh McKenzie, and a Black quarterback.

Williams did enough on the field to keep his job, but unfortunately for him—and his Black fans—after throwing for 308 yards in a loss to the Rams, he injured his back in practice before the next game. Schroeder got his starting job back. When Doug received the news, he cried during a live TV interview. How could this happen to him? he thought. He worked his way back to a starting job in a league that never really wanted him, and now it was gone. If it were anybody but Gibbs, Doug said, he would charge racism, but he trusted Joe Gibbs.

Black fans felt his pain. They knew he had been wronged. The local Black-owned radio station, WOL, asked listeners to send in letters of support. By the time the Super Bowl rolled around, they had collected fifty thousand letters, which they placed on a scroll that ran twenty-one city blocks.

In the last game of the season, a meaningless contest against Minnesota, with Washington already having clinched the NFC East and a playoff spot, Gibbs inserted Williams back into the lineup. Doug led the team to a victory that game, and then Coach Gibbs made one of the riskiest and most controversial quarterback decisions in NFL history: he named the Black backup the starter right before the playoffs. Doug instantly knew what this meant. This game was bigger than he was. This was for his people. "I think a Super Bowl would mean more for me, not so much for a personal standpoint, (but) for black America."

THE MOUNTAINTOP

As Doug marched to the Super Bowl, he drew inspiration from Martin Luther King Jr. On top of his locker, he taped the motivating words, "I have a dream. I have been to the mountain-top." Drawn from King's "I Have a Dream" speech and his last speech, "I See the Promised Land," which the civil rights leader passionately presented on April 3, 1968, the day before his assassination in Memphis, the combined quotes symbolized the importance of how Williams saw his own role in the ongoing movement for Black equality. Doug wasn't fighting for legislation. He was battling for Black folks to have their dignity as they moved through a society that consistently tried to keep them down. "The mountaintop" was Doug telling his Black followers that, like King, he had seen the promised land, and that promised land looked like a world where the Black quarterback syndrome was eliminated. He'd get to that Super Bowl.

After a wild card playoff-weekend bye, the Redskins headed to Chicago for a January 10 showdown with the Bears. Nearly a decade removed from his historic game with Vince Evans, Williams came back to Soldier Field poised to take another step toward history. This time, the biggest prize was on the line. But the pundits hardly gave him a chance. The Redskins came to town as 4.5 point underdogs partly because, as the experts said, Williams was their quarterback. That season, he was 0–2 as a starter but 3–0 coming off the bench. Moreover, as reporters wrote, the Redskins relied on running the ball to set up the pass, but the Bears had the best run defense in the NFL. At some point, Washington would have to lean on Williams to win the game, and pundits did not think he had what it took to win a playoff game. Several writers, in fact, thought so little of Doug's chances of success that they predicted Coach Gibbs would bench him.

Making his climb to the mountain even harder was the fact that the route to the promised land might as well have had him scaling Mount Everest. Soldier Field turned into an icebox at minus-four degrees with a wind chill of minus twenty-three. It wasn't that it was just freezing cold—the unpredictable howling winds could make it nearly impossible to play football. When that wind was swirling, kickers had no control of their kicks, quarterbacks would have their throws sail 5 yards off course, and receivers waited for a pass praying it came close enough for them to get their mitts on the pigskin. One would have to have a rocket launcher of an arm to cut through that wind. Doug Williams had just that. He also had a growing number of Black Americans in his corner to keep pushing him. This included Alyne Payton, the mother of Bears star running back Walter Payton. She, like millions of Black Americans, wanted a Black quarterback in the Super Bowl. It just so happened that Alyne Payton was willing to root against her son's team even when it was the last game of his career.

Coach Gibbs's unwavering faith in Doug paid huge dividends. With the run game shut down as predicted, and down 14–0 in the second quarter, Gibbs turned the game over to his Black quarterback, figuring that the team could take advantage of Williams's live arm and the wind, which was now at their backs. Williams led his team to two second-quarter touchdown drives to tie the game, including a late-quarter 69-yard drive where he threw the ball every time and punctuated the aerial assault with an 18-yard touchdown to tight end Clint Didier. After an electrifying third-quarter punt return by speedy cornerback Darrell Green that put Washington up 21–14, the defense closed the deal. For the second time in his career, Doug Williams was heading to the NFC title game.

Reporters surrounded the Black quarterback and peppered him with questions. Williams got the usual. And for a Black quarterback, *the usual* meant inquiries about the game and about race. He answered the ones about football just fine, but after hearing one about dispelling the notion of the lack of Black intelligence, Williams calmly answered, "How many times you going to ask me about that?" It was a rhetorical response. He knew they would never stop. He knew that in 1978 as a rookie, and he knew that in 1988 as a veteran. But as Williams climbed the mountaintop, the interrogation would become more suffocating.

By this time, the question of race in sports—or more specifically, the lack of Black leadership—had been hovering around America for nearly a year. It was the sports version of the ozone layer. In this case, the pollution was the prejudice, and it seemed like American sports was not ready to rid itself of prejudice.

Eight months prior, during an ABC *Nightline* special honoring Jackie Robinson, Al Campanis, the vice president and director of player personnel for the Los Angeles Dodgers, went on a racial tirade that shocked the sports world. When host Ted Koppel asked the onetime teammate of Robinson about the lack of Black leadership in sports, Campanis concluded, "They [black men] may not have some of the necessities to be a field manager or perhaps a general manager." A befuddled Koppel asked, "Do you really believe that?" Without a second's thought, Campanis doubled down. "How many quarterbacks do you have? How many pitchers do you have that are Black?" he asked. When Koppel chided him for his racist garbage, Campanis kept spewing trash. "Why are black people not good swimmers?" Campanis asked himself, to which he replied to his own racist question with a racist answer, "Because they don't have the buoyancy." Whether it was a coach, manager, general manager, or quarterback, Campanis was suggesting that Black men did not have the mental capacity to lead. All brawn and no brains. Koppel and his other guest, writer Roger Kahn, schooled Campanis and the American public on the history of racism and ugly "single-mindedness" that had kept Black men out of leadership. The Dodgers executive exposed an ugly truth about American sports.

Beyond getting Campanis fired, his words ignited a debate across the nation about racism in sports. Why weren't there Black managers in baseball or head coaches in football? Newspapers and TV shows conducted studies and interviews to find answers. Black leaders like Jesse Jackson and his Operation PUSH stepped into the fray to mend fences and build opportunities for Black men in leadership. Jackson threatened to lead a nationwide boycott of the MLB until they agreed to an affirmative action plan to hire Black managers. But pro football would not budge. Arguing that "I'm certain we'll have a black head coach when an owner thinks that coach can help him win," NFL commissioner Pete Rozelle said he could not and would not force NFL owners to hire Black men. It would be another fifteen years when famed Black lawyer Johnnie Cochran threatened a Black boycott of the NFL until the league implemented the Rooney Rule to aid in the hiring of minority coaching candidates. In those eight months between when Campanis made his remarks and Williams's march to the Super Bowl, nothing changed in football. In fact, the racial tension tightened.

On January 15, 1988, to celebrate Martin Luther King Jr.'s birthday, a local Washington, DC, TV station sent a crew to sports bars to ask diners about King and what he had meant to America. They soon stumbled on the nationally known CBS sports TV host Jimmy "the Greek" Snyder. Known more for his tips on sports betting than his treatises on bigotry, Snyder eventually found himself in the same turmoil that Campanis clumsily stumbled into. When the reporters asked him about equal opportunities in sports, an unprovoked Snyder complained about the push for Black coaching candidates and predicted, "If they [black people] take over coaching like everybody wants them to, there's not going to be anything left for the white people." He wasn't done. In explaining Black athletic success, something he was never asked to do, Snyder dipped into an old, tired trope and suggested that Black athletes were "bred" to be better. "This goes all the way back to the Civil War," Snyder said, "when during slave trading the slave owner would breed his big black with his big woman so that he could have a big black kid." Snyder's segregationist soliloquy just two days before the NFC Championship started another national discussion about racism and leadership in sports, placing the most visible Black man in leadership smack-dab in the middle of the controversy. Doug had to get the job done.

Doug's phone rang at 5:37 a.m. It was game day of the NFC Championship. Who would call him at that time? Eddie Robinson? Coach Gibbs? A teammate? A shocked Williams answered the phone. The ring had not woken him up, because he could not sleep much that night. He knew what that game meant. And the person on the other end could not sleep much either. He also knew what that game meant. It was Rev. Jackson. No, not Rev. Jesse Jackson, the Black man running for president, but Jeffrey Jackson, a Black reverend in Chicago and a friend of Doug. That distinction did not bother the American public. They ran with the former, the famous one, and everyone believed that Jesse Jackson called Doug Williams. It made perfect sense to the media and to the American public that Jesse Jackson would call Doug Williams. As the two most visible Black leaders, they were tied at the hips. If a Black quarterback could win the Super Bowl, could a Black man win the presidency? Miracles happened. Jesse Jackson did not call Doug Williams before the game, but he too understood the meaning of the game and what it meant to Black America. He was fighting for the same thing. The other Rev. Jackson simply wanted Doug to relax and play his game. He wanted him to win too.

Maybe his nerves got the best of him? Maybe it was the Vikings' defense? Perhaps a bit of both? Whatever it was, Doug Williams did not play his best game. Even when including a first-quarter touchdown that sailed 42 yards, at one point in the third quarter, Williams was only 4 of 17 passing for 69 yards, and he had missed eleven of his last twelve throws. All total in the game, he was only 9 of 26 throwing for 119 yards. That part does not matter. When he needed to be great, he was great. By the third quarter, his left hand was busted up and bloody, and then if that was not enough, he took a jolting hit from a Vikings defender that nearly knocked him out of the game for good, but Williams was staying in this game by any means necessary. He had to win.

In the fourth quarter of a tied 10–10 contest, he took his team down the field for a 70-yard game-winning drive that culminated with a 7-yard touchdown to receiver Gary Clark. On that score,

Clark was supposed to run a corner route, but when Clark noticed the Vikings were in an outside zone, he improvised and ran to the middle of the field. Williams saw it, and in a split second, he lasered a pass to Clark. That was the type of in-game adjustment a Black quarterback was not supposed to be able to make. Doug Williams was brain and brawn. Doug Williams was heading to the Super Bowl, and Black America was coming with him.

The very next day after Williams beat the Vikings, he was the grand marshal of a local MLK Day parade. He told that screaming crowd, "I'm just glad that I am going to be one part of Martin Luther King's dream." King never dreamed about a Black man leading an NFL team to the Super Bowl, but he would have understood the moment. When King was assassinated on April 4, 1968, there had only been two Super Bowls played, both won by the Green Bay Packers. Perhaps King knew that Packers safety Willie Wood had played quarterback at USC before being switched like so many other Black quarterbacks. When King was assassinated, no Black man had started at quarterback in the modern NFL. Marlin Briscoe was still five months from making history. But King understood the power of sports and Black representation on sports. He looked for leaders like Jackie Robinson, Bill Russell, and Hank Aaron to be symbols of integration and American democracy. King supported Muhammad Ali's stance on the Vietnam War, and he helped Black Olympians like John Carlos and Tommie Smith craft their boycott stance of the 1968 Olympics. Understanding that much, it's clear King would have understood the magnitude of the moment of Doug Williams making it to the Super Bowl. This was Black history in the making.

Only Spike Lee could have written a better Super Bowl script for Doug Williams. Black history surrounded the momentous event. The day after Williams beat the Vikings, it was MLK Day. The day after he won the Super Bowl, Black History Month commenced. The Washington Redskins were Black Americans' team. Based on an ABC poll, an estimated 60 percent of Black Americans were rooting for Washington and Williams. That number should be much higher. Today, you can't find a Black person who was not rooting for Williams and Washington. A change had come. A few decades prior when Washington was the last team to integrate (1961) and still played Dixie at their games, Black folks boycotted the team. They called them the Washington Rednecks and said their team colors were maroon and Caucasian. But with Williams leading the squad to the big game, Washington's jerseys might have well been red, black, and green.

BLACK CHAMPION

FOR THE TWO WEEKS LEADING UP TO THE SUPER BOWL, BLACK America built this game into one of the most important sporting events in history. There was the 1936 Olympics when Jesse Owens won four gold medals on his way to smashing Hitler's notions of Aryan superiority. There was the day in 1947 that Jackie Robinson broke the baseball color barrier. Now there was Super Bowl XXII, January 31, 1988, when Doug Williams started for the Washington Redskins. Before the game, the number one selling shirt in the DC area was a shirt with the words TOUCH OF CLASS and an image of Doug Williams in front of DC's skyline. The phrase came from Williams and his manager, who tried to market their Black quarterback star as a humble yet heroic athlete. It worked. Stores sold out of the sweatshirts that were going for twenty-two dollars and the ten-dollar shirts. These were more than just fashion statements. For a certain generation of Black folks, TOUCH OF CLASS recalled how Black folks had to persevere through prejudice with dignity. As one Black fan put it, "Doug Williams has the old-fashioned ideas that our parents tried to teach and that we'd like to instill in our children today, but it's almost corny. We'll never have too many Doug Williamses." Or as another Black fan imagined, "Doug Williams should be the prototype, not based on what he does on the field, but the impact of what he does off of it. I just don't think I know of a finer example, even though I've never met him."

As Washington got set to duel John Elway and the Denver Broncos, Doug Williams became the most sought-after man in America. Everyone wanted to know one thing from Doug: What was it like to be the first Black quarterback to play in the Super Bowl? The constant questioning about race irritated Doug back when he was a rookie, and it still bothered him a decade later. It put an extra burden on him that a guy like John Elway, who came into the league protected by a shield of whiteness, did not have to carry. Nobody ever asked Elway what it was like to be white. No matter how hard Doug tried to deflect from the race question, the reporters kept coming at him like Lawrence Taylor. And just like facing LT, Doug knew that eventually there was no escape. He'd have to stand tall. No matter how many times Doug got asked about race, he decided to keep it cool. Even when he thought he heard, "How long have you been a Black quarterback?" This was bigger than Doug Williams.

He tried to limit Black fans' expectations for the game so he could go out and win for his team. "I just happen to be a Redskin, a quarterback and a black," he told the press. "I'm just trying to deal with the football game. After the game—black, white, green or yellow—we'll deal with that then." But he also knew he had to say something for his people. "I know it will mean a lot to the black community to have a black quarterback start in the Super Bowl for the first time," he told the press before the game, "but my goal now is just to get there as an individual. I'll worry about the rest of it later." Besides, it was better to answer those questions after a victory. In one of his last interviews, he told the press, "I'm here, I'm Doug Williams. I can't hide. This will be something for all America to witness."

Nothing would stop Williams that game. Not the emergency root canal he had to have the day before the game. Not the major knee injury he suffered in the first quarter when he slipped on the field and sat out a series. Not watching John Elway get the Broncos on the board first with a 56-yard bomb. Not being down 10–0 in the second quarter. Not all the pressure to win the game for his team and his race. Doug Williams was winning that Super Bowl. He had something to prove.

They said the Black quarterback could not lead a team. Williams had faced a lot of adversity in his life; being down 10–0 in the Super Bowl was nothing to him. He was the quarterback of forty-four other teammates and twenty million Black Americans. It was time to bounce back and put all the bigotry to rest. With 14:17 left near the start of the second quarter and trailing the Broncos 10–0, from their own 20-yard line, Williams surveyed the field. Washington lined up in their customary H-back set, with a fullback and running back in the I formation, a tight end on the line, another hybrid tight end/fullback providing extra blocking to the right, and two receivers split to either side. The Broncos lined up in man-to-man bump-and-run coverage. Easy money for Doug. He took five steps back, watched his receiver beat the Broncos defender, and lofted a beautiful pass to a wide-open Ricky Sanders for an 80-yard touchdown. It was now 10–7.

They said the Black quarterback didn't have the courage to stay in the pocket. On third and 2, from the Broncos' 27-yard line, Williams sent a receiver in motion. That little chess move told him all he needed to know. The Broncos were blitzing and playing man-to-man. He had a play called that took time to develop, so he was going to have to stay in the pocket and wait for receiver Gary Clark, who ran a deep post corner route, to hit his break for the end zone. The stereotype said the Black quarterback would bail the pocket and take off running in the face of the blitz. Williams stood tall, held the safety in place with his eyes, and placed his pass where only his man could catch it. Touchdown! It was 14–10 Washington.

After two straight touchdowns, Williams's precision throws had softened the defense, just where Washington wanted them. On their next possession, Washington scored on a 58-yard Timmy Smith run to drive the lead to 21–10. On the Broncos' next possession, Washington forced another punt. The rout was officially on. And Joe Gibbs was going to let Williams lead the show.

They said the Black quarterback had no touch. With 4:34 left in the half and starting from their own 40-yard line, Williams uncoiled a missile. He missed his intended receiver badly and almost threw an interception. It was the type of pass that got critics salivating. They were waiting to pounce. The naysayers wanted to tell him his previous throws were all a fluke. But on the next play, he hit Ricky Sanders in the middle of the field for a first down. Then, throwing from the I formation, Williams sent Sanders in motion, from right to left, to get another bead on the defensive alignment. After Smith's 58-yard run, Williams knew the Broncos were susceptible to a play-action pass, so Williams did just that. The fake to the running back fooled the defense and forced the linebackers to move forward, giving him the space to hit a streaking Sanders for a 50-yard toss that nestled into Sanders's hands like a newborn baby: 28–10, Washington. But Doug Williams wasn't done yet.

They said Black quarterbacks couldn't read a defense. After an Elway interception, Washington got the ball back with 2:14 and continued to push the pace. After a 43-yard run by Smith, it was Doug's turn. In Washington's last drive of the half, with 1:09 left, facing third and 4 from the Broncos' 8-yard line, as Doug took his quarterback drop, he saw the Broncos' defenders fly to Sanders, taking away his first option. The defense thought they had him. But Williams was a student of the game. He knew what was coming and where to go next with his throw. He quickly found tight end Clint Didier for a touchdown.

In total, Williams went 9 of 11 passing with 228 yards and four touchdowns in the second quarter. In that second quarter, Washington scored more points in a quarter than any team in Super Bowl History. Doug finished the game 18 of 29 passing for 340 yards and four touchdowns, and he won the game's MVP. Not bad for a Black quarterback.

As he left the game at Jack Murphy Stadium in San Diego, he headed right for Eddie Robinson, the man who worked so hard to get a Black quarterback to this point. Elated, Robinson said, "The NFL eliminated one of its stigmas today." He continued, "Doug won the Super Bowl today because he performed like a winning quarterback. It wasn't a matter of black or white. It was a matter of skill and courage and intelligence, but not color. And that's what makes it good." Doug knew what this victory meant to the other quarterbacks who looked just like he did. "I never had an opportunity to watch a black quarterback in the Super Bowl, but now I think players like Don McPherson [Syracuse] and Rodney Peete [USC] and all the others see they have the opportunity. They see doors are open," Williams said after the game.

McPherson never got his chance, but Peete was a backup for the Carolina Panthers when they made the Super Bowl in 2004. And Doug, Vince, and a whole host of other Black quarterbacks were there to cheer him on. That was the year when, led by the Black pioneers, including Doug, Vince, James Harris, Warren Moon, and Marlin Briscoe, the Black quarterbacks started the Field Generals, a group of Black quarterbacks to support and encourage Black quarterbacks. Joe Gilliam would have been there too, but he died Christmas night 2000 of a drug over-dose. He never had the support or resources a Black quarterback needed to battle the branches of bigotry trying to hold him back. That could never happen again. The Field Generals made sure the current players understood the history. They also wanted to give guys like Donovan McNabb, Steve McNair, Daunte Culpepper, and Shaun King the emotional support they would need as Black quarterbacks in the NFL. One had to know how to properly deal with the racist fans and prejudiced pundits all the while preparing for linebackers like Ray Lewis, who wanted to take their heads off. The group also reached down to help the younger generation climb. Every Super Bowl, the Field Generals put on a free clinic for young Black quarterbacks. They taught them about leadership in life and proper quarterbacking techniques, and they instilled in them a powerful message: don't switch positions. That had to be said. At some point in their careers, every Black quarterback was told to switch.

Doug not only paved a way for future Black quarterbacks by winning the Super Bowl. In the moment, many believed he cleared a path for Black Americans. As one writer aptly put it before the big game, "For blacks, this is not merely a football game; it is a milestone for our race." Another added Doug's performance "was more the example than the exception of how superbly many Blacks have functioned as scientists, teachers, engineers, corporate lead-ers, administrators, businesspersons etc. whenever given a chance to participate in a career previously denied them." For that partic-ular writer, Doug's game told Black Americans to "believe in your dreams, your worth and potential regardless of how much racism and other adversities may try to convince you to do otherwise." Another observed, "The pride he has instilled in Blacks in general and young Blacks in particular makes him a truly genuine Black hero."

With Black History Month following Doug's triumph, it was a no-brainer for many Black kids across the country to celebrate Williams as their hero along with Martin Luther King Jr., Rosa Parks, and George Washington Carver. Even Black members of Congress got into the act. In March, Los Angeles congressman Augustus Freeman Hawkins, who also happened to be California's first Black representative, issued an official letter into the *Congressional Record* from a Black LA resident that celebrated Williams's accomplishment: "Williams' extraordinary triumph has relieved the frustration and pain felt by so many blacks. A feeling of satisfaction, indeed elation, reigns."

For that generation of Black Americans, Williams was their Joe Louis, their Jackie Robinson, their Rosa Parks, their Martin Luther King Jr. In a year when Jesse Jackson was taking on the Democratic nominee, Williams was proof that Jackson could win. And Doug knew it too. He acknowledged, "Black America, everywhere I go, comes up to me and says, 'Hey, we're pulling for you to make it to the top because we've always been on the bottom.' So, I accept this, that I am to football and the quarterback position what Jesse Jackson is to politics." For many Black Americans, it felt like Doug was their first Black president.

But Williams also quickly became another stark reminder of the Black quarterback syndrome. After his record-setting Super Bowl victory, he did not get the financial spoils that should have come his way. There were no major endorsement deals, and there was no big contract befitting a Super Bowl hero. And after injuries to his knee and back during the 1988 and 1989 seasons, Washington didn't want him back, and neither did any other team, despite being healthy heading into the 1990 season. Doug's career was done. On his way out, he had one last hope. "One thing I'd like to see in my lifetime is the end of the black quarterback syndrome."

In the end, although he did not have the gaudy numbers and did not make the Hall of Fame, Williams remains a legend in the Black community. For Black folks, it was never about his stats, it was always about his symbol. Seeing Doug do it meant that anything was possible. Doug Williams provided hope to so many folks who faced the daily ills of America's racism. And because of that, Williams will always be fondly remembered as a hero whose popularity rivals the best and brightest of Black Americans.

EPILOGUE

As the 1985 Bears wreaked havoc on opposing offenses and rapped their way to a Super Bowl victory, Vince Evans shuffled around Denver with his head down. That should have been him out there, not Jim McMahon, he thought to himself. But now he was a car salesman, a real estate agent, a meterman checking how much electric conduit a nuclear power plant might need, anything but a quarterback. He tried every team. He wrote letters. He made phone calls. Most went unanswered. Those who replied said thanks, but no thanks. They had no need for Vince Evans's services. Two years prior, he was a million-dollar man. The only player with a contract guaranteed by Lloyd's of London. But now he was throwing to kids at a local park. What happened?

When the Chicago Blitz signed Evans for the 1984 season, he was supposed to revolutionize football. Head coach Marv Levy planned an open attack to play to Vince's strengths and would let him throw all over the field. He could run when he wanted to. No more Corvettes parked in the garage. If this worked, he'd be the first true dual threat in pro football. But that never came to fruition with the Blitz. As Evans quickly learned, he was plagued by the same problems with the Blitz as he was with the Bears. A new coach meant a new offensive system to learn, which meant it would take Evans more time to pick up the intricacies of a scheme. But there was more to his downfall than that. This was the USFL; there was always something else.

The Blitz was a terrible team because they weren't really the Chicago Blitz. They were the Arizona Wranglers. Dr. Ted Diethrich, who owned the team the previous year, swapped his Blitz franchise, who went a respectable 12–6 in 1983, for the Arizona Wranglers, who finished the season 4–14. Chicago went to Arizona, and Arizona came to Chicago. Starting with a bad team and dismal home attendance, the Blitz's new owner, Dr. James Hoffman, overpaid to lure Bears backup players to the Blitz, believing that would attract hometown fans. He spent in the wrong areas. They should have built a better offensive line. Instead, they scrapped together a line with spare parts. In the end, they had an offensive line as reliable as an elevator in the Cabrini-Green housing projects. Without protection and adequate practice time, the speedy Evans never got on track. He threw for 2,624 yards in fourteen starts but finished last in efficiency. Unfortunately for the Blitz, their fan attendance ranked near the bottom of the league too. The team folded at the end of the season.

After the Blitz went bust, Vince headed west and tried his luck with the Denver Gold. That didn't pan out either. With the Gold's new head coach, Mouse Davis, an offensive genius who is credited for bringing the run-and-shoot offense to pro football, Evans was in the perfect offense for his talents. The run-and-shoot was a pass-first offense that used four speedy receivers who each had an option to go deep on every play. The scheme had never been tried in the NFL, but when implemented by Mouse Davis at the lower levels of college, the CFL, and the USFL, the run-and-shoot seemed unstoppable. The year prior to accepting the Gold job, as the offensive coordinator for the USFL's Houston Gamblers, Davis hit pay dirt with rookie quarterback Jim Kelly, and the two broke the all-time pro football passing record with 5,311 passing yards. With Evans's big arm and his speed, those in the know believed he would finally get to show pro football what he could do. Although he struggled in his first game, going 14 of 45, he soon got the Gold on a five-game winning streak and into first place in their division by the beginning of April. This included a victory over the Arizona Outlaws and Doug Williams on ESPN. It was the last time the two Black quarterbacks played against each other. Less than a month later, Evans lost his grip on his starting job. There was no telling what the future held for him. Would he run it back with the Gold or try his hand somewhere else? He got his cold answer.

The USFL went bust before the 1986 season. The NFL took what they wanted from the scraps that the USFL left and discarded the rest. What about Vince Evans? Teams thought there was nothing they could do with a Black quarterback who did not want to switch positions. He was left in the scrap heap too. As the 1986 season went by with no takers and 1987 started the same, Vince thought he was done. But then he got one last chance. This was the story of his career. He always seemed down, but he was never out. After week 2 of the 1987 season, the NFL players went on strike.

Like the 1974 strike, which saw Black quarterbacks Joe Gilliam, James Harris, and J. J. Jones take their chances as scabs to finally get a legit shot to compete, the 1987 strike also induced multiple Black quarterbacks to cross the line. In came guys like Willie Totten (Bills), a record-breaking quarterback from Mississippi Valley State who, along with receiver Jerry Rice, helped rewrite college record books; Tony Robinson, who the state of Tennessee let out of prison on a work release to play for Washington; Reggie Collier (Steelers); and Vince Evans, who signed with the Los Angeles Raiders. In his three starts during the strike, Evans went 1–2 in the win-loss column, but he played well enough that when the full-time Raiders came back, Evans was one of the few players to stay with his team. Players hated him for crossing the line, but those players did not know how hard it was for a Black quarterback to stick in the NFL. After he spent weeks explaining his situation, his teammates eventually understood why he crossed. But by the time they came around, it did not matter. He didn't play the rest of the year after the strike, and then the Raiders cut him before the 1988 season.

Soon, most fans forgot about Vince Evans. And why wouldn't they? Doug Williams had just won the Super Bowl, and the league had two Black quarterbacks who were superstars in Warren Moon and Randall Cunningham. By the late 1980s, Moon and Cunningham had reached a crossover appeal to white fans that no Black quarterbacks had touched before them.

Today, while Doug Williams has remained an icon, Vince has largely been forgotten. He became remembered as an erratic quarterback who was not very good. That's too bad, because he made it possible for the fast quarterbacks to get a shot. He made it possible for the innovative offensive coordinators to dream about the possibilities of having a dual-threat flamethrower. And for a quarterback that was supposedly no good, Evans broke another important barrier: he became a career backup. Before Evans, if a team had no intention of starting a Black quarterback, they would not keep him on the team. Black quarterbacks did not get to collect lucrative checks for holding a clipboard. Prior to Vince, that was a privilege only reserved for mediocre white men.

Back in 1977, when Jimmy Carter was still president, they told Vince Evans to switch positions if he wanted a career in the NFL, but there he was in 1995, forty years old, still playing during Bill Clinton's tenure. By the time 1995 rolled around, the Raiders had cut him each season from 1987 to 1995, only to bring him back.

He played sparingly as a backup but got one start in 1993 against the Chiefs, making him the first Black quarterback to start under a Black head coach when Art Shell turned him loose. Two years later, when Vince was the oldest active player in the league, the Raiders tabbed him to start against the Indianapolis Colts on October 22. Invincible Vince turned into Vintage Vince.

"Hit them with the short stuff," head coach Mike White told Vince, "then we'll go with the slam dunk." Slam dunk? That was the deep ball, and Vince could always rear back and let one loose over the top like Dominique Wilkins. As a younger player, he was always looking to the slam dunk, but now as a seasoned veteran, he knew that first he had to play the short game like Muggsy Bogues. After dinking and dunking the Colts for the first half, Vince bombed the secondary and hit speedster Rocket Ismail for touchdowns of 46 yards and 73 yards. That day, Evans had his best passing game of his career, going 23 of 35 for 335 yards. "I feel renewed. I feel like my competitive juices are as intense right now as they were when I was 22. I feel great, man," he claimed after the game. What could have been?

It took some time, but in the years that followed, Evans made it possible for Black backup quarterbacks like Rodney Peete, Tyrod Taylor, and Josh Johnson, who was drafted in 2008, to stay on NFL rosters despite never being considered starting material. Between 2021 and 2023, in fact, Johnson played for four teams, only in an emergency role. He even played in the 2023 NFC Championship game for the 49ers, who signed him off the street just weeks prior to the game just in case they needed a quality veteran. In his own way, Johnson is living a Black quarterback's dream too.

Evans continues to have an impact on the game today. How? One word: *speed*. Evans was Randall Cunningham before Randall Cunningham. Michael Vick before Michael Vick. Lamar Jackson before Lamar Jackson. Jalen Hurts before Jalen Hurts. That was evident during Super Bowl LVII on February 12, 2023, when Patrick Mahomes led the Kansas City Chiefs against Jalen Hurts and the Philadelphia Eagles. Thirty-five years after Williams made history as the first Black quarterback to start a Super Bowl, the match between Hurts and Mahomes marked the first time two Black quarterbacks started against each other in the Super Bowl.

While Mahomes, who is a gunslinger built in the mold of Doug Williams, won the game, Hurts's start had a bigger impact on future Black quarterbacks. And he has Vince Evans to thank. Like Evans, Hurts is considered a speedster, one built more for a running back or a receiver than a quarterback, but like Evans, Hurts told the critics no. For far too long, pundits, GMs, and coaches have looked at quarterbacks like Evans and Hurts and suggested they switch positions. Hurts believed in his own abilities more than he did stereotypes about Black quarterbacks. And so did the Eagles, who built around his mind, arm, and legs. By proving a team can win with a Black dual-threat quarterback, Hurts has been a pioneer too.

Just months after Mahomes won his second Super Bowl with his all-world arm and Hurts mesmerized audiences with his precision passes and punishing runs, three of the first four teams in the 2023 NFL draft selected Black quarterbacks. When the Panthers grabbed Bryce Young first overall and the Texans followed with C. J. Stroud with the second pick, it marked the first time two Black quarterbacks were nabbed first and second in the same draft. But the most intriguing pick belonged to the Indianapolis Colts, who shocked experts when they selected Anthony Richardson. At six foot four and 250 pounds, Richardson is an even bigger version of Vince Evans and Jalen Hurts. And the Bears have a quarterback built just like Richardson in Justin Fields. The game is definitely changing. The NFL is finally seeing the future of quarterbacking. And the future is Black.

ACKNOWLEDGMENTS

THIS BOOK IS DEDICATED TO MY MOM, MARY MOORE, WHO LOST her battle to pancreatic cancer in 2020. I'm so blessed that I got a chance to tell her about this project before we lost her. Your son made it!

To my wife, CC, thank you for all the love and support and allowing me to pursue my dreams. You're an amazing partner and the perfect mom. To my awesome kids, Amaya, Grant, and Isla, who had to put up with me giving them lessons on Black quarterbacks, Daddy loves you. Amaya, keep shooting and working hard. Grant, keep asking questions. Isla, you have the *it* factor. And don't forget to dribble. To Willie, thanks for always being a father to me.

To my siblings, Zoey, Zenobia, and my big brother, Lance, who got me hooked on sports, thanks for letting me be me. To my aunts, Monica, Vicki, and Nancy, I really appreciate you checking in on us during these hard times.

To my friends from day one, Damion, Larry, Mark, and to no-jump-shot Todd, who not only lost the touch on his jump shot but became a fouler on the court, thanks for always having my back. To the fellas, Alex, Jeff, Marlo, and my first Black quarterback, Ahje, thanks for allowing me to hang.

I want to give a shout-out to my Grand Rapids friends. To the Camping Crew (Tracy, handyman Chad, Beca, fishing Sammy,

Mindi, Rafa, Stacy, Daniel, Janay, and Andrew, the Gary Pettis of the crew), thanks for taking care of our family and letting me read during our camping trips. To Chris, thanks for talking basketball with me. Corey B., thanks for all the great cards. You still owe me a Warren Moon. To Yazeed, although your shoe game is lacking, I appreciate all the stories about Gary, Indiana, and Starter jackets.

To *The Black Athlete* podcast crew, Derrick White and Carl Suddler, thanks for allowing me to be your friend and talk sports, scholarship, and junk 24-7. We all know who the GOAT is. I could not have written this book without the help of Derrick, who listened to me talk about this project for three straight years.

Over the years, I have had the pleasure of meeting amazing journalists who have supported my work. Thanks to Howard Bryant for helping me shape the idea of this book. To Kevin Blackistone for encouraging me to write the book. To Morgan Campbell, my speed guru. To Yussuf, for letting me write for First and Pen. To Dave Zirin for putting me on. To Andrew Maraniss for always giving me time to talk writing. To Doug Farrar for schooling me on NFL offenses. To Jack Silverstein, my go-to Bears historian.

When I got my job at GVSU in 2008, I had no idea that I'd be here forever, but like I tell people all the time, the school has let me grow and supported my work in every way. I want to give a special thanks to my history department. I can't name everyone, but I just want to give a shout-out to Paul Murphy, my office neighbor, for listening to me every day and supporting me on this project.

A special thanks to all the folks on Twitter who supported my work over the years. I wrote this book with you in mind. I especially want to thank the good card folks, Jason Schwartz and Jeff Ash, for sending me cards of Black quarterbacks over the years.

If I forgot you, I owe you a pack of cards.

WORKS CITED

Introduction

"monument of racism": "NFL Called 'Monument of Racism,'" *Boston Globe*, November 15, 1979.

BOUND FOR STARDOM: Mike Downey, "Bound for Stardom," *Chicago Sun-Times*, September 21, 1979.

"run like the cops are after him": John Schulian, "Skins' Evans More Than a Pretty Face," *New York Daily News*, November 16, 1980.

rural Louisiana: Doug Williams, *Quarterblack: Shattering the NFL Myth* (Chicago: Bonus Books, 1990), 65.

"Being a black quarterback": Jim Murray, "The New Stereotype," *Los Angeles Times*, November 26, 1974.

"There will be no speeches": Mike Tierney, "An Unheralded but Historic Happening in Chicago," *Tampa Bay Times*, September 26, 1979.

"'We HAVE Overcome'": Raymond Richardson, "First Game in Chicago," *Tri-State Defender*, October 6, 1979.

"This is the glamour position": Dave Wolf, "Eldridge Dickey's Special Mission," *Sport*, December 1966, 41.

"There are, of course": Phil Musick, "Steelers' Gilliam Proves His Point," *Pittsburgh Press*, December 13, 1972.

"had to swim the moat": Kevin Lamb, "Evans and Williams: NFL's Color Co-ordinators," *Chicago Sun-Times*, September 30, 1979.

"loosey-goosey": Charles Maher, "Why No Black Quarterbacks in Professional Football," *Los Angeles Times*, March 27, 1968.

"combination of black jargon": Doug Grow, "Williams' Critics Say He's Stupid," *Minneapolis Star*, November 14, 1980.

"Sure, I wanted a chance to play quarterback": Ocania Chalk, "Pro Football's Caste System," *Black Sports*, September 1971.

"The cornerback areas": Jack Olsen, "In the Back of the Bus," *Sports Illustrated*, July 22, 1968.

"That's the trouble with Negro quarterbacks": Sam Skinner, "Is He a Quarterback or a Flanker?," *San Francisco Chronicle*, July 16, 1968.

"There have been great strides": Sam Lacy, *Fighting for Fairness: The Life Story of Hall of Fame Sportswriter Sam Lacy* (Centreville, MD: Tidewater, 1998), 127.

Dan D. Dodson observed: "The Negro Quarterback: He Wants a Chance," *High Point Enterprise*, September 21, 1969.

"Historians will remember": Tierney, "Unheralded but Historic Happening."

Chapter 1

Kenny Washington and Bob Waterfield: Ned Cronin, *Los Angeles Daily News*, December 9, 1942.

On integrating the Rams: Louis Moore, *We Will Win the Day* (Lexington: University of Kentucky Press, 2021).

"Kenny was the greatest long passer": Jackie Robinson, "Jackie Robinson Remembers Kenny Washington," *South San Francisco Enterprise Journal*, November 3, 1972.

On the history of the T: Murray Olderman, *The Pro Quarterback* (Hoboken, NJ: Prentice Hall, 1966).

"regular" offense: "Flaws in T Formation Style Explained by Veteran Coach," *Springfield Leader and Press*, November 30, 1947.

Shaughnessy "did more to establish": Doug Farrar, *The Genius of Desperation: The Schematic Innovations That Made the Modern NFL* (Chicago: Triumph Books, 2018), 4–10.

"They are fakers": Clark Shaughnessy, "Football for Morale," *Esquire*, August 1942.

"The T is a great formation": "Aubrey Praises Lujack," *Des Moines Tribune*, October 29, 1946.

On innovation and the T formation: Tom Bennett, *The Pro Style: The Complete Guide to Understanding National Football League Strategy* (Hoboken, NJ: Prentice Hall, 1976).

Black speed?: "The Rise of the Dark Stars," *Vanity Fair*, July 1935.

"We have plays that would allow Washington": "Rams Switch Washington to Quarter," *Valley Times*, July 23, 1946.

"He threw the ball so hard": Robinson, "Jackie Robinson Remembers."

"'Ready, 75, 14'": "Big Named Stars Are Not on First Team," *Honolulu Advertiser*, August 15, 1946.

"today little green-eyed": Bob Hoenig, Inside Outlook, *Hollywood Citizen-News*, October 22, 1946.

"Bernie, we've decided": John Danakas, *Choice of Colour: The Pioneering African-American Quarterbacks Who Changed the Face of Football.* (Toronto: James Lorimer, 2007).

"Willie can pitch a football": State Sidelines, *Ludington Daily News*, November 26, 1952.

"They are shoving things at Willie": George S. Alderton, Sport Grist, *Lansing State Journal*, August 14, 1953.

"A lot of blacks from around Chicago": "Black QBs: A History of Crossed Signals," *Boston Globe*, January 25, 1988.

George Connor on Willie Thrower: "Connor Says Pride Won for Packers Over the Cowboys," *Muncie Evening Press*, October 30, 1968.

"become the first full-time Negro": Art Daley, "First Negro QB Regular in Pros Brackins' Goal," *Green Bay Press-Gazette*, February 16, 1955.

"clever quarterback": Bill Nunn Jr., "Texas Eleven has Veteran Team Back," *Pittsburgh Courier*, September 4, 1954.

"There are certain things you can't talk about": Quarterback Club, *Green Bay Press-Gazette*, November 10, 1955.

"He wasn't bad until he made the ball club": "Charlie Brackins: Born Too Soon," *Green Bay Press-Gazette*, September 16, 1979.

Chapter 2

History on Chaneyville can be found at the Pride-Chaneyville Library in the Special Collections section. The collection includes interviews, photographs, yearbooks, and a master's thesis by Lorraine June Hawkins, "Rural Communities and Land Use in East Baton Rouge Parish," and another historical research project from Hawkins entitled *Chaneyville*, all of which I used to describe the community of Chaneyville.

"it doesn't have a name": "The Grambling Rifle," *Newsweek*, November 21, 1977.

"My daddy told me": Tom Jackson, "Baddest Outlaw in Oklahoma," *Inside Sport*, March 1984.

"jam sandwich": Doug Williams, *Quarterblack: Shattering the NFL Myth* (Chicago: Bonus Books, 1990), 60.

unpaved gravel roads: "Williams Is Favorite Son of Little Chaneyville," *Tampa Bay Times*, November 6, 1979.

"great fear in our community": Williams, *Quarterblack*, 65.

Doug's family: "Well-Armed Pioneer," *Sports Illustrated*, February 1, 1988.

"When I was real young": Williams, *Quarterblack*, 62.

"They would break things": "Williams Is Favorite Son."

Doug and baseball: "Keep on Throwing Is Williams' Motto," *Shreveport Times*, November 11, 1977.

For more information on his upbringing: *A Football Life*, season 8, episode 10, "Doug Williams," aired December 7, 2018, on the NFL Network.

Chapter 3

Dudley vs. Grimsley: "Neighbor Versus Neighbor," *News and Record*, October 4, 2002.

"That's just beauty": Kevin Lamb, "Disciplined Spontaneity," *Pro*, November 1981.

For a history on Greensboro: William H. Chafe, *Civilities and Civil Rights: Greensboro, North Carolina, and the Black Struggle for Freedom* (Oxford, England: Oxford University Press, 1981).

"Sometimes, I didn't understand": Skip Myslenski, "Vince Evans' 20/20 Vision," *Chicago Tribune*, August 2, 1981.

"whip" him every day: Jerry Kenion, "The Vince Evans Story," *Greensboro Daily News*, January 15, 1977.

"It is unthinkable": Chafe, *Civilities and Civil Rights*.

"Students will make the change": "For Students, It's New Year's Day," *News and Record*, August 5, 1971.

General discussion about Black athletes in Greensboro: "A Chip off the Old Block," *Greensboro Record*, May 18, 1979; "Greensboro Pros Look Back," *Greensboro Record*, May 18, 1979; "Easy Road to Success," *Greensboro Record*, May 18, 1979.

Chapter 4

Rommie Loudd and George Scott: Mike Rather, "The Black Quarterback," *Touchdown*, 1969 All-Pro Football Annual.

"just as accurate deep": Lee Mueller, "A&M's Onree Jackson Tagged 'Above Normal' QB Prospect," *Birmingham Post-Herald*, November 15, 1968.

"Willie Mays of pro football": Rather, "The Black Quarterback."

"[James Harris]": Doc Young, Good Morning Sports, *Chicago Defender*, January 5, 1977.

Hank Washington as the next Black quarterback: John Crittenden, "Washington Set to Buck Quarterback Color Line," *Miami News*, December 21, 1966.

"It seems we have learned": Take Ten, *Chicago Defender*, December 31, 1966.

"Too cocky" quotes: "That Too Cocky Negro Quarterback," *Michigan Chronicle*, April 15, 1967.

"For you Hank Washington": Bill Nunn Jr., "Shame on Pro Image," *Pittsburgh Courier*, April 1, 1967.

"While this is no secret": Claude Johnson, "Pro Squads Discriminate Against Tan Quarterbacks," *Philadelphia Tribune*, September 15, 1964.

"To us, this has a larger meaning": Dave Wolf, "Eldridge Dickey's Special Mission," *Sport*, December 1966.

"We know that one of these days": Jack Murphy, "Merritt Grooming Dickey as First Negro Pro Quarterback," *San Diego Union*, September 15, 1967.

"Negroes form a solid slice": Vincent Johnson, From the Bench, *Mobile Register*, August 21, 1963.

"alienating your Negro community": Larry Merchant quote was reprinted in Clip Board, *Evening Sun*, April 6, 1967.

Al Davis and the "black militant" group: "How Raiders View Exhibition Games," *Press Democrat*, August 31, 1968.

Eldridge Dickey on the Black militant group: Sports Corner, *Houston Forward Times*, August 10, 1968.

"I have set a goal": Joe Booker, "Eldridge Dickey, Bearing the Cross," *Houston Forward Times*, October 5, 1968.

"That brother is going to be out of sight": "As I See It: Back to Black with the Lord's Prayer," *Sun Reporter*, July 26. 1969.

"We prefer our quarterbacks": "Blanda's Last Shot," *Oakland Tribune*, August 4, 1968.

For more on the history of Eldridge Dickey: *The Eldridge Dickey Story*, film directed and produced by Malik A. Rasheed (2008), www.eldridgedickey.com.

Chapter 5

Five Black quarterbacks: Straight from the Huddle, *New York Daily News*, August 5, 1972.

"Black America has been waiting": Brad Pye, "Can Walton Quarterback Rams to Win?," *Los Angeles Sentinel*, August 3, 1972.

Karl Douglas starts: "Ineptness Silences Douglas and Colts," *St. Petersburg Times*, August 5, 1972.

"detrimental effect on white children": "Orleans Father Sues to Block School Mixing," *Daily Advertiser*, March 9, 1960.

Doug on his white teammate: Doug Williams, *Quarterblack: Shattering the NFL Myth* (Chicago: Bonus Books, 1990), 66.

Chaneyville's integration compliance: "Changing Chaneyville Name Does Harm," *Morning Advocate*, August 25, 1981.

"We built it ourselves": Chaneyville Collection at Pride-Chaneyville Public Library, Pride, LA.

"Find you another safety": Doug Williams, *Quarterblack*, 70.

"Jefferson Street Joe": "Broadway Joe, Meet Jefferson Street Joe," *Black Sports*, February 1972.

"He can throw the ball": Ellis Johnson, "TSU Faces Quarterback Supreme in Joe Gilliam," *Houston Chronicle*, September 30, 1971.

Williams on Gilliam: Doug Williams, *Quarterblack*, 70.

For Doug's high school career, see: Football Preview, *Morning Advocate*, September 5, 1972; "Chaneyville Outlook Dim," *State Times*, September 5, 1972; "Smith and Williams Connect on 3 TD's for Chaneyville," *Morning Advocate*, September 16, 1972; "Chaneyville Overwhelms LSSD Mustangs, 46–6," *State Times*, September 23, 1972.

Black athletes on going to Dudley: "A Chip off the Old Block," *Greensboro Record*, May 18, 1979; "Greensboro Pros Look Back," *Greensboro Record*, May 18, 1979; "Easy Road to Success," *Greensboro Record*, May 18, 1979.

butted heads with the coach: "The Trojans Wanted Him," *Greensboro Record*, September 12, 1975.

On white and Black coaches in Greensboro: "Easy Road to Success."

Vince goes to Smith: "Eagles Fly with Young but Challenging Squad," *Greensboro Record*, August 27, 1971.

"one of the best I ever saw": "Vince Evans: Greensboro Native's Dream Just Never Died," *Greensboro News and Record*, September 20, 1993.

Evans's senior season: "Experience Strong Suit for Title-Hungry Eagles," *Greensboro News and Record*, August 29, 1972.

Smith vs. Page: "Vince Evans: Greensboro Native's Dream."

Chapter 6

Watching USC as a kid: "Evans May Run Off with Job," *Los Angeles Times*, August 31, 1975.

Vince on spurning NCC: Skip Myslenski, "Vince Evans' 20/20 Vision, *Chicago Tribune*, August 2, 1981.

"I wrote a letter to the athletic department": "Evans May Run Off with Job," *Los Angeles Times*, August 31, 1975.

On going west: "Trojan Horse a Colt," *Independent Press-Telegram*, June 8, 1975.

"Not many people get drafted": "Vince Evans Story—Tale of a Trojan Hero," *Los Angeles Sentinel*, October 17, 1974.

For information on John McKay, see: John McKay, *McKay: A Coach's Story* (New York: Atheneum, 1975).

Jimmy Jones as a Black hero: "Positively Jimmy Jones," *Black Sports*, November 1971.

"He's big and he can run": Loel Schrader, "Ryan's Fastball Has Them Guessing," *Independent*, September 2, 1974.

Panthers' defense knocked out Pat Haden: Brad Pye, "The Vince Evans Story—Tale of a Trojan Hero," *Los Angeles Sentinel*, October 17, 1974.

Chapter 7

Doug on going to a white school: "Quarterback Contrast in Black and White," *Newsday* (Nassau edition), November 10, 1974.

"When a boy comes to Grambling": "Robinson Says Football No. 2," *Houston Chronicle*, October 29, 1974.

"if Martin Luther King scored": George Frazier IV, "100 Yards and 60 Minutes of Black Power," *Esquire*, October 1, 1967.

Eddie Robinson's life and coaching philosophy: Eddie Robinson, *Never Before, Never Again: The Autobiography of Eddie Robinson* (New York: Thomas Dunne, 1999).

Sammy White on recruiting: Mark Ribowsky, "I Saved Tarkenton's Career," *Black Sports*, October 1977.

On Black power: Mickey Herskowitz, "A Two-Way Street at Grambling," *Houston Post*, November 1, 1968.

Eddie Robinson on civil rights: Robinson, *Never Before, Never Again*, 111–12.

"We as black coaches": "Grambling Mentor Cites Coaching for Success of Black Quarterbacks," *Journal Times*, November 24, 1974.

Sports Illustrated on the wing T: "A Wide Open Season," *Sports Illustrated*, September 19, 1960.

Mike Howell being a quarterback: "Grambling Mentor Cites Coaching."

Robinson on seeing Harris for the first time: Jerry Izenberg, "The Promise," *Staten Island Advance*, January 30, 1969.

Coach Yeoman on Vida Blue: "A Bolt of Lightning," *Time*, August 23, 1971.

Robinson on teaching his offense: Barry Farrell, "James Harris Speaks Very Softly," *Sport*, October 1975.

"it's important to me": Herskowitz, "A Two-Way Street."

Harris wanting to switch positions: Steve Guback, "James Harris: Thoughts on Being a Black Quarterback," *Evening Star*, May 28, 1972.

"A quarterback just can't expect to play": "A Slow Start," *Corvallis Gazette-Times*, September 30, 1975.

Scouts on Harris: "Scouts Say Grambling's Harris Will Be First Negro at Pro Quarterback," *Commercial Appeal*, December 3, 1968.

On John Rauch's system: John Rauch, "Bills' System Demands Thinking Players," *Buffalo Evening News*, August 8, 1969.

Rauch on Harris: John Rauch, "Bills Paid the Price," *Buffalo Evening News*, August 18, 1969.

Harris and his Blackness: Larry Felser, "Only 3 Pro Games Behind Him, But Harris May Be Bills Starter," *Buffalo Evening News*, September 9, 1969.

Larry Felser told readers: Larry Felser, "Rauch Will Be Watching Harris," *Buffalo Evening News*, August 15, 1969.

Harris to start: Larry Felser, "Jets Had Bills in Mind," *Buffalo Evening News*, September 13, 1969.

Robinson on Rauch and Harris: "Grambling Coll.: America's Black Football Factory," *Sun*, November 11, 1969.

On Robinson having a type: Paul Attner, "Doug Williams: I Guess I'm a Pioneer," *Washington Post*, reprinted in *Pensacola News Journal*, November 26, 1977.

Southern won't recruit: "Team Formations Won't Be Blamed," *Shreveport Journal*, November 13, 1973.

Doug trying to quit: Doug Williams, *Quarterblack: Shattering the NFL Myth* (Chicago: Bonus Books, 1990), 74.

Gilliam gets the start: "The NAACP Lauds Gilliam," *Tennessean*, September 14, 1974.

Harris gets the start: Jim Murray, "Rosenbloom's Folly," *Los Angeles Times*, August 24, 1975.

The year of the Black QB: Robert Chrisman, "Whiter the Black Quarterback," *Los Angeles Times*, January 12, 1975.

Chapter 8

"Within the next 10 years": "What They're Saying," *New York Times*, November 3, 1974.

Gilliam on quarterbacks: "Black Quarterbacks Making Mark," *Journal and Courier*, November 9, 1974.

Stats on formations: "Triple Option, Veer, to Be Most Popular Formation," *Marion Star*, September 4, 1974.

Schembechler on quarterbacks: Sam Lacy, "Real Quick Now, Who Are These Guys," *Afro-American*, January 12, 1974.

Yeoman on quarterbacks: "Color No Longer Barrier When Playing QB," *Orlando Sentinel*, January 1, 1989.

Chapter 9

"I must not be any good": Doug Williams, *Quarterblack: Shattering the NFL Myth* (Chicago: Bonus Books, 1990), 75.

"My problem is": "Robinson Says Football No. 2," *Houston Chronicle*, October 29, 1979.

The cerebral quarterback: "Grambling Stops Jackson State," *Shreveport Times*, October 27, 1974.

"Dandy Doug": Jim McClain, "Grambling Rambling," *Times*, December 8, 1974.

Chapter 10

Description from Carlos Pennywell: "Tigers' Passing Fancy," *Shreveport Journal*, September 9, 1975.

"the biggest game of my career": "Grambling Coach Says OSU 'Biggest Test,'" *Oregonian*, October 3, 1975.

"We've got to realize": "A Slow Start," *Corvallis Gazette-Times*, September 30, 1975.

"They have pro-size people": "Grambling Got the Butterflies," *Albany Democrat-Herald*, October 4, 1975.

Description of the game: "Tigers Stun Oregon State," *Times*, October 6, 1975.

Parnell Dickinson on Black quarterbacks: "Parnell Dickinson on All-American Team," *Greenwood Commonwealth*, December 19, 1974.

Results of the Grambling vs. Mississippi Valley game: "One-Sided Shootout," *Shreveport Journal*, October 20, 1975.

Getting injured: Doug Williams, *Quarterblack: Shattering the NFL Myth* (Chicago: Bonus Books, 1990), 77–78.

Pennywell on training with Doug and playing against Grambling: Billy McIntyre, "Deep at Quarterback," *Times*, August 12, 1976.

Talking with James Harris: "Another Grambling Trailblazer," *New Orleans States Item*, November 24, 1976.

Chapter 11

Evans on Pat Haden and his upcoming season: Loel Schrader, "Trojan Horse a Colt," *Press-Telegram*, June 8, 1975.

"He's a better runner than passer": "Far West," *Popular Sports Kick-Off*, 1975; "Pacific Eight," *College Football 1975 Annual Preview*.

McKay on the quarterback battle: Jeff Prugh, "USC Still No, 1," *Los Angeles Times*, August 26, 1975.

McKay on Evans's throwing: "Evans May Run Off with Job," *Los Angeles Times*, August 31, 1975.

Evans on Coach Fertig and the previous season: Skip Bayless, "Vince Evans' Unending Fight to Be No. 1," *Los Angeles Times*, October 9, 1976.

Evans loses starting job: "McKay to Start Stanford at Quarterback," *Arizona Daily Star*, November 12, 1975.

UCLA beats USC: "UCLA Drops Ball, but Holds Roses," *Los Angeles Times*, November 29, 1975.

"Grand Canyon": "USC Is Right on Pitch," *Sports Illustrated*, November 29, 1976.

McKay leaving USC: "For Texas A&M," *Daily Press*, December 17, 1975.

Evans on hate mail: Vince Evans, *Chicago Sun-Times*, July 24, 1977.

Evans on criticism: Bayless, "Vince Evans' Unending Fight."

Evans on the color syndrome: Vince Evans, *Chicago Sun-Times*, July 24, 1977.

"I didn't get much guidance": Bayless, "Vince Evans' Unending Fight."

Rams quarterback competition: Doug Krikorian, "Great Quarterback Debate Heating Up," *Los Angeles Herald-Examiner*, August 16, 1976.

"Wheaties coverboy": Doug Krikorian, "Pat Haden Is Everything a QB Shouldn't Be," *Sporting News*, December 17, 1977.

James Harris on his time with the Rams: Chuck Knox and Bill Plaschke, *Hard Knox: The Life of an NFL Coach* (San Diego: Harcourt Brace Jovanovich, 1988), 158.

Evans on Coach John Robinson: Bayless, "Vince Evans' Unending Fight."

Evans on his excitement for Robinson: "Is It the Coach or the Passer?," *Los Angeles Herald-Examiner*, September 2, 1976.

On John Robinson and offense: "USC Will Be Passing More," *Progress Bulletin*, January 7, 1976.

Evans on his excitement for Robinson: "Is It the Coach or the Passer?"

"Vince is an excellent athlete": Loel Schrader, "USC's Robinson Off and Running," *Press-Telegram*, January 12, 1976.

Hackett on watching film: Curt Sylvester, "Bo's Not Laughing at USC's Evans," *Detroit Free Press*, December 29, 1976.

"throw with a lighter touch": "Is It the Coach or the Passer?"

Hackett and Evans on their work together: Bayless, "Vince Evans' Unending Fight."

Hackett on Evans at USC: "Evan's Ex Coach Sure Vince Will Star," *Chicago Tribune*, August 19, 1979.

Evans on training with Hackett: Vince Evans, *Chicago Sun-Times*, July 24, 1977.

Preseason information on 1976 USC: "Pacific Eight," *College Football 1976 Annual Preview*.

Preseason expectations: Dick Miller, "Trojans Are Deep at Almost All Positions," *Los Angeles Herald-Examiner*, September 6, 1976.

"He played very well": Dick Miller, "Opening Game Jitters Part of SC's Problem," *Los Angeles Herald-Examiner*, September 13, 1976.

"I'm rooting for Vince": Dick Miller, "Now Trojans Are up for the Ducks," *Los Angeles Herald-Examiner*, September 18, 1976.

"Venus de Milo passing": "Evans Boils Purdue," *Los Angeles Herald-Examiner*, September 26, 1976.

"a complete quarterback": "Evans Fall Guy, Autumn Whiz," *Los Angeles Herald-Examiner*, November 4, 1976.

"He played magnificently": "Quarterback Duel," *Los Angeles Herald-Examiner*, November 16, 1976.

couldn't hit the Grand Canyon: "USC Is Right on Pitch," *Sports Illustrated*, November 29, 1976.

"This was the greatest thrill" and *"That game film is art"*: Dave Moore, "Jekyll and Hyde Routine," *Daily Trojan*, January 5, 1977.

Chapter 12

"The Black Dominance": "The Black Dominance," *Time*, May 9, 1977.

Tony Dungy on playing quarterback: William C. Rhoden, *Third and a Mile: The Trials and Triumphs of the Black Quarterback. An Oral History* (New York: ESPN Books, 2007), 47.

"Briscoe. Up.": Dick Connor, "Briscoe Used to Handicaps," *Denver Post*, October 27, 1968.

Briscoe starting: "'Magician' to Get Starting Call for Broncos Sunday," *Rocky Mountain News*, October 1, 1968.

Briscoe on dealing with being a starter: Dick Connor, "Two Paying for New Fame," *Denver Post*, October 3, 1968.

On the decision to start Briscoe: "Little Magician to Wave Wand for Broncos on Sunday," *Rocky Mountain News*, October 6, 1968.

"first Negro quarterback": "Briscoe Breaking Line Is Incentive," *World Herald*, October 30, 1968.

Bill Walsh's plans for Briscoe: Dick Forbes, "Defensing the Magician," *Cincinnati Enquirer*, October 5, 1968.

Briscoe's play against the Bengals: "Broncos Pull Out 10–7 Win Over Bengals," *Cincinnati Enquirer*, October 7, 1968.

"He showed a lot of poise": "Briscoe Impresses San Diego," *Denver Post*, October 21, 1968.

"'black magic'": "Bronc Magic Works Again," *Rocky Mountain News*, October 28, 1968.

WORKS CITED

Briscoe beats the Dolphins: "Miami Succumbs to Briscoe Magic," *Denver Post*, October 28, 1968; Leonard Kahn, "Pro and Kahn," *Rocky Mountain News*, October 28, 1968.

John Rauch on Briscoe: Rick Lucas, "'Laugh-in' Turns into Near Horror Show for Oakland," *Denver Post*, December 9, 1968.

Stram remarked that Briscoe: "Broncos Give Chiefs 30–7 Win," *Denver Post*, December 15, 1968.

On Briscoe's successful passer: Irv Moss, "Briscoe Ranks High in Broncs QB Stats," *Denver Post*, December 10, 1968.

"white Gullivers": Connor, "Briscoe Used to Handicaps."

Bobby Layne on Briscoe: Jim Graham, "Sizing Up Quarterbacks," *Denver Post*, December 20, 1968.

"I never think of them": Dick Forbes, "Defensing the Magician."

Briscoe compares height to Bart Starr: Dick Connor, "Briscoe to Be AFL's First Negro QB?," *Denver Post*, September 27, 1968.

"I really don't feel small": "Breakthrough for Black Quarterback," *Ebony*, January 1969.

Gillman on Briscoe: Phil Collier, "55–24 'Poor Game' for Chargers," *San Diego Union*, October 21, 1968.

Wally Lemm on Briscoe: George White, "Coaches Laud Houston Quarterback," *Houston Chronicle*, November 18, 1968.

"A quarterback who runs": Murray Olderman, *The Pro Quarterback* (Hoboken, NJ: Prentice Hall, 1966).

"I've got to learn when to scramble": "Broncos Looking to 1969," *Denver Post*, December 15, 1968.

"Marlin scrambles": "Breakthrough for Black Quarterback," *Ebony*, January 1969.

Bobby Howard on Briscoe: Collier, "55–24 'Poor Game.'"

His teammates on Briscoe's scrambling: "Scrambling Briscoe Hard for Receivers," *Denver Post*, October 5, 1968.

Briscoe as a scrambler: Connor, "Briscoe Used to Handicaps"; Wally Provost, "Heroic Briscoe Uncertain of Starting Role," *Omaha World-Herald*, October 28, 1968.

On Briscoe passing while scrambling: Chet Nelson, Sports, *Rocky Mountain News*, November 26, 1968.

"And all the screaming": "Improving Broncs Still Lean," *Denver Post*, December 15, 1968.

Briscoe on being cut: "Harris Had Tough Job," *Buffalo News*, September 10, 1970.

"That would seem like a cop-out": Skip Bayless, "Vince Evans' Unending Fight to Be No. 1," *Los Angeles Times*, October 9, 1976.

Matthew Reed as an NFL prospect: Mike Roberts, "Grambling's Success, Dismay," *Evening Star*, September 26, 1972.

Reed on his future: Darrell Williams, "He's a Quarterback," *Atlanta Journal*, August 25, 1972.

James Harris on Reed: "NFL Missed Out on a Good Guy," *Fort Worth Star Telegram*, February 29, 2004.

On Reed not making it: Adam Hunsucker, "Dual Threat Pioneer Reed Enjoyed Great Run," *News Star*, July 15, 2014.

"Although he made great strides": Joe Stein, "No Draft Tries the Souls of Scouts and Players," *Sporting News*, February 26, 1977.

Evans on playing quarterback: "Evans: 'I Can Play Quarterback,'" *Chicago Tribune*, May 8, 1977.

Finks on Evans: "Evans Will Get Shot at QB Job," *Chicago Tribune*, May 5, 1977.

On Evans's unique deal: "Evans Gets Bears Pact—and QB Guarantee," *Chicago Tribune*, June 2, 1977.

Chapter 13

"Vince Evans, the USC star": Doc Young, Good Morning Sports, *Chicago Defender*, June 6, 1977.

On Gillman as an offensive innovator: Doug Farrar, *The Genius of Desperation: The Schematic Innovations That Made the Modern NFL* (Chicago: Triumph Books, 2018), 31–35.

Evans struggling in preseason and Evans on race: Vince Evans, *Chicago Sun-Times*, July 24, 1977.

Bo Rather on Vince's athleticism: "The Long Wait," *Los Angeles Times*, October 25, 1978.

Evans feels the pressure: "Evans Plays for Returns," *Chicago Sun-Times*, September 16, 1977.

Evans on why he returned kicks: Tony Blackwell, "Gloomy Outlook for Chi Bears' Black QB," *Michigan Chronicle*, January 28, 1978.

"This is a break for me": Rick Talley, "Evans Only Wants a Chance to Showcase His Talent," *Chicago Tribune*, July 30, 1978.

On Ken Meyer: Rick Talley, "This Bears Coach Will Know the Score," *Chicago Tribune*, May 21, 1978.

"He hasn't tamed that howitzer": "Third Down and Long," *Chicago Sun-Times*, October 6, 1978.

"If I'm not playing": "The Long Wait."

Vince Evans plays quarterback: "The Unbelievable Happened," *Chicago Metro News*, November 25, 1978.

"We showed we had confidence in Evans": "Bears Conceal Quarterback Selection," *Tennessean*, November 22, 1978.

Evans not a quarterback: Ricky Talley, "Bears Corner Humiliation Market," *Chicago Tribune*, December 5, 1978.

Chapter 14

"In high school, you're called a quarterback": "The Grambling Rifle," *Newsweek*, November 21, 1977.

The summer before his Heisman campaign: "A Day in the Life of Doug Williams," *Shreveport Journal*, September 23, 1977.

"Hey, Mr. Heisman!": "Doug Williams: Statistics Are His Game," *Times*, November 10, 1977.

"I don't want to brag": John Adams, "Mr. O Versus Mr. D," *Clarion-Ledger*, September 6, 1977.

Whitney Young Classic: Eddie Robinson, *Never Before, Never Again: The Autobiography of Eddie Robinson* (New York: Thomas Dunne, 1999), 163–67.

WORKS CITED

The Morgan State game: Al Harvin, "Williams Aids Heisman Trophy Bid," *New York Times*, September 18, 1977.

"*I guess that's what it means*": Larry Carmody, "Grambling Quarterback Leads Route of Morgan State," *Newsday*, September 18, 1977.

"*cool drop-back style*": Norm Miller, "Williams Flips Lift Grambling," *New York Daily News*, September 18, 1977.

On the New York press and Doug: "Grambling's Doug Williams Leaves N.Y. Press in Awe," *Town Talk*, September 19, 1977.

Jeff Rude on Doug Williams: "A Day in the Life."

"*candle lights to the bright lights*": Gerry Robichaux, "Keep on Throwing Is Williams' Motto," *Shreveport Times*, November 11, 1977.

"*Being a black quarterback*": "Grambling QB Eyes FL," *Jet*, December 1977.

national player of the week: "Williams Is Named Co-Back of Week," *Shreveport Times*, November 9, 1977.

"'*There goes another one*'": "Doug Williams: Statistics Are His Game."

On Doug and passing during the season: "Keep on Throwing Is Williams' Motto."

"*I guess I'm a pioneer*": "Doug Williams: Guess I'm a Pioneer," *Washington Post*, reprinted in *Pensacola News Journal*, November 26, 1977.

Will a team draft him: Ron Rapoport, "91 TDs and All It Takes for NFL—Unless Williams Is Wrong Color," *Chicago Sun-Times*, reprinted in *Press and Sun-Bulletin*, November 29, 1977.

Chapter 15

Moon on leaving for Canada: "Racial Issues Help Land Moon," *Edmonton Journal*, April 13, 1978.

"*Right now, the situation of a black quarterback*": "Black Quarterback Moon Is CFL Success Story," *Vincennes Sun Commercial*, April 14, 1978.

"*Doug Williams walks the earth*": Ron Rapoport, "91 TDs and All It Takes for NFL—Unless Williams Is Wrong Color," *Chicago Sun-Times*, reprinted in *Press and Sun-Bulletin*, November 29, 1977.

"*He's got a big league arm*": Ron Reid, "He's Already in the Big Leagues," *Sports Illustrated*, October 31, 1977.

Scouting report on Doug Williams: "Cavanaugh Cream of Quarterback Crop," *Green Bay Press-Gazette*, April 25, 1978.

"*They say Bradshaw isn't too smart*": Skip Bayless, "A Black Hope at Quarterback," *Los Angeles Times*, November 23, 1977.

McKay on race and the draft: Dave Anderson, "Smile a While with John McKay," *New York Times*, January 6, 1980.

"*He can rifle the ball*": "Just Another Super QB," *Chicago Tribune*, October 20, 1978.

The Bucs draft Doug: "Bucs Make Williams No. 1 Choice," *Tampa Tribune*, May 3, 1978.

"*If anybody passed him over*": Dave Anderson, "Smile a While with John McKay," *New York Times*, January 6, 1980.

"*Doug is apple pie*": "Bucs Bot 'Apple Pie' Arm," *Tampa Tribune*, May 3, 1978.

"*I think of myself as a quarterback*": Norm Miller, "Do Not Color this Quarterback," *Daily News*, June 24, 1978.

"my burdens": Derek Reveron, "Rookie May Become First Black Pro," *Ebony*, January 1979.

"Man, go up there": "Bucs Williams Handles the Pressure as NFL's 1st Black Rookie Quarterback," *Chicago Sun-Times*, reprinted in *Detroit Free Press*, October 22, 1978.

Chapter 16

Hearing racism at the Bucs game: Michael A. Hall, "Hey, Tom!," *Tampa Bay Tribune*, December 26, 1980.

"the first black quarterback": Ralph Wiley, "Playing with Pen," *Oakland Tribune*, December 29, 1978.

Johnny Carson joke: "An Outsider Looks at 0–26," *Bradenton Herald*, December 5, 1977.

"I think they wanted a slave": Doug Williams, *Quarterblack: Shattering the NFL Myth* (Chicago: Bonus Books, 1990), 91.

"taking advantage of this poor little black boy": "Doug Williams Is Passing," *People*, November 19, 1979.

"I'm the first black quarterback": "Williams Aware of Extra Pressure," *Sentinel Star*, July 23, 1978.

Doug on the Black community rooting for him: Jim Selman, "Unlike Rickey Bell, Less Heat on Doug," *Tampa Bay Tribune*, July 25, 1978.

"I was lost": Ken Rosenberg, "Doug Williams Has Always Been a Winner," *Football Digest*, January 1980, 38–45.

Morris Owens on Doug: "Just Another Super QB," *Chicago Tribune*, October 20, 1978.

Johnny Unitas on Doug's throwing: "The Odds Were Against Him," *New Press*, August 31, 1979.

"a dime a dozen": Larry Keech, "Rapidly Maturing Evans," *Greensboro Daily News*, November 30, 1980.

"first black quarterback to mess up": "Day of the QB," *Tampa Tribune*, August 31, 1978.

Players talking after the first game: "Locker Room," *Tampa Bay Times*, September 3, 1978.

On Doug's popularity: "Old Master Tortures Buc's Best," *Tampa Bay Times*, October 2, 1978.

"Just keep cockin'": "Just Another Super QB," *Chicago Tribune*, October 20, 1978.

"Right then and there": Rosenberg, "Doug Williams."

Jokes about Doug: "Williams Says He's Just the Starter," *Los Angeles Times*, January 28, 1988.

Ahmad Rashad noticed: Rosenberg, "Doug Williams."

"Color Blind" McKay: "Color Blind McKay," *Los Angeles Sentinel*, November 2, 1978.

On criticism of being dumb: John Feinstein, "Doug Williams: The You-Know-What Quarterback," *Washington Post*, reprinted in *Arizona Republic*, October 4, 1980.

On his critics: Jim Selman, "Tampa Bay's Doug Williams: 'Judge Me by My Performance,'" *Football Digest*, March 1981, 48–53.

Watermelon in a box: Doug Williams, *Quarterblack*, 93–94.

Chapter 17

The Bucs' dominating defense: Ron Martz, "Selmon Bros," *Sporting News*, November 24, 1979.

WORKS CITED

The Bucs rebuilt offense: Mike Tierney, "Points Starved Bucs Hit Pay Dirt," *Sporting News*, October 1979.

"I learned to have patience": Jim Selman, "Above Everything Else, Williams Is a Quarterback," *Tampa Bay Tribune*, July 10, 1979.

On improvements to the Bucs' offense: "Doug Williams Shatters Myth That Blacks Can't Quarterback," *Bay State Banner*, August 30, 1979.

"Doug Williams is really maturing": "Tampa Bay Bucs Upset Los Angeles," *Stuart News*, September 24, 1979.

Evans wants to start: Kwame's Sports Whirl, *Chicago Metro News*, May 26, 1979.

"There's no question that I can play": "Judgement Time for Vince Evans," *Chicago Defender*, July 23, 1979.

A changed Vince Evans: "Vince Evans: No. 1 Against All Odds," *Chicago Tribune*, September 16, 1979.

Vince on his religion: Frances White, "Vince Evans, 'Quarterback of the Future,'" *Chicago Metro*, November 15, 1980.

How Vince changed his life: "Vince Evans' 20/20 Vision," *Chicago Tribune*, August 2, 1981.

Teammates on an improved Evans: "Vince Evans: The People's Choice and Players," *Chicago Tribune*, September 14, 1979.

"I used to be proud of how hard I could throw": "Vince Evans: No. 1."

How Vince improved: "Bound by Stardom," *Chicago Sun-Times*, September 21, 1979; "The Bomb," *Chicago Sun-Times*, September 21, 1979.

Quarterback controversy: "Who Will Start," *Chicago Tribune*, August 25, 1979.

Noah Jackson on Vince: "Bears Wait for a QB to Take Job," *Chicago Sun-Times*, August 6, 1979.

After the Jets game: "Evans May Be One Good Game from No 1," *Chicago Tribune*, August 13, 1979.

Evans on being a Black role model: Kevin Lamb, "Evans and Williams: NFL's Color Co-ordinators," *Chicago Sun-Times*, September 30, 1979.

ARMSTRONG IS A RACIST: "Armstrong Is a Racist," *Chicago Metro News*, August 18, 1979.

Evans against the Vikings: "Payton Kept Vikes on the Run," *Minneapolis Star*, September 10, 1979.

"The axiom says": "Evans Will Be the Bears' Man in Dallas," *Chicago Sun-Times*, September 15, 1979.

"That's not a bad way to go": "Evans Will Be the Bears' Man."

"it makes you want to pop your buttons": "Bears Passing Takes Off with Evans at Controls," *Chicago Sun-Times*, September 18, 1979; "Evans Earns Bears Starting Role," *Chicago Sun-Times*, September 18, 1979.

Evans on his reunion with McKay: Dave Nightingale, "Bears Evans Too Busy for Reunion," *Chicago Tribune*, September 26, 1979.

On the meaning of the game: Bob Oates, "Black Quarterbacks Making History," *Los Angeles Times*, September 18, 1979; Ron Rapaport, "Color? Bears and Bucs Fans Don't See It," *Chicago Sun-Times*, September 25, 1979; Brad Pye, "Check the Records," *Los Angeles Sentinel*, September 20, 1979.

"I don't put color into the situation": Raymond Richardson, "First Game in Chicago," *Tri-State Defender*, October 6, 1979.

"That's not fair": Lamb, "Evans and Williams."

"Coach McKay knows": Mike Tierney, "Bears Evans Too Busy for Reunion."

"One token pass": Don Pierson, "Loss Leaves Bears Snarling," *Chicago Tribune*, October 1, 1979.

Game notes: "Buccaneers Bop Bears," *Tampa Bay Times*, October 1, 1979.

Evans gets a staph infection: "Vince Evans Probably Out for the Season," *Chicago Tribune*, October 6, 1979.

Evans on getting sick: "Spring Vets Camp Brings Bear Smiles," *Chicago Tribune*, April 26, 1980.

Evans on God saving him: "Evans Shows He's Extraordinary," *Los Angeles Times*, September 27, 1981.

"Satan put me here": Joe LaPointe, "Test of Faith," *Detroit Free Press*, November 21, 1979.

Chapter 18

Evans earns starting job: "Vince Evans to Start," *Chicago Defender*, October 14, 1980.

"There have been numerous raps": John Schulian, "Skins' Evans More Than a Pretty Face," *New York Daily News*, November 16, 1980.

Coach Monte Clark on Evans: "Hurting Time," *Detroit Free Press*, October 19, 1980.

"They weren't showing much respect": "Bears Battle Lions in Key Matchup," *Detroit Free Press*, October 20, 1980.

Making of Vince Evans: David Israel, "It Was the Making of Vince Evans, QB," *Chicago Tribune*, November 28, 1980.

Optimism for Vince Evans: "Evans Makes 'Wait Til Next Year' Sound Almost Good," *Chicago Tribune*, December 8, 1980.

"Yeah stigmas": "Bears 'Con-Vince-d'—Evans Is for Real," *Charlotte Observer*, December 9, 1980.

Throwing to the halfback trend: Norman MacLean, "Why Today's Runners Must Be Receivers," *Football Digest*, December 1981, 52–58.

New-look offense: Don Pierson, "Marchibroda Doesn't Shun a Challenge," *Chicago Tribune*, September 6, 1981.

Offensive philosophy: "Marchibroda Welcomes Bear Challenge," *Chicago Tribune*, September 6, 1981.

"return from Las Vegas": "Bears New Aide Walks in Smiling," *Chicago Tribune*, February 24, 1981.

Marchibroda questioning if Vince could read defenses: Mike Kiley, "Vince Evans Primed to Succeed," *Chicago Tribune*, August 30, 1981.

Marchibroda on Vince: "Marchibroda Welcomes Bear Challenge."

Evans in the preseason: "Vince Evans: Precisely on Target," *Herald and Review*, September 3, 1981.

Celebrating Vince: "Vince Evans Day," *Chicago Metro News*, May 16, 1981.

Midseason struggles: "What Changes Can Be Made," *Chicago Tribune*, November 6, 1981.

Evans struggles: Don Pierson, "Armstrong Takes Heat off Evans," *Chicago Tribune*, November 25, 1981.

Evans loses confidence: Don Pierson, "Evans, 'All I Can Do, Is What I Can Do,'" *Chicago Tribune*, December 11, 1981.

Ditka hired: "Halas Game Plan Complete, Hires Ditka," *Messenger-Inquirer*, January 21, 1982.

Ditka has a system: Kevin Lamb, "Ditka Does Dallas with His Bears at Heart," *Tampa Tribune*, September 11, 1982.

Evans and the new coordinator: "Evans to Get New Tutor," *Chicago Tribune*, January 28, 1982.

McMahon on playing quarterback: "Mike Ditka Starts Shaping New Look Bears," *News Tribune*, May 9, 1982.

Evans on his faith: Ray Richardson, "Faith Makes Evans No. 1," *Chicago Defender*, August 4, 1982.

"Vince is my No. 1": "Ditka Claims Evans Is No. 1 Quarterback," *Times-Mail*, July 31, 1982.

Ditka contemplating who will start: "Bears Hit a New Woe Against Colts," *Chicago Tribune*, September 5, 1982.

"Anytime you have to give up a job": Don Pierson, "It's Avellini," *Chicago Tribune*, September 8, 1982.

"I really don't understand why": "Bears Humiliated by Saints," *Chicago Defender*, September 20, 1982.   \

"The unfairness of the situation": "Evans Wants to Know His Status," *Chicago Defender*, September 21, 1982.

Chapter 19

"You're better than that": "I'm Sorry," *Tampa Tribune*, October 16, 1979.

Doug Williams on Bucs fans: Against Bucs, *Tampa Times*, October 15, 1979; Locker Room, *Tampa Times*, October 15, 1979.

"The social barriers": "Doug Williams Takes Two Barriers in Stride," *New York Daily News*, January 4, 1980.

"the average black family": Jim Smith, "Doug Williams Tries to Play for All," *Newsday*, January 5, 1980.

Alan Goldstein, "Williams Must Conquer Plantation Thinking," *Baltimore Sun*, January 6, 1980.

"chimpanzee at quarterback": Hubert Mizell, "Bucs Defense and Offense," *Tampa Bay Times*, September 22, 1980.

Being booed: "Williams Late Scramble Turns Boos into Cheers," *Tampa Times*, September 12, 1980.

his victory prevented a "lynching" and *"EVERYBODY TALKS"*: "Williams' Arm Needs Radar Rod," *Fort Worth Star Telegram*, September 18, 1980.

Doug's grammar: Skip Bayless, "Doug Williams: A Phenomenon?," *Dallas Morning News*, September 19, 1980.

Doug on his grammar: John Feinstein, "Williams: The You-Know-What Quarterback," *Arizona Republic*, October 4, 1980.

Doug on his critics: Doug Grow, "Williams' Critics Say He's Stupid," *Minneapolis Star*, November 18, 1980.

McKay on race: "Dallas Just Outplayed Us," *Dallas Morning News*, September 22, 1980.

WORKS CITED

"Just judge him as a quarterback": "McKay Blasts Critics," *Clarion-Ledger*, September 23, 1980.

"All right, John": Hubert Mizell, "Bucs Defense and Offense Take Blame for Letdown," *St. Petersburg Times*, September 22, 1980.

"Now is there any question": "Williams Quiets Critics," *Fort Worth Star Telegram*, November 17, 1980.

On the 1982 strike: "They're Playing for Keeps," *Newsweek*, September 20, 1982.

"a company man": Doc Young, Good Morning Sports, *Chicago Defender*, December 1, 1982.

"I was taught" and *"more than a handshake"*: "Williams: Handshakes Not the Answer," *Tampa Tribune*, September 4, 1982.

"Many wondered": Hey, Tom!, *Tampa Tribune*, September 26, 1982.

Doug heads home to Chaneyville: "Williams Heads Home Seeking Peace of Mind," *Tampa Tribune*, September 28, 1982.

"Let me negotiate": "Williams Says Bucs Would Vote to Play," *Tampa Tribune*, November 9, 1982.

McKay on Doug: John Underwood, "Gone with the Wins," *Sports Illustrated*, October 19, 1983.

Janice: Doug Williams, *Quarterblack: Shattering the NFL Myth* (Chicago: Bonus Books, 1990), 83–90.

"You know I fought": "Bucs Williams May Sit Out," *Tyler Morning Telegraph*, July 12, 1983.

Negotiating his contract: Doug Williams, *Quarterblack*, 106–115.

Fans support Doug: "18 Quietly Sign in for Williams," *Tampa Bay Times*, July 17, 1983.

Polling the fans: Mike Tierney, "It Was Close, Doug, but Poll Says $600,000 Too Much," *Tampa Bay Times*, July 17, 1983.

Letters about Doug: Hey, Tom!, *Tampa Tribune*, July 24, 1983.

Doug signs with Oklahoma: "Williams Meets One Last Time with Tampa Area Media," *Bradenton Herald*, August 17, 1983.

"Tampa Bay let the black folks down": Tom Jackson, "Baddest Outlaw in Oklahoma," *Inside Sport*, March 1984.

Doug on race and Tampa: John Underwood, "Gone with the Wins," *Sports Illustrated*, October 19, 1983.

"To Many Blacks": Peggy Peterman, "To Many Blacks, the Bucs Got the Season They Deserve," *Tampa Bay Times*, December 19, 1983.

"If Vince Evans": Doc Young, "Vince Evans, Quarterback," *Chicago Defender*, September 10, 1983.

"The Black community": Ferman Mentrell Beckless, Reckless Beckless Perspectives, *Chicago Metro News*, 1983.

Vince frustrated in quarterback role: "Evans Deals with Disappointment," *Chicago Tribune*, October 2, 1983.

"I frankly don't care": Don Pierson, "While Ditka Burns, Bears' Players Fidget," *Chicago Tribune*, October 16, 1983.

Ditka picks a quarterback: "McMahon Is It," *Chicago Tribune*, November 8, 1983.

"He had wanted to make contributions": "Former USC Quarterback a Starter for USFL," *Los Angeles Times*, January 30, 1985.

Vince goes to the Blitz: "For Vince Evans, It's Fun in the Sun," *Chicago Tribune*, January 26, 1984.

Black quarterback syndrome: Leanita McClain, "The Black Quarterback Syndrome," *Chicago Tribune*, December 7, 1983.

Chapter 20

On Arizona: Doug Williams, *Quarterblack: Shattering the NFL Myth* (Chicago: Bonus Books, 1990), 120.

"I got to be perfect": "Williams Corralled," *Arizona Republic*, June 26, 1985.

Making his way back: Doug Williams, *Quarterblack*, 127.

On going to Washington: Doug Williams, *Quarterblack*, 134.

On possible trade to Raiders: "His Time Hasn't Passed," *Washington Post*, September 14, 1987.

"this gentleman's demonstration": Courtland Milloy, "Not Just a Passing Fancy," *Washington Post*, September 7, 1987.

"I had to look around": Christine Brennan, "Williams Settles into Starting Role," *Washington Post*, November 20, 1987.

"For black fans": Patrice Gaines-Carter, "Fans' Dreams Fulfilled by Williams' Start," *Washington Post*, November 24, 1987.

On Jesse Jackson: "New Leader in Washington," *New York Times*, November 23, 1987.

Crying: "NFC Notes," *Journal News*, December 6, 1987; "Williams: Laughing Eases the Pain," *Spokesman Review*, December 20, 1987.

Letters from fans: "Weather Won't Sack Redskins Parade," *Washington Post*, February 3, 1988.

On getting to the Super Bowl: "Williams Says He's Just the Starter," *Los Angeles Times*, January 28, 1988.

"How many times": Elmer Smith, "Doug Williams Isn't a Has Been," *Philadelphia Daily News*, January 11, 1988.

Campanis controversy: "Jesse Jackson Appears Pleased," *Morning Call*, June 11, 1987; "Rozelle Says He Can't Force Clubs to Hire Blacks," *Morning Call*, June 11, 1987.

Reverend Jackson call: Don Pierson, "Williams Key Passes Foil Vikings," *Chicago Tribune*, January 18, 1988.

MLK parade: "King Honored," *Washington Post*, January 19, 1988.

On Black support: "Black, White, Left, Right, Hail Redskins," *Washington Post*, January 30, 1988.

TOUCH OF CLASS: "Redskins Memorabilia Bring in a Touch of Class," *Washington Post*, January 25, 1988.

"old-fashioned ideas": Lynda Richardson, "Fans React to a Touch of Class," *Washington Post*, January 30, 1988.

Meaning of the game: "Williams Says He's Just the Starter."

Impact on Black quarterbacks: "Redskins Williams Gets Second Shot at Super Bowl," *Detroit Free Press*, January 17, 1988.

On the game and race: Tom Archdeacon, "Williams' Performance Speaks of Bowl Records," *Miami News*, February 1, 1988.

What the win meant to the Black community: "MVP Williams Wows 'Em in DC," *Washington Post*, February 1, 1988.

Doug as a hero: Juan Williams, "Many Blacks Blocked for Williams' Triumph," *Palm Beach Post*, February 4, 1988.

In Congress: "Doug Williams, a Joe Louis of Our Times," *Congressional Daily*, March 29, 1988.

On Jesse Jackson: "Redskins Williams Gets Second Shot."

Black quarterback syndrome: Doug Williams, *Quarterblack*, 187.

Epilogue

A new chance in Denver: "Vince Evans Thinks Denver May Be His Place," *Birmingham Post-Herald*, February 28, 1985.

With the Raiders: Jim Murray, "He Never Fit a Color Code," *Los Angeles Times*, July 28, 1988.

Complications with teammates: "NFL Strike, Vince Evans and 55 Other Raiders Are Taunted," *Los Angeles Times*, September 24, 1988.

"Hit them with the short stuff": "Evans Strong Arm Vexes Colts," *Indianapolis Star*, October 23, 1995.

On Super Bowl LVII: Louis Moore, "Patrick Mahomes, Jalen Hurts Complete Eddie Robinson's Black QB Vision," First and Pen, February 12, 2023, https://firstandpen .com/eddie-robinsons-vision-opened-the-door-for-patrick-mahomes-jalen-hurts-in -super-bowl-lvii/.

INDEX

INDEX

INDEX

LOUIS MOORE IS A HISTORIAN OF African American history and sports history. He has appeared in media outlets, including *USA Today, Sports Illustrated*, the *New York Times*, the *Chicago Tribune*, the *Washington Post, Time*, NPR, CNN, the Huffington Post, Deadspin, and *Rolling Stone*. His research was cited in Brian Flores's landmark lawsuit accusing the NFL of racial discrimination, and he has appeared live on CNN, MSNBC, BBC Sports, and CBC to discuss issues involving the Black athlete. He also appeared in VICE Sports' documentary *Fear of the Black Quarterback*.

PublicAffairs is a publishing house founded in 1997. It is a tribute to the standards, values, and flair of three persons who have served as mentors to countless reporters, writers, editors, and book people of all kinds, including me.

I. F. STONE, proprietor of *I. F. Stone's Weekly*, combined a commitment to the First Amendment with entrepreneurial zeal and reporting skill and became one of the great independent journalists in American history. At the age of eighty, Izzy published *The Trial of Socrates*, which was a national bestseller. He wrote the book after he taught himself ancient Greek.

BENJAMIN C. BRADLEE was for nearly thirty years the charismatic editorial leader of *The Washington Post*. It was Ben who gave the *Post* the range and courage to pursue such historic issues as Watergate. He supported his reporters with a tenacity that made them fearless and it is no accident that so many became authors of influential, best-selling books.

ROBERT L. BERNSTEIN, the chief executive of Random House for more than a quarter century, guided one of the nation's premier publishing houses. Bob was personally responsible for many books of political dissent and argument that challenged tyranny around the globe. He is also the founder and longtime chair of Human Rights Watch, one of the most respected human rights organizations in the world.

.   .   .

For fifty years, the banner of Public Affairs Press was carried by its owner Morris B. Schnapper, who published Gandhi, Nasser, Toynbee, Truman, and about 1,500 other authors. In 1983, Schnapper was described by *The Washington Post* as "a redoubtable gadfly." His legacy will endure in the books to come.

Peter Osnos, *Founder*